The Complete Book of
Gold Investing

To my three children,
Joseph, Julie and Joshua,
who are worth more than all the gold in the world.

The Complete Book of Gold Investing

Jeffrey A. Nichols

DOW JONES-IRWIN
Homewood, Illinois 60430

DOW JONES-IRWIN
Homewood, Illinois 60430

This publication is designed to provide accurate and
authoritative information in regard to the subject matter
covered. It is sold with the understanding that the
publisher is not engaged in rendering legal, accounting, or
other professional service. If legal advice or other expert
assistance is required, the services of a competent
professional person should be sought.

*From a Declaration of Principles jointly adopted by a Committee
of the American Bar Association and a Committee of Publishers.*

ISBN 0-87094-755-9

Library of Congress Catalog Card No. 86–72576

Printed in the United States of America

1 2 3 4 5 6 7 8 9 0 K 4 3 2 1 0 9 8 7

In this book I attempt to give readers an overall survey of the gold market, providing a practical and sophisticated guide to gold investment and trading. My chief aim is to help the investor and trader understand the complex workings of that market and maximize his or her profits. Beginners can gain a well-rounded introduction to the complex world of gold, and professionals can look to a definitive overview of recent trends in that market.

Anyone with a disposable income should invest some of it in gold—from the individual who buys a single gold coin to the institutional investor dealing in millions. Significantly, since the gold market is international in scope, my book—while covering the issues of importance to American readers—also will appeal to a worldwide audience.

I have not intended this to be an economic discourse on the alleged coming financial collapse or a polemic on the need to turn to gold as insurance in bad times. And I have not forecast gold's future price.

This book provides readers with a clear and comprehensive explanation of the "tools" of the trade necessary for successful gold investment and trading. It details fundamental analysis (the study of gold supply and demand factors), explores the relationship between gold prices and the economy, and reviews technical or "chart" analysis (how past prices provide clues to the future). After explaining what influences the price of gold using these analytical tools, I review the many gold instruments now available, such as bullion coins, physical metal, "paper" gold programs, gold mining equities, futures, options and so on.

Equally important, I have organized the material to serve the needs of each type of reader, from neophyte to professional. Each reader can readily select information relevant to his own holding or trading objectives, concentrating on the chapters that concern him most.

I believe that my work will be a timely guide to investing and trading in gold for the growing number of investors and professionals who are adding precious metals to their personal and/or institutional portfolios.

Finally, an undertaking of this sort is a major challenge and I am grateful to many in the industry for their positive feedback. In particular, I should like to especially thank the Gold Information Center—Investment Service; my thanks also go to Goldman Sachs & Co./J. Aron Division and others for their special interest.

Jeffrey A. Nichols

CONTENTS

Oscillators. Relative-Strength Indexes. Point and
Figure. Contrary Opinion. Warehouse or Depository
Stocks. Open Interest. Commitment of Traders.
Market Volume. Ratios. Summary.

PART ONE

Introduction

CHAPTER ONE

Who Should Own Gold—And Why?

"When we have gold, we are in fear;
When we have none, we are in danger."

John Ray, English Proverbs

More than a decade has passed since the unrestricted owner-ship of gold was legalized again in the United States. Yet, it remains a mysterious medium for most American investors, and one that a great many misunderstand. Only slowly are investors in this country coming to appreciate the metal's vir-tues—as a hedge against inflation, as a vehicle for diversifica-tion and enhancement of portfolio performance, and as an insurance policy against the risks associated with paper assets such as stocks, bonds, money-market instruments, and the like.

While many investors, particularly pension funds and other institutional buyers, scorn gold as unconventional or nontradi-tional and hence unfit, there is no other single asset, from a global point of view, to which the word "traditional" better applies. After all, gold's investment tradition spans millennia. It has long been coveted by emperors, kings, sultans, and sheiks, and since time immemorial it has been a favorite invest-ment of millions of others as well, whose blood was less "blue."

Looked at analytically, gold is a simple metal designated on the periodic table of elements by an atomic number of 79 and an atomic weight of 196.967. In flesh-and-blood terms, however, it clearly represents a great deal more. This is apparent at once from the way that it pervades our everyday language. "As good as gold"..."A heart of gold"..."He's got a real gold mine"— these and similar terms have long since entered the vernacular, and all of them conjure up specific and generally positive mental images.

Despite its long tradition and its excellent reputation, gold has been slow to develop as a widespread investment medium in this country. In part, this may be due to lingering doubts and suspicions from the period of more than four decades when its ownership effectively was banned. From 1933 until 1974, Americans were prohibited from buying, selling, or owning gold in any form other than jewelry and collectible coins—and during those years, they developed misconceptions and misgivings. More recently, such clouds have been dispersing, and more and more Americans are now adding gold to their portfolios.

Who should own gold? And why? The answer to the first question is easy: Nearly everybody—everybody, at least, with savings and discretionary income, whether that income is $15 million a year or $15,000. One important premise of this book is that there is a place for gold and gold-related assets in virtually every American's savings and investment program. As for why someone should own gold, the answer may vary from one investor to another, but essentially there are two fundamental reasons: safety and income.

Only during relatively brief intervals of harsh government proscription, such as the period from 1933 to 1974 in the United States, has gold's traditional role been curbed or displaced. And even then, the restrictions have tended to be limited in scope. During the time when U.S. gold investors were suffering repression, for example, gold remained a popular and widely used investment tool elsewhere in the world, serving millions as a cautious nest egg in a portfolio and others as a hedge against inflation or similar insurance against political disorder. In my view, gold is the traditional investment vehicle par excellence—and after the episode of disuse in the United States, it is coming into its own here, as well.

The resurgence of gold in this country was triggered by a combination of political and economic factors starting in the late 1970s. Geopolitical tensions were running high, fueled by the American hostage crisis in Iran and the Soviet invasion of Afghanistan. This, combined with the extraordinary surge in world inflation and the associated appreciation in the price of gold itself, served as the magnet that first began to attract the

American investor to this market in a serious and significant way. At the same time, some institutional money managers, influenced by modern portfolio theorists, were starting to recognize that the performance of a conventional stock and bond portfolio often could be improved by including gold.

Some investors hold gold sacrosanct, viewing it as the one secure asset in an insecure world. Fearful that conventional financial assets—even our very currency—may be in dire jeopardy and that hyperinflation or worse may lie ahead, the "gold bug" puts his trust in gold and gold alone. But you need not be a gold bug, or rely on the gold bug's logic and emotions, to conclude, as I do, that gold has a legitimate place in your investment program. While I believe that gold should be a part of almost everyone's portfolio, I do not maintain that it holds any theological significance or messianic promise. Note that I said it should be a *part* of a portfolio. Just how big a part depends on your individual needs, desires, fears, and expectations. It is yet another premise of this book that gold investment can be supported by a cool and objective analysis of the yellow metal's attributes and also by the lessons of portfolio theory and experience.

HIGH RETURNS AND LOW VARIANCE

Portfolio theory counsels the investor not only to pursue maximum returns but also to seek a minimum variance—in other words, the least possible exposure to one-sided risk. A central tenet of modern portfolio theory, the "efficient portfolio" concept, focuses on the idea that risk can be reduced by diversification. An efficient portfolio is one in which the expected rate of return is maximized for any given level of risk and uncertainty. Here, the risk is measured by the dispersion or variability of possible future returns. A portfolio can be made "efficient" by minimizing the risk associated with any given level of return. In down-to-earth language, all of this can be summed quite simply: "Don't put all your eggs in one basket." In other words, a modern portfolio should be diversified and spread between "hard" and "soft" assets. "Soft" assets include common stocks, bonds, commercial paper, bank certificates of deposit, money market accounts, and the like. A soft asset is a representation, receipt, or claim for a physical item, while a hard asset is the item itself. Thus, shares in a factory are "soft," while the factory itself is "hard."

Gold has the attribute of being a highly liquid asset. While your home and the land on which it sits may rightly be considered hard assets, they normally would not be looked upon as part of your investment portfolio, since few of us would be willing to part with such assets in order to raise quick money. And real estate generally is not fully liquid. Often, it may take weeks, months, or even years to find a willing buyer for a piece of property and realize a price that you, as the seller, consider reasonable. So really, to be of immediate use, part of your hard assets should be fully liquid—and gold, which is traded worldwide and almost on a 24-hour basis, is probably the most liquid hard asset available.

In addition to its liquidity, gold also has another attribute that makes it a valuable part of a portfolio: its "contrariness." And this can be of crucial importance. In periods when the gold market has been free to fluctuate, the price of the metal has tended to move in the opposite direction from the price of "conventional" financial assets, or with little apparent correlation with those assets. This sometimes contrary nature of gold allows it to be used as a hedge against changes in the value of a portfolio. To "hedge" a portfolio means to protect its value against fluctuation by including within it different assets whose price movements are inversely correlated: When the price of one goes up, the price of the other tends to go down, and vice versa. While the price of gold does not always move exactly opposite to the prices of other investments, it does so often enough to permit its use as a hedge against changes in the value of these investments.

You do not own any stocks? All you have is money? This means your "portfolio" is in cash, and part of almost every portfolio is. But even if your portfolio is entirely in cash, then gold can certainly serve you. Just as it has historically shown its contrariness to many other investments, gold's real value often moves as well in a fashion contrary to the value of currency—of money itself. That is what happened in 1979 and 1980, when the U.S. inflation rate soared above 12 percent, sparking a modern "gold rush." Investor demand for gold pushed the metal's price to record highs. In that extreme case, gold was a more than adequate hedge against inflation. It not only maintained its intrinsic worth, but it actually increased in real value, while the buying power of paper currencies was being eroded substantially. Gold's strong performance during the 1970s was not a fluke. It has held its real value—its purchasing power—not only over the short term but also over the centuries, while even the strongest paper currencies have fallen prey inevitably to the ravages of inflation and depreciation.

For many people, gold has been more than just a hedge against the economic uncertainty of inflation: It has meant the difference, quite literally, between life and death. This was the case, for instance, with the "Boat People" who fled from Vietnam after the fall of Saigon. Many of these people were able to survive largely because they had gold stowed away. Indeed, many immigrants from many different countries have been able to reach America—escaping repression, persecution, and even death in their homelands—because a few ounces of gold bought their freedom. Even in ordinary, less dramatic circumstances, gold has served its owners well in regions of the world less stable than the United States and Western Europe. In most countries, whether they are prone to revolution or election, governments often are forced to devalue currency—but gold retains its value through both changes in economic policy and the more dramatic political upheavals. Thus, it is sought by people around the world as a hedge against economic and political uncertainties. Such demand increases the value of gold by forcing the price higher—even for investors in the United States and Europe.

THE PYRAMID OF INVESTMENT

Traditionalists hold that a person should view his investments as a pyramid, with conservative assets at the base, more speculative holdings in the middle, and the riskiest investments at the top. In keeping with the shape of the pyramid, the greatest amount of money would be spent on the items in the base—a house, a car, and savings accounts, for example—with progressively smaller sums being allocated for items at the middle and the top. Under this approach, stocks and bonds would be placed in the middle, with gold at the very top.

While the concept of an investment pyramid makes sense, I would move at least a part of the gold, especially bullion and coins, to the bottom. Far from being blatantly speculative, gold, in my opinion, can serve as an anchor for a person's whole portfolio. As I have pointed out, it is a valuable form of insurance, especially against inflation and currency depreciation. To counterbalance the gold, an investor might consider buying long-term bonds and placing those, as well, in the pyramid's base. They would provide a hedge against deflation.

Those who can afford it might buy additional gold, perhaps in different forms, for the middle and top of the pyramid. For the middle, I would suggest some gold stocks; for the top, perhaps futures or options. How much you should spend and what form of gold you should buy will depend on both your income and your personal investment philosophy. But I feel very strongly that a truly sound portfolio should include gold in one form or another.

THE TYPES OF GOLD INVESTORS

There are three basic types of gold investors: long-term hoarders, who may hold gold or related assets for years, perhaps with no intention of ever selling them; medium-term investors, who treat gold like any other industry or investment sector, buying to achieve a capital gain and/or earn income over a period ranging from several months to several years; and short-term speculators.

The word "hoarder" carries something of a stigma—the image of an unpatriotic miser who keeps a stash of coffee while his neighbors suffer through wartime rationing. But, viewed dispassionately, with an understanding of the motives of a gold hoarder in a politically or militarily unstable country, the term starts to lose much of that stigma. The Boat People were hoarders of gold—but, as pointed out earlier, their hoards enabled them to buy their passage to freedom at a time when South Vietnam's currency was nearly worthless outside that country.

For an American hoarder, the stash of gold is a form of

protection against a devaluing currency, or simply a "nest egg" to pass on as part of an estate—but a nest egg that will not lose its real purchasing power, as might occur with many other conventional investments. All hoarders share one thing in common: They are not likely to sell except in a dire emergency. For them, gold is not a quick fix—not simply something to be held until the market rises, with the object of taking a profit at the first propitious moment.

If you are a medium-term investor, you probably think of gold just as you would almost any other investment asset: as something to buy when you perceive it to be undervalued and likely to appreciate, and then to sell at a profit. If you are a medium-term investor with a bullish view of gold—that is, you expect its price to rise—you might elect either to own the metal itself, in the form of bullion or coins, or opt to purchase gold-mining equities. Recognizing the value of gold as part of a portfolio but not dedicated to keeping it forever, the medium-term investor is willing to sell if a profitable opportunity presents itself. The medium-term investor might hold gold or gold-related assets for as short a time as a few months or as long as several years.

If you are a short-term investor, then you might be likely to trade gold futures contracts or options—investments that may be held for as short as a few minutes or as long as a few months. As a rule, short-term investments in vehicles such as the gold futures markets are highly risky ventures. Generally, though, they offer the greatest potential profit over a relatively short time span. The short-term investor is interested in gold not as a safety net or hedge investment but rather for its pure profit potential as a trading vehicle. For the short-term holder, gold is nothing more than a source of trading income.

As a rule, each level of investment involves a different portion of a buyer's investment income. The hoarder is a person who tends to view gold holdings as part of savings—as a nest egg. This is not what you might consider risk capital. Again, when I say "hoarder," I do not mean to conjure up visions of a miser in the Silas Marner tradition. I am speaking of any individual or family that saves regularly for the proverbial rainy day by setting aside a fund not earmarked for a house, car, or any other specific kind of purchase. For such an individual or family, I recommend a "golden umbrella" as part of the package of protection. I believe an investment in gold should account for a share of the savings—perhaps as little as 5 percent or as much as 25 percent, depending on the buyer's own emotional attitude toward the metal. This will increase the probability of successfully weathering the storm if that rainy day ever arrives.

The medium-term investor, on the other hand, is willing to accept some risk in order to achieve some return in the form of capital gains. But, in the case of a gold investor, he also is looking to protect his assets. If you are accustomed to making investments in the stock market, you can use those as a basis for deciding how much to invest in gold. My advice would be to determine how much you are willing to invest in any one industry group—computer stocks, natural resources, or banks and financial institutions, for example. This is how much you should be willing to invest in gold-related investments, above and beyond any gold you may be holding as a long-term nest egg.

If you are a short-term investor, you are using the most discretionary part of your income—the part you can afford to risk and lose. The short-termer who invests in the gold futures and options markets or in "penny stocks," another highly speculative vehicle, is not using gold to protect assets or as a form of insurance against possible setbacks in other parts of a portfolio. Rather, he is looking to earn as high a profit as possible in as short a time span as possible. If you are thinking of trying the short-term route with gold, by all means have the bulk of your investments in either long-term or medium-term vehicles.

Just what percentage of your portfolio should be in gold? That is a matter of debate among investment experts. Their recommendations range from as little as 5 percent to as much as 40 percent or even higher. But increasingly, experts agree that precious metals belong in every modern portfolio. Moreover, investors in the gold market have some pretty impressive company. Just as large institutional investors such as pension funds and insurance companies will be fellow shareholders in a blue-chip stock, some institutions also are holders of gold. But, in the case of gold, the scale of institutions is much larger than even the largest pension fund. Among your fellow investors will be the U.S. government, the Union of Soviet Socialist Republics, and just about every other national treasury. In 1985, the U.S. Treasury held more than 262 million troy ounces of gold bullion—by far the largest hoard of any country. As of the end of 1986, the Soviet Union held an estimated 70 to 80 million ounces. Unlike the United States, which sells relatively little gold, the USSR has been a consistent seller since 1953. But while the Russians regularly market a portion of their annual gold-mine output, they still have managed to increase their holdings in most years by retaining a portion of domestic mine production for official reserves. The fact that so many nations with widely varying economic ideologies are heavy investors in gold suggests that the citizens of these countries, where allowed to do so, likewise should participate in the market.

The question for you, an individual investor, is not whether you should participate in the gold markets, but to what extent. Before you can answer that question intelligently, you will have to study the various uses of gold and learn how to evaluate the potential of gold as an investment as well as some of the risks that are involved. You also will have to determine your personal investment objective. Are you a hoarder? A medium-term investor? Or, are you seeking an immediate return? Last but surely not least, how do you invest in gold? You are the only person who can answer questions dealing with your personal view of the world. However, this book will help you learn the ropes when it comes to investing in gold and gold-related instruments.

One important note on terminology: Gold and other precious metals are measured in troy ounces. The troy ounce is a unit of apothecary weight that is equal to 31.103 grams. By contrast, a standard, British, or avoirdupois ounce is equal to 28.349 grams. Thus, a troy ounce weighs 9.7 percent more than the standard ounce—the kind we normally use to weigh almost everything else, including ourselves. All references to "ounces" in this book are to troy ounces.

PART TWO

Forecasting Gold Prices—
The Tools of the Trade

CHAPTER TWO _____

Understanding Gold's Fundamentals

"A Golden Rule is, there is no Golden Rule."

George Bernard Shaw

A book about investing in gold, especially one written by an analyst, should begin with an analysis of market fundamentals—that is to say, trends in gold supply and demand.

Before attempting analysis, it is best to define its purpose. For you, as an investor, the analysis of the gold market boils down to one thing: price—looking at where it has been and trying to explain why, in order to better understand what might happen in the future. On one level, market analysis may involve sophisticated econometric and computer models of gold's supply and demand and the interaction of inflation, interest rates, and a host of other variables that may affect the metal's price. On another level, analysis can be as simple as the action of a trader in drawing a line on a historical gold-price chart, without regard to the multitude of factors that operate in the marketplace to determine that price. As an investor, you always have to remember that both extremes of the analytical spectrum have one thing in common: Neither system can predict, with certainty, the future price of gold. The investor who forgets this invariable law is asking for serious trouble. Nevertheless, analysis is important and necessary—and, if properly done, it can raise the probability of a successful gold investment or trading program.

Although many analysts are philosophically or theologically wedded to one school of analysis or another, our approach will be more pragmatic. We will examine both the fundamental

15

and technical indicators with a strong dose of skepticism and common sense, looking to both the supply/demand analysis of a fundamentalist and the lines and figures of a chartist. Both have their place, and both can help you improve your performance as a gold-market practitioner. No one can predict the future, but solid and serious analysis, unlike reading tarot cards and interpreting crystal balls, may raise the chances of making correct investment decisions.

The use of charts, moving averages, relative strength indexes, chart patterns, and investor consensus has many adherents. In fact, if a great mass of traders and investors were to notice the same buy or sell signals, the market might be hit by a simultaneous flurry of orders. Like someone shouting "Fire!" in a crowded movie theater, a simultaneous outbreak of buying or selling can stampede the market in whatever direction the technical signal dictates. As a result, the predictions of technical analysis sometimes become self-fulfilling prophecies.

Although the technical school of thought can often move the gold market, such a move cannot be sustained for very long unless there are fundamental reasons for that move. Once the technicians have placed their orders and the market has satisfied the prophecy, the fundamentals will reassert themselves. For this reason, no one should overlook the charts when attempting a short-range analysis of the market. But, for the medium and long range, we start with the fundamentals.

SUPPLY AND DEMAND

In order to understand gold's fundamentals, we have to deal with two basic questions: Where does it come from—in other words, what is the supply? And where does it go—what is the demand? It is easy to brush off the first question with the jocular observation: "It comes from a gold mine." Actually, though, mine production is only one of three sources of the gold that enters the marketplace. Secondary supply—old industrial scrap, coin melt, dishoarded jewelry, and the like—and sales by the Soviet Union and other centrally planned economies are also important sources, as shown in Exhibit 2-1. A final note: Periodically, central banks have also been important suppliers to the international gold market pool—acting at times

EXHIBIT 2–1 World Gold-Mine Production by Country or Region, Primary Supply
(thousands of troy ounces)

Year	United States	Canada	South Africa	Other Market Economies	Total Market Economies	USSR and COMECON Bloc	Total World Mine Supply
1970	1,747	2,409	32,164	4,550	40,870	7,220	48,090
1971	1,495	2,261	31,389	4,530	39,675	7,420	47,095
1972	1,450	2,079	29,245	5,001	37,775	7,620	45,395
1973	1,176	1,698	27,495	5,132	35,501	7,820	43,321
1974	1,127	1,698	24,388	5,596	32,809	8,020	40,829
1975	1,052	1,654	22,938	5,292	30,693	8,220	38,156
1976	1,048	1,692	22,936	5,503	31,179	9,425	40,604
1977	1,100	1,734	22,502	5,700	31,036	9,565	40,601
1978	999	1,735	22,649	5,692	31,075	9,685	40,760
1979	964	1,644	22,617	5,467	30,692	6,400	37,092
1980	970	1,563	21,631	6,036	30,200	2,900	33,100
1981	1,378	1,673	21,122	6,716	30,889	9,000	39,889
1982	1,466	2,081	21,355	7,428	32,330	6,500	38,330
1983	2,000	2,400	21,900	9,400	35,700	3,000	38,700
1984	2,200	2,700	22,000	10,000	36,900	4,000	40,900
1985	2,500	2,800	21,600	12,100	39,000	10,000	49,000
1986*	2,900	3,200	21,800	13,000	40,700	11,000	51,700

*1986 estimates.

SOURCE: American Precious Metals Advisors; Chamber of Mines of South Africa; J. Aron/Goldman Sachs Precious Metals Research; U.S. Bureau of Mines; U.S. Central Intelligence Agency.

as buyers and at other times as sellers. I have chosen to discuss central bank involvement in the market toward the end of this chapter.

Since it takes years of exploration, planning, financing, and development before a gold mine can be brought onstream, mine production—also known as primary supply—is a relatively inelastic source, changing little from one month to the next, or even from year to year, in response to a changing price. When the price of gold shot up in 1979 and 1980, exploration and mine development also increased. But it took several years—until the mid-1980s—before their output really began to rise in a meaningful way. Mine production in the non-Communist nations in 1977 was 31 million ounces. By 1983, it had increased to almost 36 million ounces, a 15.2 percent jump. By 1986, mine output had risen to roughly 40.7 million ounces, a 31 percent increase over the level of output in 1977. But during that time span, the price of gold had more than doubled, from an average of $148 per ounce in 1977 to the $340 to $400 range during most of 1986.

Even though the increase in mine production may appear to be slight, there have been important changes in the mining picture. During the 1970s, there was a gradual *decline* in mine production: It fell from an average of 41 million ounces per year in the late 1960s to only 30.2 million ounces in 1980. Also, there has been a shift in the location of much of this mining exploration and development. South Africa continues to be the leading gold-producing nation, but many of the newly developed mines are in Canada, the United States, Brazil, Australia, and other countries.

Although the last decade has seen a proliferation of new mines, the gold investor need not be concerned by such an apparent abundance. A mine is a finite, depleting resource: There is only so much gold in any particular hole in the ground. Many older mines are running out of high-grade ore, and over time, they will become uneconomical to operate. And, unlike many of the older mines, the newer ones typically are smaller, low-grade operations with limited reserves and fairly short lives. Without the incentive of further substantial increases in the price of gold, total world gold-mine output should begin to ebb again during the 1990s.

Investors should consult publications from the U.S. Department of Interior's Bureau of Mines for a convenient review of annual mining activity. Other good sources of information are the South African, Canadian, Brazilian, and Australian institutions; the Gold Institute, a private industry group based in Washington, D.C.; and the excellent annual review of Consolidated Goldfields, which is titled simply *Gold*. (See Appendix D, Information Sources about Gold and Gold Investments.)

SECONDARY SUPPLY

While the gold supply from mines tends to change only slightly from year to year, the amount that is obtained from the other major sources can vary dramatically from week to week, and even from day to day.

The first of these is secondary supply—metal that has been sold for recycling. This can come from old jewelry, scrapped computer parts and electronic equipment, dental fillings, and a wide range of other gold products. Unlike mine production, this source is very price elastic—that is to say, sensitive to changes in the metal's price, even in the short run. In 1977, when the average price of gold was around $148 per ounce, about 4.5 million ounces came from secondary sources, compared with mine production that year of 31 million ounces. In 1980, when the average price per ounce was up to about $612, more than 21 million ounces came from secondary sources, while mine production actually declined slightly, dipping to just over 30 million ounces. The following year, when the price dropped to $459, secondary supplies fell to 10.5 million ounces. Exhibit 2-2 details the annual supply of gold from secondary sources.

In 1982, the price of gold dropped to an average of $376, but total secondary supply showed a surprising jump to 11 million ounces. There was yet another gain in secondary supply of roughly a half million ounces in 1983, when the price of gold rebounded to an average of $424. But secondary supply fell by approximately a million ounces during 1984, coinciding with a drop in gold prices. As prices drifted lower yet in 1985, the secondary supply fell by another million ounces, to 9.5 million.

The flow of secondary supply sometimes lags behind mar-

EXHIBIT 2-2 Secondary Gold Supplies (millions of troy ounces)

1977	1978	1979	1980	1981	1982	1983	1984	1985	1986
4.5	5.7	10.9	21.2	10.5	11.1	11.5	10.5	9.5	8.5*

*Preliminary estimate/projection.
SOURCE: American Precious Metals Advisors; J. Aron/Goldman Sachs.

---

ket moves in price, as holders of scrap material—whether it is old jewelry or industrial equipment—retain their metal, awaiting higher prices. During 1982, some of the metal entering the secondary market came from people too late to capitalize on the higher prices of the preceding years—people who had held on, waiting for higher prices, but were ultimately disappointed.

In general, it is safe to say that scrap supply is a function of price: The higher the price, the greater the supply. But, as the reservoir of scrappable material is depleted at a given price level, unusually large amounts probably will not come onto the market until the next higher significant price level is reached.

The more than 21 million ounces of gold recycled in 1980 drained the available supply at that year's prices. It is reasonable to expect that secondary supply will not again reach the 20-million-ounce annual rate until the price of gold rises toward or above its historic peak. Although a vast quantity of scrap is still potentially available, fewer people are willing to release it without the incentive of substantially higher prices.

The price of gold in U.S. dollars appeared low in 1984–85, but the unprecedented strength of the dollar versus virtually every other currency made the gold dear to large numbers of buyers around the world when expressed in their own local currencies. Exhibit 2–3 shows how the price of gold expressed in the yen and in the U.S. dollar has dropped sharply since 1980—but how the decline is not nearly as sharp when the price is expressed in the pound sterling or the deutsche mark.

The flow of secondary supply from one country to another depends to a great extent on the local currency price of gold—how many pesetas, lire, dinars, cruzados, or yen, for example, the seller will receive. High prices in the currencies of many countries, particularly of indebted developing countries, have

EXHIBIT 2–3   Price of Gold in Six Major Currencies, March 1979 to March 1986 (monthly data—actual prices)

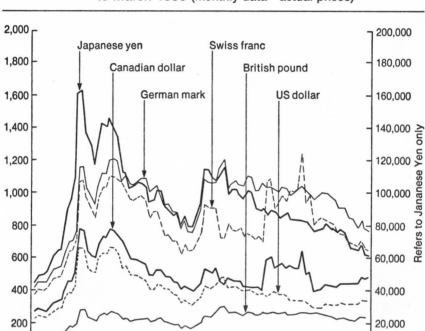

SOURCE: Gold Information Center—Investment Service, 1986.

helped maintain the flow of secondary supply near 10 million ounces per year despite the apparent weakness in the metal's dollar price.

The flow of scrap is governed not only by the price of gold but also by a need for hard cash, which makes for "distress selling" in many developing countries where economic circumstances have become increasingly difficult (and local currency prices are also very high). This factor has supported a higher rate of scrap flow in recent years than a simple look at the gold price in U.S. dollars might suggest.

Another element in the scrap picture is the increasing flow of metal from scrapped industrial equipment. This recovery of gold from obsolete electronics, telecommunications, and computer equipment continues even in times of low gold prices, because the technology of recovery has advanced and the recycling business has developed substantially since the late 1970s. Even so, the recovery of scrap from these sources may diminish during the next few years because this kind of equipment has contained less gold since 1980. Manufacturers began to curtail their use of gold, or to substitute other metals, following the extraordinary price rise early that year.

What does all this mean for the investor? Total secondary supplies are likely to increase in a meaningful fashion only if the price of gold rises dramatically in the future. Certainly, the price must rise well above $500 per ounce before growth in the secondary supply again becomes an issue.

But, at some price level, the flow of scrap again may become great enough to restrain a further increase or even reverse the price. The substantial flow of secondary supply during 1980 was a major reason for the steep price reversal that followed. As an investor, you must watch the flow of scrap, especially at high price levels, because it is one of the fundamental indicators of a possible price reversal.

THE THIRD SOURCE

There is one other major source that furnishes gold for the market, and it is the hardest of all to forecast. Major amounts of gold come each year from sales by nations with centrally planned economies—especially the Soviet Union. Several of these countries—the Soviet Union, the People's Republic of China, and North Korea—are blessed with important mine deposits. Our interest, though, is not how much they produce but rather how much they sell.

Unlike the long-term trend in Western gold mining or the flow of scrap, sales from these countries appear to be dictated in many instances more by their foreign-exchange needs than by the price of the metal. This is not to suggest that the centrally planned countries ignore the market. Like shrewd traders, they try to sell at as high a price as they can. If their foreign exchange and their balance of payments will permit, they may reduce their sales at times of price weakness, and during short-term

EXHIBIT 2-4 The Centrally Planned Economy Picture

	1980	1981	1982	1983	1984	1985
USSR Grain Imports (in billions of U.S. dollars)	1.52	1.71	2.32	0.983	2.3	1.7
Centrally Planned Gold Sales (in millions of ounces)	2.9	9.0	6.5	3.0	4.0	10.0
Average Comex Spot Price (in U.S. dollars)	611.97	458.49	375.59	423.45	360.40	317.60

SOURCE: American Precious Metals Advisors, Inc.; U.S. Department of Agriculture.

intervals—day to day or week to week—prices and market conditions may dominate their sales. But, overall, it would appear that foreign-exchange requirements and balance-of-payments trends are the dominating influences.

Exhibit 2-4 demonstrates how sales from these nations in any given year are not correlated closely with the metal's price. In 1980, when the price of gold hit its peak, centrally planned economy sales totaled only 2.9 million ounces—off sharply from the previous year's figure of 6.4 million. In 1981, although the price of gold had dropped sharply from the 1980 high, centrally planned economy gold sales rose to 9 million ounces. They declined to 6.5 million ounces in 1982, then dropped sharply to 3 million ounces in 1983, even though gold prices recovered that year. The lack of correlation was apparent again in 1984, when gold prices dropped but centrally planned economy sales rose anyway, to 4 million ounces—and especially in 1985, when those sales rose dramatically to 10 million ounces, despite continued softness in market prices.

While price appears to bear little relationship to the quantity of gold sold by the centrally planned countries, the size of the grain harvests in the Soviet Union and elsewhere in Eastern Europe do provide a fairly good determinant. Statistics from the U.S. Department of Agriculture on U.S. grain sales to the Soviet Union give an indication of how abundant the harvest was each year in the centrally planned nations. In 1980, those sales totaled $1.52 billion. The following year, the total was

$1.71 billion. And in 1982, the total was $2.32 billion—a record level at the time. In 1983, a time when gold sales from centrally planned countries dipped to only 3 million ounces, grain sales by the United States to the Soviet Union totaled only $983 *million*—the lowest figure in nine years.

Grain sales, however, are only part of the picture. In nations with centrally planned economies, the overall balance of payments is the underlying reason why gold sales vary from year to year. If the governments of those countries have sufficient foreign exchange to cover their import requirements, there is no reason to sell gold, regardless of how much grain they may purchase from the West. In recent years, a declining volume and value of Soviet oil exports has been a major factor in the deterioration of that country's overall trade position, and along with poor harvests may help explain the step-up in Soviet gold sales in 1985 and 1986. One information source overlooked by many professional analysts is the quarterly report from the Bank of International Settlements headquartered in Basel, Switzerland—an institution known as the central banks' central bank. This report provides an overall indication of the dollar value of deposits held in Western bank accounts by the centrally planned nations. When these deposits are low, the nations are more likely to be sellers of gold.

In recent years, the Soviet Union (like many developing countries) has been using gold to collateralize loans from international banks rather than raising funds by actually selling the metal. As a result, even the traditional relationship between poor grain harvests or heavy foreign currency needs and rising gold sales may be weakening.

As in the case of the Golden Rule cited by George Bernard Shaw, there is no rule—there is only opinion—when it comes to interpreting centrally planned gold sales. For the investor looking at this source of gold, there is only one rule: WATCH OUT!

OFFICIAL TRANSACTIONS AND HOLDINGS

Central banks, national monetary authorities, and other official agencies such as the International Monetary Fund (IMF) may at times be yet another important supplier of gold to the marketplace. But, at other times, central banks may be net buyers,

EXHIBIT 2–5   Official Gold Holdings,* Selected Countries and
Regions (year-end data—millions of ounces)

Country or Region	1979	1985	Change
All Countries	944.44	948.89	+ 4.45
Industrial Countries	789.06	786.49	− 2.57
Developing Countries	152.98	157.38	+ 4.40
Africa	18.79	14.05	− 4.74
Asia	32.28	35.97	+ 3.69
Middle East	33.42	37.75	+ 4.33
Latin America	30.93	32.48	+ 1.55
United States	264.60	262.65	− 1.95
Germany	95.25	95.18	− 0.07
Switzerland	83.28	83.28	—
France	81.92	81.85	− 0.07
Italy	66.71	66.67	− 0.04
Belgium	34.21	34.18	− 0.03
Japan	24.23	24.23	—
South Africa	10.03	4.84	− 5.19
India	8.56	9.40	+ 0.04
Indonesia	0.28	3.10	+ 2.82
Portugal	22.13	20.23	− 1.90
Brazil	1.70	3.10	+ 1.40
International Monetary Fund	106.83	103.42	− 3.41
European Monetary Co-Op Fund	85.29	85.71	+ 0.42
Bank for International Settlements	8.60	6.69	− 1.91
World Total	1,145.14	1,144.74	− 0.40

*Reported to International Monetary Fund.
SOURCE: International Financial Statistics.

affecting the demand side of the gold balance rather than
supply. In 1980, such purchases resulted in the removal of an
additional 7.4 million ounces from the marketplace. In other
words, this sector was a big buyer of gold. By contrast, during
1983, official transactions resulted in an additional 3.5 million
ounces being placed on the market, as central banks became
important net sellers of gold. During 1985 and 1986, after a
couple of years of net official sales, central banks, as a group,
began buying gold again—currently, all indications are they will
continue to be net buyers. Net purchases by the central banks
amounted to 3 million ounces in 1985 and totaled between 4
and 5 million ounces by the close of 1986. Exhibit 2–5 provides
greater details about trends in official holdings.

Official transactions sometimes are tied to the strength or weakness of a country's currency and its ability to meet its foreign indebtedness. Though several developed countries bought gold during 1983—that is, they reduced the amount of metal otherwise available—this was more than offset by distress selling by several less developed nations. Even when a nation attempts to aid its local mining industry by buying its own gold output, as was the case in 1983 with Zimbabwe and Zaire, it sometimes is forced to sell its new purchases quickly in order to raise desperately needed foreign exchange.

Such a case demonstrates how fine the line can be between sources of supply and sources of demand. A similar situation developed in 1980, when one of the major demand factors was hoarding by Middle East buyers concerned about the combat and uncertainty in that region. This demand turned to supply when Iran sold gold in order to raise money to help finance its war against Iraq.

Some of the central banks that sold in distress in 1982 and in 1983 have now run out of gold to sell, and a few have begun to repurchase gold in order to rebuild their official reserves. Among the biggest buyers in the past year have been countries like Brazil and the Philippines, which, in the prior two years, were debtors scraping the bottom of their official reserve coffers. These countries and others with domestic gold-mining industries have more than once bought gold to shore up their international reserve positions. And because they pay for the gold in their local currency, there is no foreign exchange cost in building up their official gold reserves. Recent purchases by The Central Bank of Peru are perhaps indicative of a new trend toward increased gold holdings among the more hard-pressed, debt-ridden nations. It has been reducing its official dollar-denominated reserves and substituting gold—1986 purchases totaled $200 million. As the international debt crisis intensifies, it will be interesting to note whether other developing nations follow Peru's lead and turn, once again, to the safety of gold.

For a monthly snapshot of central bank gold transactions, the investor can read the *International Financial Statistics* published by the International Monetary Fund in Washington, D.C. This publication is available in many business and university libraries.

THE DEMAND SIDE

Official sales and purchases are only a thin slice of the overall supply/demand pie. On the demand side, fabricators' needs and private investors' purchases are far more important. In recent years, total gold demand for fabrication into jewelry and other manufactured items averaged about 35 million ounces per year. Of that total, about 3.5 million ounces went into electronic products, slightly more than 2 million ounces were used for dentistry purposes, an average of about 28 million ounces annually was consumed by the jewelry industry, and the balance went into other industrial applications. Exhibit 2–6 shows the breakdown in industrial demand, by use, since 1974.

Like most elements in the gold market, the line between investment demand and fabrication demand is usually somewhat fuzzy, at least within the jewelry sector. Analytically, it makes sense to subdivide the jewelry industry into two separate categories of demand. On the one hand, gold jewelry in developed or industrialized countries is valued principally for its ornamental worth and often is purchased as a luxury item. In less developed countries, on the other hand, gold jewelry is most often bought and held as an investment and store of wealth. Exhibit 2–6 shows how gold jewelry consumption has differed in recent years in industrialized and developing nations. Notice how much more volatile the year-to-year changes in gold use have been in developing countries, reflecting the investment quality of that demand. In 1980, in fact, demand dropped sharply in the developing countries, as purchases of gold jewelry were offset by the resale of large quantities of old jewelry back into the market. Hoarders and others were selling their gold at that time in order to take advantage of the sharp price rise. In the industrialized countries, there was a dip in consumption that year to 11 million ounces. But even the high prices were not enough to totally discourage purchases, since the primary motivation was not investment but appearance.

The recovery and renewed business expansion in many of the world's economies in the mid-1980s also led to a rise in the demand for jewelry and other manufactured items containing gold. However, that renewed demand did not translate into an

EXHIBIT 2-6 Industrial Gold Demand (in millions of troy ounces)

	1974	1975	1976	1977	1978	1979	1980	1981	1982	1983	1984	1985	1986*
Industrial:													
Electronics	3.0	2.2	2.5	2.5	2.8	3.5	3.2	3.1	3.0	3.3	3.7	3.9	4.1
Dentistry	1.8	2.0	2.5	2.5	2.5	2.8	2.0	2.2	2.0	1.7	1.8	1.9	2.0
Other	2.2	1.8	2.8	2.1	2.3	1.8	1.4	1.3	1.2	1.5	1.2	1.2	1.3
Jewelry:													
Industrial Nations	9.0	10.2	15.3	17.4	19.0	19.2	11.0	13.8	15.4	14.2	16.0	18.0	19.8
Developing Nations	(1.7)	6.6	14.9	14.9	13.3	10.5	6.8	11.4	13.6	12.6	13.5	14.0	14.2
Total Demand	14.3	22.8	38.0	39.4	39.9	37.8	24.4	31.8	35.2	33.3	36.2	39.0	41.4

Note: Periods of dishoarding are indicated by parentheses; (*) denotes estimates; figures rounded to the nearest digit.
SOURCES: American Precious Metals Advisors; Consolidated Goldfields, Ltd.; Gold Information Center—Investment Service.

increase in gold usage by all the industries producing such items. Investors can no longer assume that even a broad, well-based economic and business cycle upturn will automatically lead on a one-to-one basis to an increase in demand for gold. One important reason is the recent trend in the jewelry industry toward fabrication of lower karatage items and hollow wire and tubing for the manufacture of chains and bangles, for instance, instead of solid filaments. This has been a response to the much higher price levels that have prevailed since 1980. Even at the 1982–84 lows of less than $300 an ounce, gold remained well above even the peak prices from the period that ended in 1979. Consumer resistance—stiffened by the inability of many consumers to afford gold jewelry at the higher price levels—has led manufacturers to reduce the amount of gold they use per item.

Rings that once were made from 18- or 14-karat gold may be fabricated now from 10- or 12-karat metal. Bracelets and necklaces that used to be solid are often made now of hollow tubular metal. And buyers had better beware, for this kind of metal still qualifies as karat gold in some countries. In the United States, for example, jewelry made of 10-karat or more qualifies as real gold. Jewelry items such as these tend to weigh much less than their 1970s counterparts. As a consequence, even though the volume of jewelry sales picked up considerably in 1983–84, the amount of gold used by this industry remained well below the levels that previous history would have suggested.

In addition to the cited use of lower karatage and lighter weight jewelry, there also have been trends toward economies of usage and substitution of less expensive metals—particularly palladium in both electronic and dental applications. As a result, consumption of gold in most end-use sectors disappointed the expectations of many who, since 1983, have banked on stronger demand and economic fundamentals to sustain higher prices for the metal.

THE BALANCE—INVESTMENT DEMAND

Subtracting total demand for gold by jewelry manufacturers and other industrial fabricators from the total supply, and adjusting for official sales or purchases, leaves us with a surplus.

In the gold market, as in any market, the iron law dictates that supply must equal demand. By definition, any surplus will be equal to the amount of gold purchased by investors on a net worldwide basis. In 1983, this surplus, equivalent to investor demand, equaled roughly 20.4 million ounces—a sharp increase over the previous year's figure, which was just under 14 million ounces. In 1984 and 1985, the surpluses amounted to approximately 17 million and 16.5 million, respectively. In 1986, this surplus was somewhat smaller still—between 14 and 15 million ounces. To put the picture in perspective, if investors wanted to purchase the same quantity of gold in 1986 they had bought in the past year, it would have been impossible for them to do so. Something had to give—and that something was the price. Exhibit 2–7 shows how this investment demand has broken down recently. Looking ahead, the price outlook depends on how big the surplus of gold will be before it is fully absorbed by investors, after accounting for the other sectors of supply.

By any yardstick, the 1983 surplus was a hefty quantity for private investors to absorb, especially at a time when inflation appeared to be under control. There were high and rising interest rates and the U.S. dollar was extraordinarily strong; these factors contributed to reduce investor interest in gold. In other words, there was more gold available for investors at a time when they were least likely to be interested in acquiring it. Since the market must strike a balance between supply and demand, the price of gold dropped from 1983 into 1985 until it reached levels where investors were willing to purchase precisely the quantity available to them—the "surplus."

It is this "surplus," combined with investors' desire to acquire it, that determines the price of gold. If the surplus is large and there is little investor interest, the price will drop to a level at which it is once again attractive to investors. If the surplus is small or there is great investor interest, the price will rise through competitive bidding until it reaches a point where investors feel it is too costly to continue augmenting their holdings.

The intensity of investors' interest is determined by a number of factors: how much money people have available to buy gold, how safe they feel holding cash and other investment

EXHIBIT 2-7 Gold Investment Demand—Coins versus Bullion (millions of troy ounces)

	1979	1980	1981	1982	1983	1984	1985	1986*
Coin and Medallions	10.4	6.5	7.0	4.9	6.3	5.6	2.6	12.5
Bullion and Bars	17.3	16.1	7.1	9.0	14.1	11.6	13.9	2.8
Total	27.7	22.6	14.1	13.9	20.4	17.2	16.5	15.3

Note: Please note that, in this table, investment demand is broken down into two components—official coins, medallions, and fake coins; and bullion and bars. Because coins represent actual sales, the data here may differ from official fabrication statistics published in yearly industry reports.

*Denotes APMA projections.

SOURCE: American Precious Metals Advisors, Inc.

assets instead of gold—and, most importantly, the relative returns on other assets versus the expected return on gold as it appreciates. When the surplus is particularly large in relation to investors' willingness to add to their total holdings of gold, then the price falls. And at each successively lower price level, there are some additional investors who believe, rightly or wrongly, that the price is near a trough and the potential for appreciation warrants purchasing the metal. The process of price reduction continues until investors are willing to buy enough gold to bring the market into supply/demand equilibrium.

Let us look at examples to see how this process of price determination actually works. In 1982, as inflation in the United States and elsewhere began to ebb from the double-digit rates of the previous five years, the price of gold in London worked itself down to $296.75 per ounce on June 21. At that point, after a lackluster spring, trading on the Commodity Exchange gold futures market, one indicator of investment interest in gold, sparked up. This increase in demand was fueled in large measure by the relatively low, "affordable" price of the metal and investors' expectations that gold's potential appreciation had become competitive with yields from other investments.

Of more immediate interest is what happened to the surplus in 1986. As noted, projections for total supplies are a record of 60.2 million ounces, while total fabrication demand from all sectors is estimated at 41.4 million ounces. This tightening of the supply/demand balance suggested a mildly bullish scenario for the gold price as the year wore on. In order to balance the market, prices rose as more buyers—both governments and investors—competed for a shrinking quantity of metal. Exhibit 2–8 gives a roundup of gold's recent statistical position.

EQUITY MARKET FUNDAMENTALS

The fundamentals I have mentioned so far are those that apply to the price of gold, along with supply and demand. In analyzing the price of an equity, such as a gold-mining stock, fundamentalists will look at a company's earnings, dividends, and

EXHIBIT 2-8 Gold's Statistical Position (in millions of troy ounces)

	1980	1981	1982	1983	1984	1985	1986*
Supply:							
Primary Mine Production of Market Economies	30.2	30.9	32.4	35.7	36.9	39.0	40.7
Secondary Supply	21.2	10.5	11.1	11.5	10.5	9.5	8.5
Centrally Planned Economy Sales	2.9	9.0	6.5	3.0	4.0	10.0	11.0
Fabrication Demand:							
Industrial	6.6	6.6	6.2	6.5	6.7	7.0	7.4
Jewelry	17.8	25.2	29.0	26.8	29.5	32.0	34.0
Total Fabrication Demand	24.3	31.8	35.2	33.3	36.2	39.0	41.4
Stock Changes:							
Official Purchases or (Sales)	7.4	4.5	1.0	(−3.5)	(−2.0)	3.0	3.5
Net Private Investment	22.6	14.1	13.9	20.4	17.2	16.5	15.3
Total Stock Changes	30.0	18.6	14.9	15.9	15.2	19.5	18.8
Total Demand (Fabrication plus Stock Changes)	54.3	50.4	50.0	50.2	51.4	58.5	60.2

Note: Figures in parentheses represent dishoarding or sales.
*APMA forecasts; figures rounded to the nearest digit.
SOURCE: American Precious Metals Advisors, Inc.

production costs and other business factors. For someone who invests in the equity markets, these are quite clearly important considerations in determining whether the per-share price of a stock is reasonable. But, as I will point out in Chapter 8, Gold-Mining Equities, the price of gold also can play a very important part in determining the value of an individual stock. Before you invest in any gold-related instrument, be it equities, gold bullion, gold futures, or options, it is important to first understand and analyze the metal and its fundamentals.

Although fundamentals are what govern the behavior of a market over the longer term, perhaps even several years, they are not formed of bedrock—or even fabricated in gold. If you had analyzed the gold market in late 1979 and early 1980, you would have perceived several factors that were fundamentally bullish for gold prices—that pointed to the likelihood that those prices would increase, as indeed they did. As I mentioned earlier, there was military conflict, inflation was high, and the value of many currencies was depressed. All these factors contributed to a rising demand for gold. At the same time, gold-mining production had been dropping for a decade. Your fundamental analysis would have pointed rightly to higher prices—though not, perhaps, to such a strong gain as developed. The situation in the spring of 1980, when gold prices fell, has often been termed a technical correction—one that followed a sharp upward price spike that lifted gold briefly to more than $850 per ounce. However, the correction actually reflected a change in the *fundamentals*. The high prices of the preceding months had attracted an overwhelming amount of scrap into the market and was discouraging jewelry, industrial, and even investor trade, tilting the supply/demand balance to a condition of oversupply.

Fundamentals, like the sands of the Sahara, are constantly shifting, even though they—like the Sahara—may seem motionless. Sometimes, as happened in 1980, this shift will be subtle. Technical analysis often can be useful in detecting times when such a shift is possible or even probable—when market fundamentals have to be rethought. And if you are to think as an analyst, you must constantly be prepared to rethink your position.

The London Fix

Twice each day, the eyes and ears of the international gold markets turn almost religiously toward London. What is the fix? Ah, that is the question! At one time, London was the center of global gold trading, and the Bank of England was the most important institution in the whole realm of gold. The reason was simple: The United Kingdom controlled South Africa, the world's most important source of gold, and also reigned supreme on the high seas.

The pound may no longer be "sound the world 'round," but for gold traders there will always be an England.

The twice-daily fixing of the gold price in London, a price that forms the basis for many contracts dealing in physical gold, bears about as much relationship to the hustle, bustle, and noise of U.S. gold futures exchanges as a Viennese masked ball does to a rodeo hoedown. Twice each business day, a representative from each of five major London bullion dealers—Mocatta and Goldsmid, Ltd.; Samuel Montagu & Co.; Sharps Pixley & Co., Ltd.; Johnson Matthey Bankers, Ltd.; and N. M. Rothschild and Sons—gather at the Rothschild offices and sit around a table, a procedure their corporate ancestors followed 150 years ago. The only concession to modern times is a telephone beside each seat connecting the holder to his gold trading desk.

The chairman—traditionally the Rothschild representative—calls out a price at the beginning of the fixing session. In front of each place, next to the telephone, is a small Union Jack. If the person at one of the seats wishes to buy at the announced price, the flag is pointed down; if selling is the intention, the Union Jack is raised. Aside from the chairman's announcement of the price, the only conversation is on the phones, between the representatives and their trading desks. If everyone is a buyer, the chairman raises the price until there are some sellers. Conversely, if everyone indicates an intention to sell, the price is lowered until some buying is attracted. When there are flags both up and down, each participant indicates how much metal he is willing to trade. If there is a mismatch, the chairman will make proposals to bring the quantities in line. Finally, the price is agreed upon and transmitted from the room at N. M. Rothschild to gold trading desks around the world. (It may be only

EXHIBIT 2–9 Gold Price in U.S. Dollars; London P.M. Fix—Yearly

	High	Low	Average
1970	39.30	34.95	36.19
1971	44.25	37.30	41.10
1972	70.30	44.30	58.45
1973	127.00	63.90	97.32
1974	195.25	116.50	159.25
1975	185.25	128.75	161.01
1976	140.35	103.50	124.83
1977	167.95	129.75	147.72
1978	242.75	165.70	193.23
1979	512.00	216.85	306.68
1980	850.00	481.50	612.56
1981	599.25	391.25	459.71
1982	481.00	296.75	375.79
1983	509.25	374.25	424.18
1984	405.85	307.50	360.44
1985	341.15	284.25	317.26
1986	438.35	326.55	361.83

Note: 1986 figures through October.
SOURCE: Handy & Harman.

1:30 in the morning in San Francisco, but there will be people awake and waiting.)

Recent changes in the international gold market—not the least of which has been the growth of futures trading in New York—have tended to lessen the importance of the London fix, with prices also being "fixed" in Paris, Zurich, and Frankfurt, as well as Asian centers such as Tokyo, Singapore, and Hong Kong, for example. Other markets have developed in Sydney, Australia, and Sao Paolo, Brazil. But the prices determined in these centers do not carry the circulation and importance of the London figure.

The London fixing process is an example, in microcosm, of the way the international gold market itself achieves balance. When the price is too high, it is lowered until someone is willing to buy. When it is too low, it is raised until someone is willing to sell. Like the gold market itself, the London activity must always achieve a balance, that is, a point where there are both buyers and sellers.

EXHIBIT 2–10 Where Is Gold Going? (1980–1986)

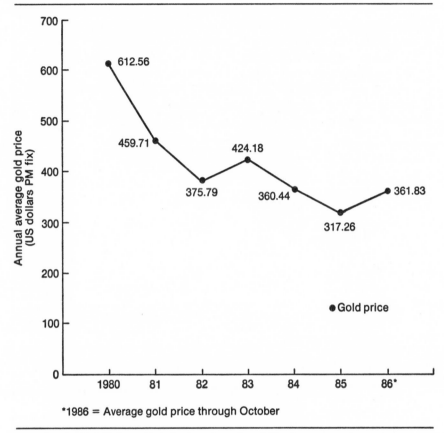

*1986 = Average gold price through October

SOURCE: Gold Information Center—Investment Service.

Jewelry

In the gold industry, "karat" refers to the purity of metal. A 24-karat piece of gold, the purest available, is 99.99 percent gold. Lesser purities are expressed in lower karat values, based on a scale where 24 karats is the highest numerical grade. Thus, a 22-karat piece would be 22/24ths, or 91.67 percent, gold. In some parts of the world, particularly the Mideast and developing nations elsewhere, government standards require gold jewelry to be no less than 18 karat—that is, $^{18}/_{24}$ths or 75 percent pure. Some countries, such as Saudi Arabia and Kuwait, even set a minimum of 21 karat, or 87.5 percent pure. In more developed countries, where gold jewelry tends to be viewed more often as an ornament rather than an investment, lower karatage metal still qualifies legally as "gold." The word "karat," as applied to gold, is not to be confused with the word "carat," which is used in the field of gemology. In the case of diamonds and other gems, "carat" refers to the weight of the stone, not its purity.

CHAPTER THREE

Gold and the Economic Environment

"If you must choose between placing your trust in government or placing your trust in gold, then gentlemen, I strongly advise you to place your trust in gold."

George Bernard Shaw

Supply and demand are the fundamentals of gold, but there are other factors that also have an impact on the price of the yellow metal—even though they cannot be classified as "supply" and "demand" per se. Interest rates, the strength of the U.S. dollar, and a host of other economic and in some cases political variables all play a role in the pricing of gold. These are what are known as *environmental factors:* They do not arise out of the mining or buying of gold, but they can influence whether a miner will continue and expand operations and whether a buyer—an industrial user; you, an investor; or anybody else—will want to buy.

One of the strongest environmental factors in the gold market is the rate of inflation. Since gold is a traditional hedge against inflation, demand for the metal increases when there is either a clear and present danger of inflation or some anticipation that inflation will pose a threat in the future. The best evidence of gold's anti-inflation role came in the price runup of 1979–80, when the U.S. inflation rate soared above 12 percent per year—or, to put it another way, the dollar was losing 12 percent of its value annually. For those fortunate enough to be holding gold instead of dollars, the value of the metal increased by more than 180 percent. This is not to suggest, however, that there is a direct relationship between the rate of inflation and gold's price performance or effectiveness as a hedge. Hedges are used not only as protection against inflation itself but also as insurance policies against an anticipated rise in the rate of inflation. And, clearly, gold responds to many other influences as well. Please note that I have been talking about the U.S. inflation rate. My decision to focus on the U.S. rate is not prompted by chauvinism. Rather, it reflects the U.S. dollar's role as an international investment alternative to gold.

THE U.S. DOLLAR

The role of the U.S. dollar as an investment vehicle, vis-à-vis other currencies, puts it in competition with gold for investment cash, just as equity shares or bonds might be seen as competitors. In 1984, the dollar soared in relationship to other currencies; that is, it took more and more French francs to buy one dollar in 1984 than it did in 1983. While the average small investor does not ordinarily trade foreign currencies, institutions do. In 1984, a great many of these large institutional investors as well as large private investors put their money into dollars—or sold other currencies, which amounts to the same as buying dollars. The return on investments in the dollar far exceeded what they perceived they could earn in the gold market. As a result, demand for gold slackened and the price of the asset dropped accordingly. The pattern moved into reverse during 1985 and 1986. The dollar weakened in relation to foreign currencies and altered the perception that dollars remained a good investment relative to gold. Gold's upward climb intensified as 1986 wore on. In August and September of that year, the dollar's decline was accentuated and the gold price exceeded $440 in London before settling back. The recent relationship between the dollar and gold is referenced in Exhibit 3-1.

The strength or weakness of the dollar is tied closely to the rate of inflation. If inflation is high, it reduces the value of the dollar. Conversely, low inflation raises the value of the currency. Which is the chicken and which is the egg? Sometimes, this is hard to determine. The investor should keep in mind that

EXHIBIT 3-1   Gold Climbs Steadily as Dollar Plummets
(1985-1986)

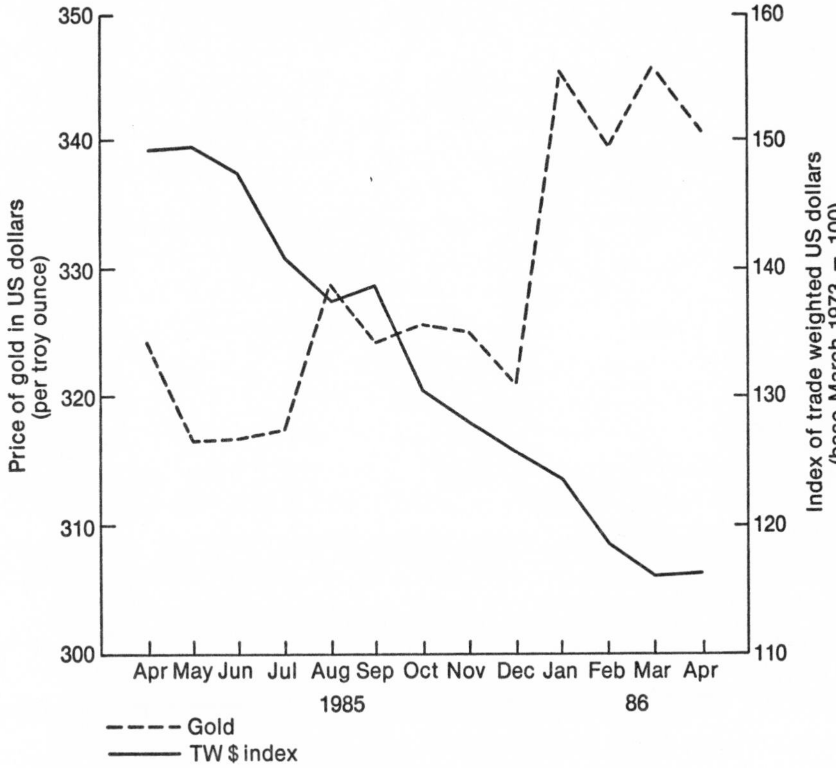

SOURCE: Gold Information Center—Investment Service 1986.

the dollar is not a finite item. With gold, on the other hand, there is only so much in the world. To date, man has been unable to create any more (although there are still attempts to find the "philosopher's stone" which alchemists claim can turn lead into gold). Dollars, on the other hand, are the creation of the U.S. government, just as francs are created by the French and pounds sterling by the British. Though various regimes may pledge not to print money willy-nilly, there is no guarantee that those who come to power next will not reverse policy and once again "turn on the presses."

INTEREST RATES

For a period of several years starting in the early 1980s, investors were dealing not only with low inflation rates and low expectations of impending inflation but also with the fact that investments other than gold were offering returns that substantially exceeded the inflation rate. Even simple passbook savings accounts were paying annual interest in excess of inflation, and money-market accounts were paying interest several percentage points higher.

Some investors view gold as a "sterile investment"—one that does not offer any income in and of itself. (In Chapter 12, Options—the Techniques, I will explain how gold investments can yield profits.) For the average gold investor, whether the instrument is bullion, mining shares, or even futures, profits are achieved by observing the simple adage: "Buy low and sell high." If the gold market will not cooperate, you cannot apply this adage to your investment. A money-market account, on the other hand, does cooperate: It will pay whatever interest rate is advertised. But even if an investor perceives a chance to profit from the traditional buy-low, sell-high technique, the level of that return on investment is also an important consideration.

If you expect the price of gold to appreciate 8 percent in the coming year and your local bank's money-market account is paying 10 percent, no one would consider you a fool for investing in the money-market account instead of gold. You could, however, justify a gold investment on grounds that you were buying the metal or gold-related instruments as part of your "nest egg"—that is, acquiring gold not for an immediate return, but as a more or less permanent part of your estate.

GOLD AS A BAROMETER OF TENSION, ANXIETY

Is gold still to be regarded as a barometer of tension and anxiety? This question has preoccupied many investors over the past few years. In fact, in the past 10 years, prior to 1982, the price of gold has shown a distinct tendency to be swayed by international events much as it had done in the waning years of the Roman Empire. Recently, gold's price stability during certain geopolitical conflicts (such as the U.S. invasion at Grenada or the Libyan crisis) has surprised investors by seemingly ignoring such events.

When the Soviet Union invaded Afghanistan, an act that almost coincided with the taking of U.S. hostages by Iranian religious fanatics in late 1979, gold reacted dramatically to international political uncertainty as it began its meteoric climb from less than $300 to more than $800 per ounce in less than one year. But in 1982 and in 1983, at the time of the Falklands War between the United Kingdom and Argentina and when a Korean civilian jetliner with a U.S. congressman aboard was shot down by the Soviet Union, the price of gold actually fell. In the subsequent years from 1984 to 1986, when the United States invaded Grenada and during the culmination of the Libyan crisis, gold's price was relatively stable—it fluctuated only a few dollars in either direction. These incidents prompted newspaper articles at the time to suggest that gold had lost its role as a barometer of international tension and anxiety.

What differentiated these two episodes—first in 1979-80 when gold shot up and say in 1983 when it fell—was the relative threat that these incidents posed to the world economy and the U.S. dollar. A crisis in the Middle East (particularly one which had the potential to disrupt the world's supply of oil), and which some believed could pull the United States and the Soviet Union into direct military confrontation, sent investors scurrying for a golden security blanket as they shied away from an already unpopular dollar at the time. By 1983, however, the U.S. dollar was again rising on the global foreign exchange market and was, at least temporarily, upstaging gold as a store of value and "safe haven" asset. So, in this circumstance of a "lesser order" crisis, it was the U.S. dollar that benefited at the cost of gold.

In the past few years, international crises have had an inconsistent influence on the price of gold. For gold's price to move sharply upward in the face of world tensions requires that the fundamentals and economics of gold be supportive as well. During the period 1983 onwards, this has not been the case. But now that the dollar is falling, U.S. monetary policy is expanding, and the supply and demand balance in the gold market is tightening, we may expect to see gold once again play its traditional role as a hedge against geopolitical tensions.

THE OIL CONNECTION

In much the same way that international crises have not had a consistent impact on the price of gold over past years, the relationship between oil and gold has been changing. For many years, oil prices were viewed as a reliable indicator of the fortunes of gold, with these precious metals tracking changes in the price of oil. But over the past year or two, gold had exhibited remarkable resilience and maintained a steady market level despite a precipitous slump in oil prices. This is shown in Exhibit 3–2. So, what is the significance of the recent breakdown in the link between oil and gold? And what, if any, are the consequences of lower oil prices for the future of gold?

The conventional wisdom might have projected that the gold prices touch increasingly lower market levels in tandem with oil. In 1985 and 1986, lower oil prices acted as a dampener on inflationary expectations by masking the underlying expansionary bias of the U.S. economy—policies of easy money, bulging federal deficits, and more recently, a depreciating dollar. But these factors contributed to the propping up of the gold price despite oil price weakness. In addition, lower oil prices influenced gold in other ways:

- Lower oil prices stimulated business activity and personal consumption expenditures in the United States and abroad, and some of this increased demand for raw materials was channeled into gold.
- Lower petrodollar earnings caused expectations of increased social and political tensions within and among some of the oil exporting nations. This was apparent not only in the Middle East, but also among some of the other oil debtor countries in Latin America and Africa, whose hard-pressed economies could not accommodate more reductions in domestic economic activity. Because gold has had a long tradition in these parts of the world,

EXHIBIT 3-2   Gold's Remarkable Strength Relative to Oil
(1985-1986)

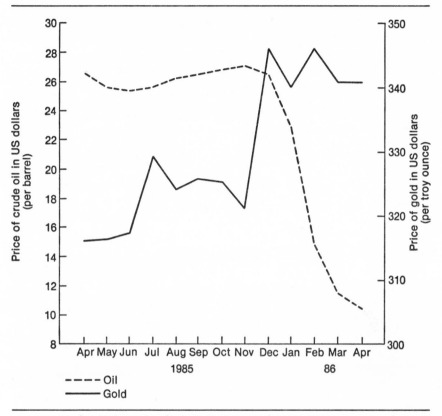

SOURCE: Gold Information Center—Investment Service 1986.

whenever the governments there feel threatened with political instability, they invariably turn to the safety of that monetary asset.

- Most significant, however, is the possibility of default on the loans extended by the large international banks to heavy debtors like Mexico and Nigeria and to energy-related industries in the United States and elsewhere in the industrialized world. Concerns about the possible damage to the stability of the international banking and financial systems arising from an inability to service these debts work to gold's advantage. Such situations generally force the Federal Reserve and other central banks to pursue policies of monetary growth and low interest rate in order to limit the adverse impact of a possible international debt crisis. Evidence of this during 1986 was the orchestrated reduction in international interest rates as the central banks of West Germany, Japan, and the United States acted in concert to lower their official discount rates in early March and again later in the year.

What these last two examples tell us is that we cannot view gold as a barometer of global tension and anxiety without consideration of the host of other fundamental and environmental factors that interact in determining its price.

LOOKING AT THE ENVIRONMENT

Each of the environmental factors I have outlined has an effect on the price of gold. However, they are not causes in and of themselves. As I have pointed out, even though inflation was low beginning in 1984 through 1986 at an annualized rate of 3.5 percent, there still was inflation—and the value of the dollar was being eroded. Interest rates may be high at a given moment, but a shrewd investor will always find some way to make money in the gold markets. The dollar may be strong, but gold prices generally change faster than exchange rates, and the changes can often be more dramatic.

Gold prices are not determined by any one of these environmental factors any more than they are dictated by supply and/ or demand, in and of themselves. The key question is: How much do people want gold? And that, in turn, depends on how they perceive the future of inflation, or interest rates, or the dollar. Humans set the price of gold—or any other good or commodity. Always remember that. Gold does not float in a vacuum. As an investor, you must study other investors and try to discern their views on economic, political, and social conditions in the world. Environmental factors may help explain how they came to hold the views they do, but these are not the causes. You have no assurance that a given view will follow automatically from a given environmental situation.

Now that you have learned the fundamentals of the gold market and the market environment, your next step as an analyst is to take a closer look at the market's behavior—and to do that, we call upon *technical analysis.*

CHAPTER FOUR

Technical Analysis—A Primer

"There are lies, there are damn lies
And there are statistics."

Benjamin Disraeli

It is not completely clear whether Disraeli was placing statistics in the same category as lies and damn lies or whether he was trying to set them apart as the one exception in a world of falsehoods. In either case, statistics should be treated carefully. In the hands of the skilled, they can mislead. In the hands of the uneducated, they can be downright costly.

But statistics are the basis for technical analysis and, at least on a short-term basis, technical analysis can serve as a very useful tool for the gold investor. While fundamental analysis may help us decide whether or not to invest in gold with a medium- to long-term time horizon, technical analysis helps us pick the right moment to invest and the best time to take profits. If you are interested in trading with a short-term orientation, technical analysis is indispensable.

There are several methods of technical analysis—but just as you should not be wed to either technical or fundamental analysis, you also should not tie yourself exclusively to any single technical method. Arthur Sklarew, one of the most respected experts in the field, maintained in his *Techniques of a Professional Commodity Chart Analyst* that a technical analyst should use what he calls the "Rule of Multiple Techniques." Stated simply, this directs the analyst not to rely on just one technical signal but rather to seek confirmation from several different signals. If a simple "high-low-close" bar chart points to a pending change in the direction of gold prices while other technical tools fail to indicate the same potential change, then it probably is best to be cautious and perhaps disregard the bar chart for the time being. You must look to other charts and technical tools for confirmation of what you perceive from the high-low-close bar chart.

Most of the techniques I will talk about in this chapter seem addressed specifically to investors in the gold futures markets—but technical analysis also can apply to gold-mining equities, options, and bullion (although obtaining data on bullion markets is not as easy as it is for futures or equities). Just as you can prepare a high-low-close bar chart of Commodity Exchange gold futures trading, you also can compile one on ASA, Ltd., a closed-end gold-mining mutual fund, or Homestake Mining Company, a major U.S. mining firm, or on options prices or the twice-daily London gold bullion price fix. Although a technical tool may seem to pertain only to the futures markets—for example, gold depository inventories or open interest—these statistics also provide an overall indication of how much interest investors are showing in gold, regardless of the investment vehicle, at any given time.

Even if you feel that your interest in gold involves some other sector of the market such as mining equities or gold bullion coins, I encourage you to look through this chapter. Most of the techniques I will be describing here apply to all the various gold markets, and they will give you a better understanding of what to expect from these markets in the future.

THE BAR CHART

Technical analysis generally begins with construction of charts and graphs which give a visual picture of the market. The high-low-close bar chart is one of the most popular and certainly the simplest form of charting. For an example of a daily high-low-close bar chart, see Exhibit 4–1, page 50, which represents a month of gold futures trading on the Commodity Exchange (Comex) in New York. (Such a chart also could be used to illustrate the high-low-close for trading in an individual gold-mining equity or a gold-based mutual fund.) The vertical line for each trading day shows the total range for that day, that is, the highest and lowest prices, while the small horizontal line

---

EXHIBIT 4–1 Daily High-Low-Close Bar Chart

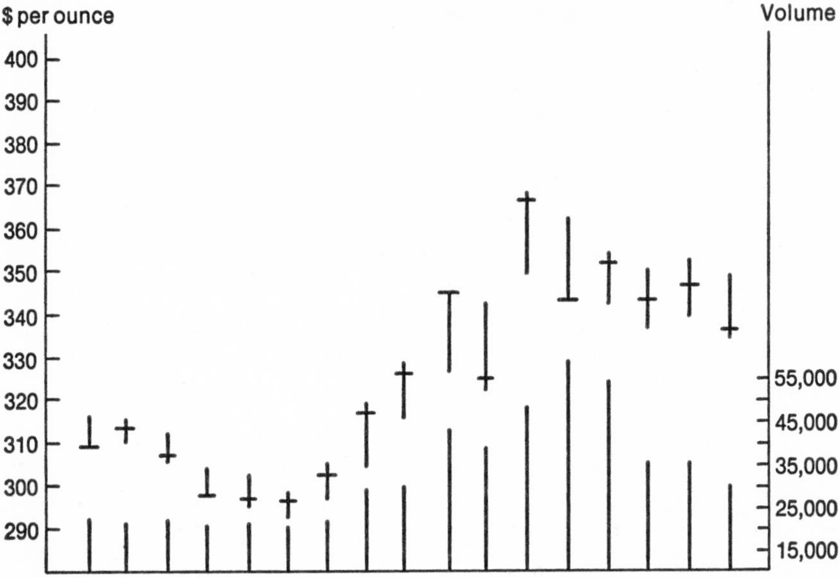

intersecting the vertical bar indicates the settlement price for the day. The settlement price, often referred to simply as the closing price, is the official price established by an exchange committee and represents the level which, in the committee's view, best reflected the market at the end of the trading day. More importantly, this is the price used to mark outstanding contracts to the market—the price at which they can be settled— and is used to determine who will face margin calls the next day.

Simply looking at a bar chart will give you a quick picture of the direction of a market as well as how volatile it is—how wide the trading range is—on an intraday basis and also over a period of many days and weeks. If the daily vertical line is a short one, this tells you the price range was narrow that day. You also could plot the daily volume—the number of futures contracts traded each day—on such a chart, by using a different vertical scale on the right side of the page, as I have done in Exhibit 4–1.

The daily vertical line represents the volatility. As a rule, the longer this line is, the greater the volatility and the higher the volume for the day.

If you are interested in following gold's performance through high-low-close bar charts of daily, weekly, and monthly prices, you can subscribe to one of several chart services covering the commodity futures and/or stock markets (see Appendix D, Information Sources about Gold and Gold Investments), or you can do the charting yourself. To draw a bar chart, take a piece of graph paper and draw a horizontal line near the bottom and a vertical line near the left-hand side. The horizontal line will be your time scale. If it is to be a daily chart, for example, each box would equal one day. For a weekly or monthly chart, each box would represent a longer time period. The vertical line is your price scale. Normally, you can let every 5 or 10 spaces equal one, five, or ten dollars. That should give you ample room to enter gold prices each day, week, or month to reflect trading on U.S. futures exchanges, or the daily London fixes. If you are charting the prices of gold-mining equities, a smaller scale might prove more workable—say, 50 cents per box or even 25 cents. A serious analyst updates a high-low-close bar chart daily.

FINDING TRENDS

Now that you have constructed a bar chart, you have a basic tool for identifying market trends. If a quick look at the chart shows that the price of gold or a gold-related investment is rising, take a ruler and connect the highest point at the beginning of the move with the highest point at the end. Then put your pencil on the lowest point and draw a second line roughly parallel to the first, connecting the lowest point at the beginning of the trend with the lowest point at the end. If the market is indeed in an uptrend, this will give you a channel. (If the two lines are not parallel, then you have uncovered a chart formation such as a triangle, rectangle, flag, or pennant—subjects I will explain a little later in this chapter.) Exhibit 4–2 shows a parallel channel in an uptrending market. A downtrending market would show a downward-sloping channel. These chan-

---

EXHIBIT 4–2 Bar Chart with Channel

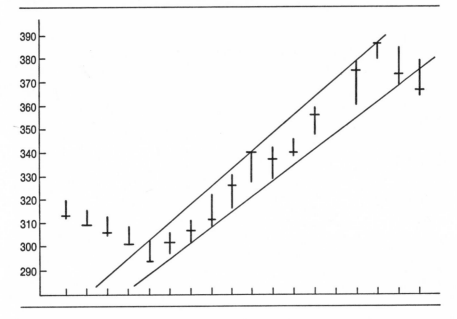

---

nels are excellent indicators of where trading "stop orders" should be placed—a topic I will cover in Chapter 10, Futures—the Techniques.

MINOR TRENDS

Channels such as these which last for several weeks, months, or years are defined as major trends. Within these major trends, there usually will be what technicians call "minor-trend patterns." Often, these will form a zigzag within a major-trend channel. Even if the market is not in a noticeable major uptrend or downtrend, minor trends still may be detectable. If the minor trend shows ascending highs and ascending lows—each high over a few days or weeks is higher than the previous high, while each low over the same period is also higher than the previous low—this is actually a gradually uptrending market. It may not be of Everest proportions, but nevertheless it is uptrending. If, on the other hand, there are descending highs and

EXHIBIT 4–3   Major and Minor Trend Lines:
Weekly High-Low-Close Bar

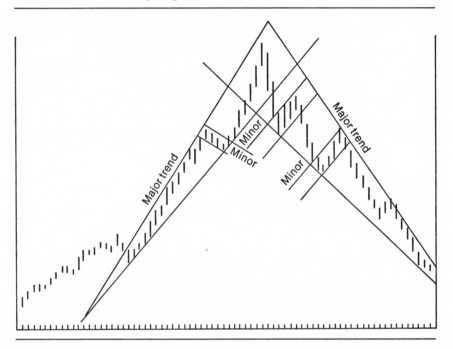

lows over the same period, it is a gradually downtrending market. Such markets may not require immediate action, but they should be watched carefully, perhaps using some of the other techniques I will discuss shortly. Exhibit 4–3 shows examples of both major and minor up- and downtrends.

KEY REVERSALS

One of the things a chartist looks for is a *key reversal* of a trend. This occurs after prices move in one direction—say, lower—over a period of time; then, in one single trading day, a new low for the move or trend is established before prices turn higher and the gold market closes at a higher price for the day. A key reversal, as the name suggests, could represent the start of a new trend. If the new high price at the close on a key-reversal day is higher than the previous day's high, the day is called an

EXHIBIT 4–4 Key Reversal

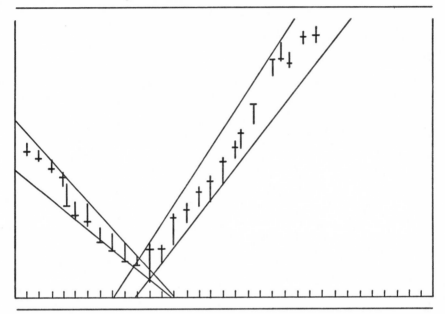

outside day—an occurrence which indicates strongly that a basic change might take place soon in the market. If the new high is higher than the previous settlement price but not higher than the previous day's high, and the low is higher than the prior day's low, it has been an *inside day* and is not as significant.

The most significant change in a bar chart comes when the highs or lows for a particular day not only exceed the previous day's activity on an outside day but also penetrate a channel. Exhibit 4–4 shows such a breakthrough in a channel on the Comex gold market.

BAR CHART FORMATIONS

Trend lines and channels are just two of the formations an analyst can detect on a bar chart. Another classic and often significant chart pattern that may be formed over a longer period of time, such as a week or a month, is a "head-and-shoulders" formation. As the name suggests, this resembles a

EXHIBIT 4–5 Head and Shoulders

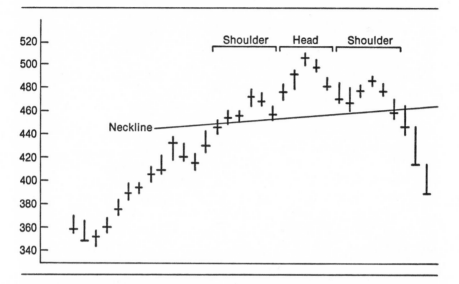

stick drawing of a man shrugging his shoulders. A head-and-shoulders formation indicates that the market's momentum—either up or down—has been broken, and a reversal may be at hand. Exhibit 4-5 illustrates such a pattern. If it were turned upside down, it would be known as a "reverse head and shoulders."

Head-and-shoulders formations are characterized by a series of three price moves, with the first and third less extreme than the one in the middle. In charting such a series of developments, you first should mark out channel lines on a high-low-close bar chart showing the three price moves to determine whether you have a true head-and-shoulders formation. Imagine the first price rally as the "right arm and shoulder" of the formation (as it faces you), the second and ultimate high as the "head," and the third high (which does not reach the high of the previous move but may be higher than the first move) as the "left arm and shoulder." Then you can draw a "neckline." This is the line that connects the lowest points of the right and left shoulders. A true head-and-shoulders formation will show prices dropping below the neckline to form a left arm—and in many cases, if the price does break down through the neckline, it indicates that the market is moving sharply lower. If this is the case, the head was indeed the high point for that market move and prices may drop back to the start of the "right arm," or near that point. A textbook on the subject would say that this formation forecasts a decline equal to the distance from the head to the neckline.

RECTANGLES, TRIANGLES, PENNANTS, AND FLAGS

Looking at a high-low-close bar chart, you will sometimes see geometric forms, or patterns that resemble common objects, rather than a parallel channel. Technicians refer to these forms as rectangles, triangles, pennants, or flags. Quite often, they are indicators not of a change in market direction but simply of a pause in that direction. They usually result from congestion in trading, that is, a period when prices appear to be hovering around one level. Whether the formation simply represents a pause or actually indicates the start of a reversal depends on the fundamental factors governing the market. But identifying these patterns is highly useful, especially in planning a short-term trading program.

A *rectangle* is an extended horizontal drift on a high-low-close bar chart, with the top of the rectangle forming a resistance level and the bottom forming a support line. Exhibit 4–6 shows a rectangle pattern formed on the Comex gold futures market. A breakout from a rectangle could be either up or down, though it probably would be in the same direction as the major trend that preceded the formation of the rectangle. When a breakout occurs, there is a good chance that the high-low-close bar chart line graphing the breakout will be as long, or almost as long, as the two sides of the rectangle itself. Thus, while this technical analysis may not tell you when the breakout will occur, it can indicate the extent of the breakout.

Technical analysts recognize three types of *triangles:* symmetrical, ascending, and descending. Exhibit 4–7 illustrates all three. A symmetrical triangle is one where the top is a downtrending resistance line and the bottom is an uptrending support line. An ascending triangle has an uptrending resist-

EXHIBIT 4–6   Rectangle

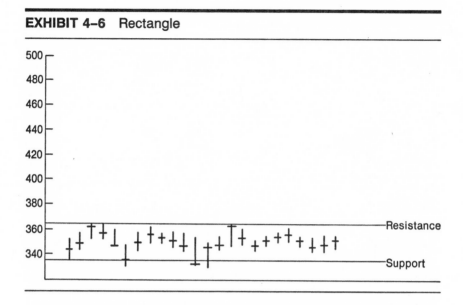

ance line along the top but a horizontal line at the bottom demarking a support level. A descending triangle has a downtrending support line at the bottom of the pattern, with a horizontal resistance line at the top. Rarely will a triangle be perfect. Just remember, when you see one forming, in all likelihood it is not a break in the former trend of the market.

A *flag* or *pennant* is a chart formation that looks roughly like a rectangle or triangle drawn around a price move. The rectangular formation is a flag, the triangular one a pennant. But unlike the rectangle and triangle formations, which are horizontal, flags and pennants are either ascending or descending. If the flag or pennant is sloping down, with the top of the longest side of the shape on the left, this is considered a "bull" formation—evidence of a temporary downtrend that constitutes a break in a continuing uptrending market. If the flag or pennant is sloping up, with the top of the longest side of the shape on the right, then it is considered a "bear" formation— evidence of a temporary uptrend. To be a true flag or pennant, the formation must have a flagpole. This is formed by a sharp move in one direction over a short time span. The flagpole for a bull flag or pennant is a spurt in price that makes up the left-

EXHIBIT 4–7 Triangles

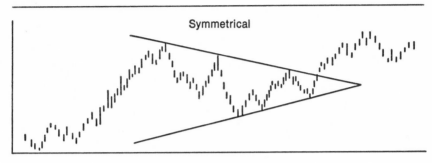

Symmetrical

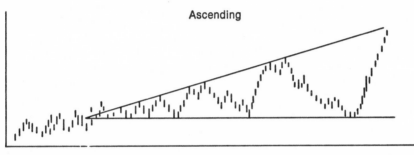

Ascending

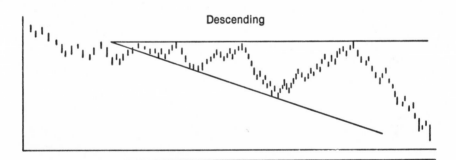

Descending

hand side of the formation. The flagpole for a bear flag or pennant is a drop in price on the left-hand side, followed by the rising flag or pennant. Exhibit 4–8 shows bull flag and pennant formations on the Comex. Note that the long sides of the shapes form downward-sloping channels. When prices broke through those channels on the upside, the flag or pennant was completed.

EXHIBIT 4-8   Bull Flag Formation

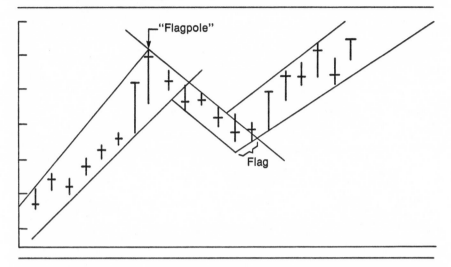

Flags and pennants are *short-term trends within a general market move going opposite to the longer term trend.* If you observe a downtrend or uptrend for which there seems to be no fundamental reason, there is a good chance you are witnessing the start of a flag or pennant, and not a reversal in the general direction of the market.

SLOPES

A slope resembles a flag, but instead of running opposite to the previous direction of the market, it goes in the same direction. It occurs after a steep move in one direction—a quick run up or down on a high-low-close bar chart. While the trend of the slope is the same, the movement is not as rapid. Exhibit 4–9 shows a slope. For the technical analyst, a slope indicates an impending reversal: It is a sign that the market is approaching an overbought or oversold condition.

In an oversold market, there are few holders of gold willing to sell at the current price level. Consequently, prices in all likelihood must rise before new sellers can be attracted. In an overbought market, there are few new buyers willing to pay a

---

EXHIBIT 4–9 Slope

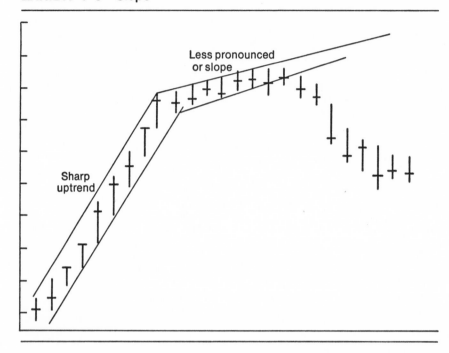

---

higher price—or even the current level—and prices will begin trending lower. When prices break out of a slope and the market begins reversing the trend, the prices often rise or fall beyond the starting point of the slope and continue in the new direction until they reach the next price-congestion area.

DOUBLE TOPS, DOUBLE BOTTOMS

Occasionally, the price of gold will form a new high for a move, retreat, and then head back up to the vicinity of the previous high. If the price fails to break through into higher territory and abruptly drops, this is known as a *double-top* formation. The mirror image of this is known as a *double bottom*. Double tops and double bottoms are indications that the market does not have enough fundamental impetus to continue in whatever direction it was headed before the extremes were reached. It is almost as if the market has run out of steam. Exhibit 4–10

EXHIBIT 4–10 Double Top

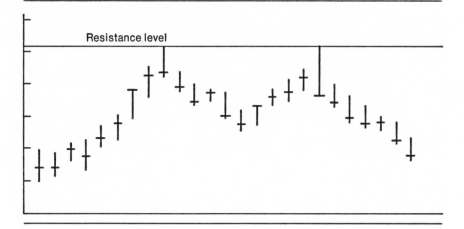

illustrates a double top. Now and then, markets may even try a third time, forming a triple top or bottom. This is an even stronger indication that the previous extremes were unsustainable—that the price has run its course and may be in the process of reversing.

GAPS

If you look at a daily price chart extending over several months, you will note that as a rule, each day's activity overlaps the range for the previous trading day. When ranges fail to overlap, this creates what chartists call a *gap*. Exhibit 4–11 illustrates what is known as a "breakaway gap"—one that occurs at the start of a trend change. Technicians classify gaps as either *common, breakaway, midway* (or *runaway*), and *exhaustion*.

The *common gap* is the most frequent, though chartists generally do not regard it as significant. This kind of gap occurs within congested periods that have few discernible price trends. Almost always, common gaps are filled immediately or within a few daily trading sessions. The *breakaway gap* is more significant because, as I mentioned, it often is the start of a new price move. Unlike common gaps, breakaway gaps usually do *not* get filled, since the gap area tends to serve as resistance. If

---

EXHIBIT 4–11   Breakaway Gap

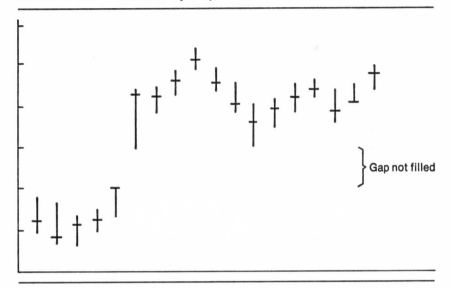

Gap not filled

---

such a gap does get filled, that suggests that the market move was not a true breakaway but only a false signal that a trend had been reversed.

Midway gaps occur part-way through a price move. They serve to break up a trend and are sometimes filled and sometimes not. In general, if your combined technical and fundamental analysis indicates that a trend should continue, then midway gaps are not particularly significant.

Exhaustion gaps often occur when a market trend has been exhausted. It is almost as if the market is making a final gasp before reversing. An exhaustion gap takes place after a trend has been firmly established. In other words, the price of gold has been increasing or decreasing over a sustained period and then there is a sudden gap. If you observe a gap in the wake of a long-established trend, you should be wary: It may be an exhaustion gap presaging a reversal. Exhibit 4–12 shows one of the best examples of an exhaustion gap: the Comex gold market in January 1980, when the price reached more than $850 per ounce.

At times, midway gaps may appear to be exhaustion gaps.

EXHIBIT 4–12 Exhaustion Gap

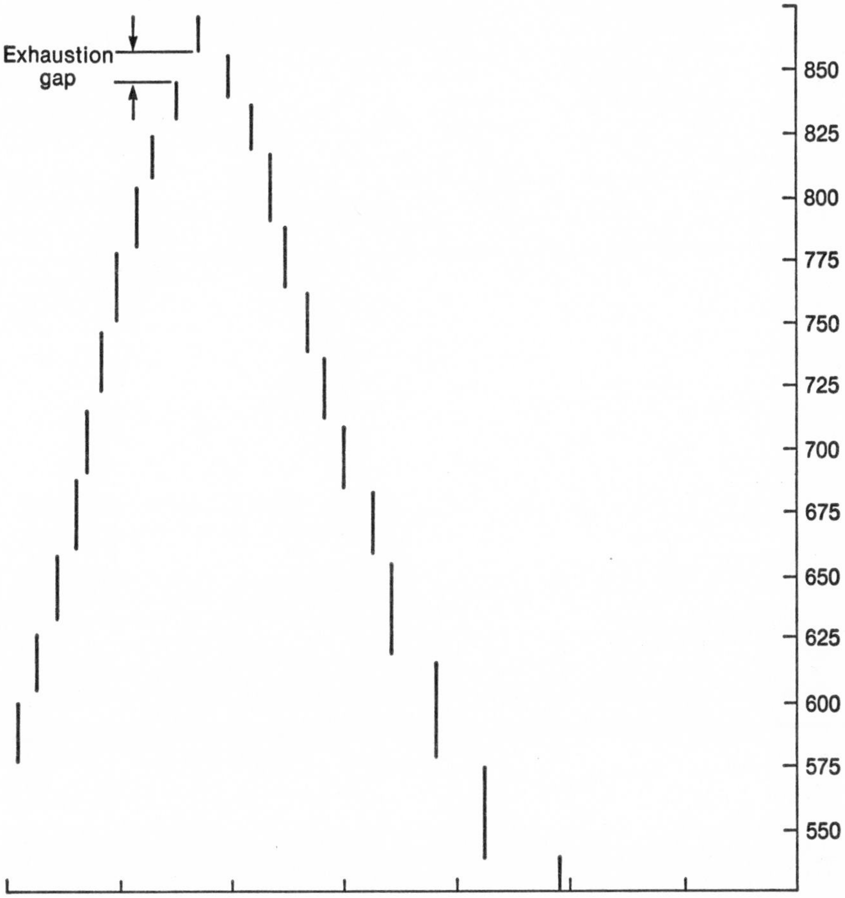

If you believe a market move has not run out of steam, that is, it has not been exhausted, then possibly the gap was just of the midway variety. Nonetheless, at such a time, the market bears very close scrutiny.

MOVING AVERAGES

The daily high-low-close bar chart is one of the simplest and most popular forms of charting. Another popular but some-

EXHIBIT 4–13 10–20-Day Moving Averages

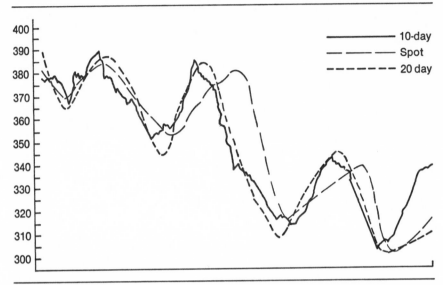

what more complex tool of the technical analyst is construction of moving-average charts. A moving-average chart compares the average price of gold or gold-related equities over a certain period of time—say, the past 5 days or the past 30 days—with the current price. Exhibit 4–13 illustrates such a chart, showing the average of 10 days' Comex spot month settlement prices (the solid line) versus the daily settlement prices (the dashed line). Each day, the moving average is calculated simply by averaging the past 10 days' prices. One of the benefits of the moving average is that it smooths out static and short-term wiggles in the price of gold, allowing the trend—if there is one—to become more readily apparent.

If the market has been moving up, both the moving-average line and the spot-price line will be moving in the same direction. If you were to add a third line—say, the average of the past 20 days, as I did with the broken line in Exhibit 4–13—then, if the market has a clearly defined trend, all three lines should move in the same direction at the same velocity. In other words, the angles of their slopes should be roughly parallel. If one of the lines diverges from the others, it could be an indication that a change in market direction is impending.

The most dedicated technicians rely on personal computers to quickly and efficiently generate a moving-average chart, making it easy to experiment with a variety of moving averages and facilitating daily updates of these useful charts.

The watcher of moving averages looks for a place where two lines cross. If the spot price or short-term moving average crosses the line formed by a longer term moving average, it often signifies a change in price direction. The longer term moving average is called the "trend line"—and the longer the period of the trend line, the more significant such a cross may be. When the two moving-average lines in Exhibit 4–13 were crossed by the spot price, that was an indication the market was turning—and, when the shorter term 10-day line crossed the longer 20-day moving average, that was an even stronger indication.

In this exhibit, I used simple moving averages—simple in the sense that the same weight has been given to each day's price when calculating the moving-average price lines. Some analysts prefer to assign a higher weight to prices from the most recent day or days, or to use a mathematical formula that will "skew" the average so the most recent prices will have more influence than the less recent ones. One approach to calculating a weighted moving average is to multiply yesterday's settlement price by 10, the prior day's by 9, the price from two days ago by 8, and so on until you have computed values for all 10 days, then add those values together and divide by 55 to get your weighted average. Proponents of weighted averages argue that the most recent trading is the most representative of the current trend, while the inclusion of older data helps smooth out a chart and keep you from being "whipsawed" by aberrant price moves. Like any system, moving averages will give you an indication of which way the market may be headed, but they are no replacement for simple common sense.

OSCILLATORS

Oscillators are measurements of the velocity with which the price of a commodity such as gold, or the price of an equity, is moving in one direction or the other. They are a measure of how fast prices are changing. The basic standard used by many technical analysts is the "net-change" oscillator. A daily net-change oscillator uses the daily closing price. To construct a chart using such an oscillator, take the daily settlement price on the Comex, for example, compare it with the prior day's settlement, and plot the difference on a chart. If, for instance, the price of gold settled at $290 today, compared with $289.50 yesterday, your first point would be a plus 0.50. If the price tomorrow on settlement were $289.75, your point to plot tomorrow would be 0.25 below today's point. To construct a five-day net-change oscillator, you would plot the net change between today's price and the settlement price of five days ago. The starting point of your chart is known as the "zero line." As long as the net changes continue in an upward pattern, they will be plotted above the zero line—while obviously, those in a downtrending market will dip below the zero line.

Net-change oscillators can be helpful in identifying potential changes in a long-term trend. Exhibit 4–14 shows the chart of a five-day net-change oscillator for the Comex gold futures market. The dotted line shows a five-day moving average for the same market. Note that the oscillator gave a signal of a pending reversal in price even before the moving average itself changed direction. That is because, in this instance, the momentum slowed before prices reversed.

RELATIVE-STRENGTH INDEXES

One tool of the technical analyst that has gained considerable new popularity in recent years is the relative-strength index. This is a measure of the buying and selling pressures behind a gold-market move. Like many technical tools, this one can be used most readily with a personal computer, but it also is available from weekly chart services.

One of the more closely watched relative-strength indexes is the one devised by J. Welles Wilder, Jr., the author of *New Concepts in Technical Trading.* Wilder's formula takes a trading period—for example, nine days—and then looks at the changes in price from day to day. The changes for all the days when the price increased are added; in a separate calculation, the changes are added for all the other days when the price decreased. Each of these sums is then divided by the number of days under consideration (nine, in my example) to get an

EXHIBIT 4–14 Five-Day Net-Change Oscillator;
Five-Day Moving Average

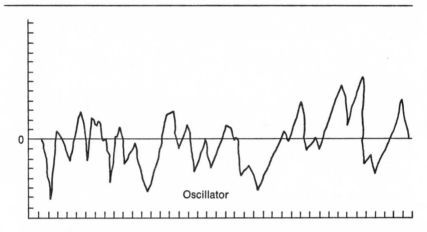

Oscillator

0

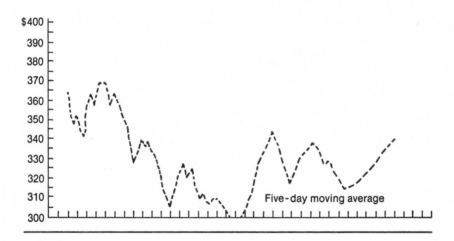

$400
390
380
370
360
350
340
330
320
310
300

Five-day moving average

average of the up-day changes as well as the down. Next, the down average is divided by the up average. Add 1 to this result and divide that sum into 100. Finally, subtract that answer from 100 and the result is Wilder's relative-strength index.

Exhibit 4–15 shows these calculations, as well as an example of a chart depicting a nine-day relative-strength index for the Comex gold futures market.

EXHIBIT 4–15   Nine-Day Relative-Strength Index Chart;
December 1982 Comex Gold Futures

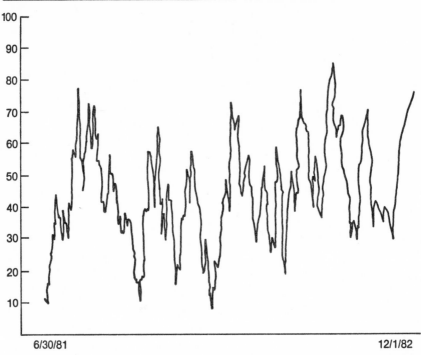

6/30/81   12/1/82

To a technician, a high index number is an indication that
the price of gold will soon begin to drop, while a low number is
a sign that the market will soon reverse and move upward. The
rationale behind this is that a high relative-strength index indicates an overbought market, while a low index number is a sign
of an oversold market.

POINT AND FIGURE

Not all analysts make extensive use of high-low-close bar
charts, moving averages, relative-strength indexes, and oscillators. Instead, some prefer to look at *point-and-figure* charts. Like
the charts and chart patterns already discussed, point-and-
figure charts can help you pinpoint changes in the direction of a

market's price, whether you are analyzing gold bullion, equities, futures, or options. And they also can give you an indication of the extent of these changes. These charts can be based on intraday prices—if you have access to such data—or end-of-day closing or settlement prices. Many day traders, or scalpers as they are sometimes called, rely heavily on point-and-figure charts. They update them frequently during the trading day, sometimes using a personal computer with access to "real-time" trading information—that is, trade-by-trade input from an exchange floor. Obviously, this approach is only for an active, full-time trader. But even if you are not a professional gold trader and you lack computer charting capabilities, you still can benefit from point-and-figure charts by subscribing to a weekly chart service and updating the service's charts by hand at the close of every trading day. This is similar to what you can do with relative-strength charts furnished by such a service.

The point-and-figure chart differs from a high-low-close bar in that it concentrates on the horizontal axis rather than the vertical. What the technician looks for in the point-and-figure chart is price congestion—periods when there is very little change in price and the gold market seems in balance between buyers and sellers. A bar chart will give some indication of congestion, because the length of each bar—whether it represents an hour's, day's, week's, or month's worth of trading—will be relatively short during congestion periods. As I noted earlier, congestion can show up on a bar chart in the form of a rectangle. Each trade in a congestion period will have little significance to someone trying to ascertain the eventual direction of the market. But a point-and-figure chart allows you to decide what constitutes a significant trade—one that reflects a meaningful change in price.

On the U.S. gold futures markets, the minimum allowable price fluctuation is 10 cents per ounce. In other words, if one contract were sold for $350.50 per ounce, the next trade would have to be at $350.60 or more, if higher, or $350.40 or less, if lower. Such minor changes are of interest only to the scalper, since a 10-cent shift is equal to only $10 per 100-ounce Commodity Exchange gold futures contract. A point-and-figure chart generally tracks larger moves. Exhibit 4–16 is a gold futures point-and-figure chart with a 50-cent reversal. No

---

EXHIBIT 4–16 Point-and-Figure Chart with 50-Cent Interval

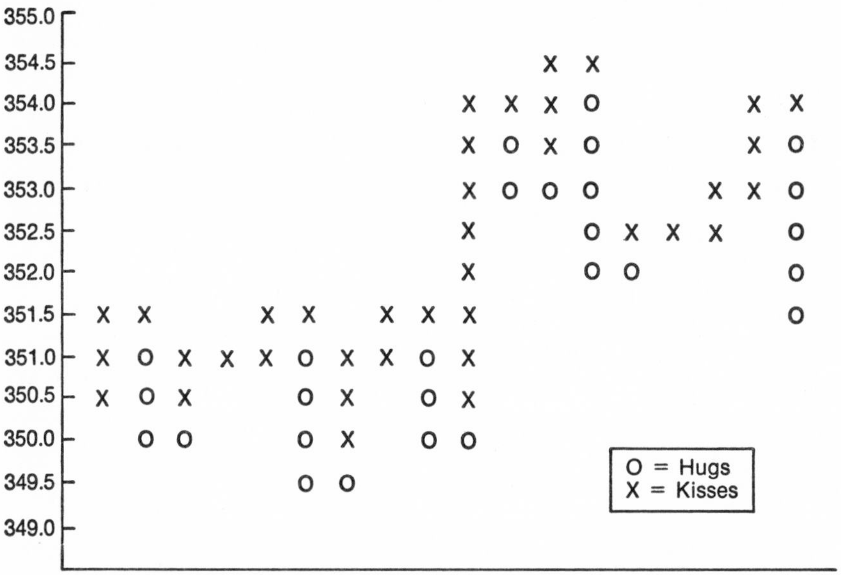

```
355.0 ┌
354.5 │                           X  X
354.0 │                     X  X  X  O              X  X
353.5 │                     X  O  X  O              X  O
353.0 │                     X  O  O  O           X  X  O
352.5 │                     X        O  X  X  X        O
352.0 │                     X        O  O              O
351.5 │  X  X        X  X     X  X  X                   O
351.0 │  X  O  X  X  X  O  X  X  O  X
350.5 │  X  O  X        O  X        O  X
350.0 │     O  O        O  X        O  O
349.5 │           O  O                   ┌──────────────┐
                                         │ O = Hugs     │
349.0 │                                  │ X = Kisses   │
      └                                  └──────────────┘
```

---

change is indicated unless the shift has been at least 50 cents above or below the prior change.

Looking at this chart, you will notice that no attempt has been made to plot the exact prices at which gold was traded. Instead, only the nearest 50-cent mark is indicated. A high-low-close bar chart or an intraday tick chart—one which marks off every single trade—would record a trade at exactly $350.60 per ounce, but this point-and-figure chart shows trades at only $350.00, $350.50, or $351.00, reflecting shifts of at least 50 cents.

To construct a point-and-figure chart, you first must decide what reversal points interest you. This will determine your vertical scale. In Exhibit 4–16, I have used a scale of 50 cents per ounce, which means that each horizontal line on the chart represents a 50-cent change in the per-ounce price of gold, corresponding to the 50-cent reversals the chart illustrates. Each time the price moved up by 50 cents or more, I have entered an "X" on the chart. If there was a reversal—that is, the price declined by 50 cents or more—I have entered an "O" on the chart.

Exhibit 4-16 shows a period of congestion where the columns of Xs and Os are about the same length until there is a series of Xs going straight up about midway across the chart, starting at $350. The technician looking at a point-and-figure chart concentrates on the number of blocks filled in along the horizontal line, using a chartist theory that when a breakout from the congestion point finally occurs, the length of the upward or downward trend will equal the number of blocks in the sideways trend. In other words, if there are five blocks sideways, the break will go either up or down for five blocks.

The reasoning behind this is that potential trades will accumulate unfilled in a congestion area, and the longer the congestion, the greater this accumulation will be. During this period, both buyers and sellers have experienced relatively small gains and losses. Take, for example, a breakout on the upside from congestion. Those who have traded during this period from the short side, holding futures contracts to sell gold, will be eager to buy to avoid turning their small losses into big ones. As growing numbers of contracts are purchased by these former holders of short positions, upward price pressure is created. In addition to the former shorts who now will be scrambling to cover positions, there also will be an even greater number of investors who wisely sat on the sidelines all through the congestion—the accumulation of orders I referred to above—who now will be willing to "jump on board" a rising market, thus increasing the upward pressure. The reverse would happen in a downward break from congestion, as holders of long positions finally sold, creating downward pressure which quickly would be joined by investors wishing to profit from a market decline. Selling short is common on the futures market, where every transaction necessarily must involve someone selling short (that is, entering into a contract to sell gold in the future). The strength of a downside breakout in the equities market is not likely to be as great as that of an upside break, since selling equities short involves the borrowing of shares, among other considerations, and it is not always possible for a small investor to borrow the stock.

Generally speaking, congestion will happen at the high or low end of a market move, since it is the result of a balanced market with equal numbers of buyers and sellers. If the market is not in balance, those looking to buy will outnumber sellers toward the low end, or those wishing to sell will outnumber buyers toward the high—and thus there will be a trend, rather than congestion. During a trend, depending on its direction, either buyers or sellers will predominate. If it is an uptrend, there will be more people interested in buying, and they will bid higher and higher for however much gold is available. If it is a downtrend, more and more people will be offering gold at lower and lower prices in order to attract buyers.

When congestion occurs at the low end of a price move, the breakout from the congestion point is likely to be to the upside, since the low prices have served to interest more buyers. Conversely, when congestion occurs at the high end, the breakout is likely to lead to lower prices as more people offer more and more gold at lower prices to attract sellers.

As a subscriber to the Rule of Multiple Techniques, I believe a point-and-figure chart has a place in a technician's toolbox but that you should not rely any more heavily on this kind of chart than on any other tool at your disposal.

CONTRARY OPINION

So far, most of the technical analysis I have talked about in this chapter has involved graph paper and mathematical computations. But not all technical tools are mathematical. Among those that are not, one of the most important is "contrary opinion."

If a consensus view were always right about the gold market, there would not be much need for this chapter. Instead of drawing charts, a public opinion poll would tell you which way the market was headed. When the majority of respondents thought prices would head higher, you would buy; if the consensus believed it would go lower, you would sell. But not everyone is right. In fact, the majority seems to be wrong most of the time—and this is the basis of contrary opinion. Since pollsters do not regularly survey the public to see how it feels about the gold market, those who use contrary opinion often look at the recommendations in investment letters from brokerage house analysts. Because of the high interest in gold, almost every major commodity and stock brokerage firm now employs at least one analyst whose main job is to make gold recommendations to clients—recommendations which often are followed.

The contrarian approach is based upon the notion that the current market price reflects the collective thinking of all the participants. If most are bullish, the price already reflects this. Taking this to an extreme, if 100 percent are bullish, and as bullish as they could be, then the current price would be at its highest possible level, since no more bulls would be left to enter the market and push the price higher. Therefore, the market could only go down. If the consensus of recommendations was to buy gold, the contrarian's rationale suggests that the market quickly would become overbought—so before new buyers could be attracted, the price would have to go lower.

There are a number of publications and services that survey commodity markets analysts on a weekly basis and report the results to their subscribers, presenting their compilations in terms of the percentage of analysts who are bullish on a given market. Generally speaking, as that percentage moves above the halfway point, it is time to start considering the possibility that a market may be in the process of becoming overbought. Using consensus opinions with this guideline, of course, is not a hard and fast method of analyzing a market. You still must consider the market fundamentals and decide whether they justify a bullish, or bearish, attitude.

WAREHOUSE OR DEPOSITORY STOCKS

There are many holders of gold around the world, but most do not divulge the extent of their hoards. Each futures exchange, however, maintains depositories where gold may be delivered in fulfillment of contracts, and the size of these warehouse inventories is made public daily. Again, stocks of gold bullion held in Comex-approved depositories are the most important, simply because they are the largest. Unfortunately, very few general-circulation publications carry information on these stocks. However, they are available from the exchanges themselves for a slight fee. Your broker will also have access to these figures.

The technical analyst takes great interest in the size of these warehouse stocks and, even more importantly, in changes in the quantity of gold held in Comex depositories. If, on a given day, there were a large increase in the size of the stocks, that would be a general indication the supply of gold available had increased—although, in many cases, it could be simply the result of a major bullion house shifting its inventory from, say, London to New York or New York to Chicago to take advantage of arbitrage opportunities arising from price differences. Generally, an increase in warehouse stocks over a sustained period—that is, longer than one or two days—should be interpreted as a bearish signal, since increases in supply may indicate a drop in demand and could foretell a drop in the metal's price. On the other hand, a decrease in depository stocks could be an indication that commercial interests are withdrawing metal, or at least could signal an interest on someone's part in taking possession of physical gold. Since this would represent a decrease in available supply (and presumably an increase in demand), a technical analyst as well as a fundamental analyst would view a decline in depository stocks as bullish.

OPEN INTEREST

Another important statistic for the technician is *open interest*— that is, the number of gold futures contracts which have not been fulfilled, either by the holder making or taking delivery or by the holder liquidating the position. (The owner of a futures contract may liquidate that position by entering into an opposite position. The holder of a contract to buy would do so by selling that contract; the holder of a contract to sell, by buying the contract back.)

Like so many exchange-related statistics, open interest should be watched closely for any changes, since it may give an indication of who is in the market. Rising open interest coupled with rising prices would be a technical signal that there are new buyers in the market initiating new positions. Rising open interest and falling prices would be viewed by the technician as an indication that there are new sellers in the market, since those entering a futures market in this situation are likely to be selling contracts short (entering into contracts to deliver gold in the future). A drop in open interest coupled with a fall in prices would be evidence of profit-taking by those who held long positions—that is, contracts to buy gold in the future—or a sign that holders of long positions are selling to stem losses they may have suffered. Finally, rising prices and falling open interest would be evidence that those who had contracted to sell in the future—"gone short"—are buying back those contracts, either because they anticipate rising prices or because they are satisfied with any profits they already may have made.

Open interest has no corresponding statistic in the gold-mining equity or bullion markets. Nor is there anything comparable to depository inventories. But both these figures give an indication of potential interest and volatility in all gold-related investments.

COMMITMENT OF TRADERS

Once a month, the Commodity Futures Trading Commission publishes a "commitment of traders" report detailing the number of positions, both short and long, held by hedgers, large speculators, and small speculators. Hedgers—commercial firms or individuals that use gold in the normal course of business—are an important feature of the gold futures market. But their trade commitments generally are governed by their business needs. A mining company usually will approach the futures market from the short side—that is, make a commitment to sell in the future—since it anticipates selling gold. A jewelry manufacturer would be expected to buy gold futures, since it will be buying physical gold in the future in order to make its products.

Large and small speculators, on the other hand, are trading gold futures simply because they believe the price will rise (if they are buying futures) or fall (if they are selling). If you took a contrarian approach, then you would view a large number of speculators holding long futures positions as a sign that the market was overbought, while a large number holding short positions would indicate that the market was oversold.

While not generally published in most newspapers, the commitment of traders report is available from the Commodity Futures Trading Commission in Washington.

The data in this report can be correlated with any conclusions you might draw from consensus reports. If the consensus was bullish, there should be a large number of speculators buying gold futures, while if the consensus was bearish, there should be a large number selling.

MARKET VOLUME

Each day, the U.S. gold futures exchanges publish their daily volume figures—tallies reflecting the number of contracts traded. These figures are published in the commodity futures tables, which appear in many daily and financial newspapers. Since the Commodity Exchange in New York is the largest gold futures exchange in the world, accounting for the lion's share of gold futures trading, the Comex volume figures are the most important for the technical analyst. On a busy day, more than 80,000 gold futures contracts might be traded; on a light day, there may be fewer than 20,000. Exchange volume totals are one of the quickest and easiest ways to determine who is active in the market.

Since the other gold futures exchanges do not attract as many speculators or commercial businesses, their volume figures are not as significant, although they tend to mirror activity on the Comex. On low-volume days in New York, it is not uncommon for the Chicago Mercantile Exchange's International Monetary Market division to have no volume at all. Some analysts will look at just the Comex volume statistics. Others may look at the total volume on all U.S. exchanges. In either case, the conclusions you reach are likely to be the same, since what you should be looking for is not necessarily the exact volume figure but how each daily, weekly, or monthly total compares with the previous period.

A high figure indicates that speculators or investors were active in the market that day. A high volume coupled with rising prices indicates there were many "new" buyers, that is, speculators initiating new long gold futures positions or entering into contracts to buy gold in the future. A high volume with declining prices indicates heavy liquidation by speculators, possibly to take profits but just as probably because they were threatened by margin calls. A low volume figure, no matter which way the price of gold is headed, usually signifies that the only participants were professional traders—either those who hold seats on the exchange or commercial firms using futures exchanges in the course of transacting their normal business.

In the equity markets, volume is reported daily for each

individual stock. Remember, the figure published in the newspaper stock tables represents the number of "round lots" traded, that is, blocks of 100 shares. To arrive at a total number of shares exchanged, simply add two zeroes to the published figure. ("Odd-lot" transactions, those involving fewer than 100 shares, are not included in these daily figures, but generally they are not sufficient in number to significantly affect the total number of shares traded.)

RATIOS

If you are interested in trading commodity future spreads—that is, entering into a contract to sell one product and simultaneously entering into a contract to buy another—then a study of ratios between the price of gold and other precious metals will be an invaluable tool for you. The trader who uses spreads is looking to profit at the same time from the rise in the price of one futures contract and the drop in the price of the other.

If you are long (have agreed to buy in the future) one gold contract and short (have agreed to sell in the future) one silver contract, you are looking for the price of gold to rise, allowing you to sell at a higher price than you initially bought—and, at the same time, you are looking for the price of silver to drop, allowing you to buy back your short contract at a lower price.

In mid-1986, the ratio between the price of gold and silver was approximately 65 to 1—that is, it took 65 ounces of silver to buy 1 ounce of gold (or, to put it another way, gold was 65 times as expensive as silver). During the previous decade, this ratio had varied widely, but this was about the highest it had gone. It reached its low point of 17.5 to 1 in January 1980, when silver and gold prices both hit their recent highs.

Spreading may also be done between gold and platinum futures. As a rule, the price of platinum will be higher than that of gold when there is strong demand for platinum in the automotive and oil-refining catalytic converter markets, the two largest users of this precious metal. During such times, the price of platinum has been more than $100 per ounce above that of gold. Conversely, during the 1982 recession, the price of platinum dropped to as much as $50 below that of gold.

Even if you are not interested in spread trading, a look at

these ratios—especially the gold/silver spread—is well worth-while, since it may give you an indication about the future direction of the price of gold. If you are interested, I have explained further how to trade spreads in Chapter 10, Futures—The Techniques.

SUMMARY

Whether you are interested in gold bullion, mining equities, futures, or options on any of these investment vehicles, technical analysis of the markets will help you make more intelligent investment decisions. Many of the technical indicators I have talked about in this chapter are taken from the gold futures markets. Because of the importance and growth of gold futures trading during the past decade, it would be foolish for the investor in any gold-backed or related instrument to overlook the influence of futures, and particularly the technical signals that may be apparent through careful analysis of these markets. (See Chapter 9, Futures—Their Origins, Purposes, and Workings, for an exhibit spotlighting this growth.)

At the start of this chapter, I advocated the Rule of Multiple Techniques. Similarly, you as an investor—whether your interest lies in futures, physicals, bullion, equities, or options—should not operate in a vacuum, oblivious to those markets that you feel do not interest you. I cannot emphasize enough the important role the futures markets play in modern gold trading. As an investor in gold, regardless of your vehicle, you must keep a close watch on the prices and activity on the Commodity Exchange in New York.

At the very least, you should follow a high-low-close bar chart of the Comex. This will give you an indication of the direction of gold bullion prices—which, in turn, has a bearing on the price, earnings, and liquidity of gold-mining equities. Many of the other technical tools, such as oscillators, relative-strength indexes, commitments of traders, and open interest, will tell you who is involved in the gold market. If the only people who seem to be interested in gold are manufacturers, this will put downward pressure on the market, since manufacturers are normally buyers of gold bullion and it is in their best interest to get their raw materials as cheaply as possible. Lower gold prices also serve to attract more people to buying jewelry, thus increasing a jeweler's sales.

If the commitment of traders report shows a high number of both large and small speculators in the market at a time of uneasiness over world political or financial events, this is a bullish signal. Generally speaking, the more interest there is in the gold market, the greater upward pressure there will be on prices. And that interest can be seen in the commitment of traders, open interest and high futures exchange volume, or heavy trading activity in mining equities. As a rule, public interest in the gold market comes only when prices are rising, and prices seem only to rise when there is public interest in buying—even though many people make money selling gold or gold futures when prices are falling.

Of course, if you subscribe to contrary opinion, you would interpret heavy buying by the general investing public as evidence that prices will drop soon because of an overbought market. Be careful, however, about becoming contrarian. Remember, the general public participated successfully in the 1976 to 1980 bull market.

Although the futures markets are often the first to indicate a change in gold prices, the way has been paved now and then by the equities markets instead. I have worked with many commodity analysts, and most are as aware of the activity and price movements of shares in companies such as Homestake Mining or Campbell Red Lake as they are of the current interest in gold futures contracts. Naturally, if your interest is primarily in equities, you probably will not keep comprehensive charts on Comex futures. Likewise, if your interest is in bullion coins, you probably will not keep a relative-strength index of the price of Homestake.

But regardless of your main area of interest, as a serious investor in gold—no matter what vehicle you choose—you have to be aware of the activity and overall trends in every segment of this market.

PART THREE

Modern Alchemy— Turning Gold into Money

CHAPTER FIVE

Tailoring a Personal Gold Program

There is no such thing as a universal gold portfolio to fit the needs of every investor, just as there is no universal portfolio of stocks and bonds that will fit the need of every investor. This book's only contention is that gold should be a part of everyone's portfolio. How much and in what form is variable from one investor to the next. And based on its track record, this advice is eminently justified. During the 15 years ending June 1, 1986, gold was a top performer among 15 major investor instruments rated by the New York investment firm of Salomon Brothers, Inc., with its performance exceeded only by the U.S. collector coins. With an annual rate of return of 15.2 percent, gold surpassed stocks, farmland, housing, and Old Masters artworks by wide margins—and even outstripped oil as an investment.

Before you decide what percentage of your investments should be in gold or gold-related instruments, and before you decide which gold instrument is the best investment for you, I suggest that you take some time to look at yourself as objectively as possible and consider how you view the world around you.

YOUR VIEW OF THE WORLD

Everyone has an opinion on what kind of shape his country is in, as well as the current state of the world at large. Gold is a global commodity—so when you get ready to choose a gold investment, you have to take time to consider your view of the current world situation. Are you expecting higher inflation in the coming months or years? Do you think the international banking system can survive, given the large amounts owed by developing nations? What is your opinion on the likelihood of world peace? What about unrest in the Mideast, South Africa, or Latin America? Remember, South Africa and some Latin American countries are major gold producers, and war or revolution in those areas can result in major disruptions of mining activity and consequent disruptions in the actual flow of gold into the world market. And, while the Mideast is not a gold-producing area, the people who live in that region have a cultural attraction to gold, and any major outbreak of violence can cause increased demand from them. In fact, it often has. What is the likelihood of another oil price explosion, such as the one in 1973 which triggered rampant inflation around the world? On the other side of that coin, the major oil price decrease in 1983 resulted in a sharp drop in gold prices. Holders sold their metal since they no longer feared inflation.

INVESTMENT OBJECTIVES

The most important question you must answer before you decide which gold investment is best for you personally is this: What are your investment objectives? As I noted in the opening chapter, there are three basic types of gold investors: long-term hoarders, medium-term investors willing to take profits where possible, and short-term speculators looking for income, not safety. Which category applies to you? In part, that depends on your view of the world as well as what types of investments you already have. If you have an essentially negative view of the world—if you fear high inflation or political and financial instability—then you are probably a long-term hoarder, and a sizable percentage of your gold investments probably should be in the form of physical metal: gold bullion coins or bars. Which would be preferable? That depends on the size of your investment. And, as a rule, I would advise most investors to make their first bullion purchases in the form of coins, since they are the most liquid and can be sold in small quantities if you later need cash.

If you do not have a negative view of the world but simply are seeking a nest egg to leave your children or grandchildren (or favorite charity), gold bullion or "paper" gold programs still may be the best investment vehicles for you, since the metal itself has kept its buying power through the ages, while a mine eventually will be depleted and a company—any company—might someday go out of business due to mismanagement or merely a depletion of its reserves.

If you want some safety but also would like some income from your investments, gold-mining equities can offer you both of these. Investing in an established mine, such as a North American company with at least a few years of operating history, can offer you security, since it is unlikely to go out of business in the near future. An even better approach may be to invest in a mining mutual fund, which combines your money with other investors' dollars and buys shares in several mining companies. There are mutual funds that specialize in South African gold mines, North American properties, and all precious metals—including gold, silver, and the platinum-group metals (platinum and palladium)—and funds that invest primarily in mining firms but also might take some of their funds and place them in other investments in an effort to diversify.

If your investment objective is the quickest possible appreciation, the gold futures and options markets or the "penny-stock" market might interest you. As a rule, you never should place more than 10 percent of your total investment capital into these highly speculative instruments. While they may yield very high profits, equally high losses are just as possible.

HOW MUCH TO INVEST?

Regardless of which gold-market instrument you select, you also have to determine how much money you should invest. To a great extent, of course, that depends on how much you have available. How much of your net worth is readily accessible, either as cash or as collateral for a cash loan, assuming that you are willing to take a loan? And how much of that cash have you dedicated already for some other project or purchase?

In the field of investment, there is a general rule of thumb that the bulk of your portfolio should be in the form of long-term holdings. In other words, you should have set aside, or should be setting aside, enough money to enable you to buy a home, educate your children, and eventually to retire comfortably. How much money? That really depends on your lifestyle. If you are fond of having caviar for lunch on the fantail of a yacht, you will need more, of course, than someone who is satisfied with a bologna sandwich on the back porch. The second part of your portfolio should be dedicated to some measure of safety—some contribution to your eventual well-being—but it also may be dedicated to growth. As I have noted previously, the final part of a portfolio can be dedicated to speculative gains. There is no iron law that everybody has to invest funds in all three categories. Everyone should have funds in the first, but the other two are really matters of personal preference. If you are comfortable simply building a nest egg, do not feel that you have to buy mining stocks or gold futures contracts. Likewise, if you have your nest egg in place and would like to enjoy some growth from a portion of your portfolio, do not feel that you also must "play" the commodity markets in order to be a well-rounded investor. There are plenty of prosperous people who have lived quite happily and successfully without ever knowing what a futures contract is.

One of the most important factors to consider before you make an investment is just how risky an instrument is. If you refer to Exhibit 5–1, which ranks the performance of various assets over time, you can easily see that gold was a good performer—over the long term—trailing only numismatic coins and easily outperforming other financial and nonfinancial assets. Exhibit 5–1 shows the rates of return associated with each asset.

Additional evidence of this is marshaled in a study conducted by the Salomon Brothers Center for the Study Of Financial Institutions, which analyzed the performance of gold when this asset is taken in isolation and when it is included as part of a diversified portfolio. The results underscored what many of us had suspected in the past few years. Gold enhanced a portfolio's performance by reducing the volatility of that portfolio and increasing the returns. For this, the Salomon Brothers Center research focused on the betas of gold and those of other investments. I explain below the progression of this analysis.

EXHIBIT 5-1 Compound Annual Rates of Return (in percentages)

	15 Years	Rank	10 Years	Rank	5 Years	Rank	1 Year	Rank
U.S. Coins	18.2	1	15.1	1	2.2	8	7.2	7
Gold	15.2	2	10.5	7	(6.6)	13	9.2	5
Stamps	14.3	3	13.9	2	(2.0)	11	14.5	4
Oil	13.0	4	1.0	15	(15.4)	15	(48.8)	15
Diamonds	10.5	5	9.7	9	2.7	7	7.5	6
Chinese Ceramics*	10.4	6	12.0	4	1.5	10	1.5	12
Bonds	9.3	7	10.6	5	20.9	1	26.0	3
Treasury Bills	9.2	8	10.2	8	9.0	3	7.1	9
Old Masters*	8.5	9	10.6	6	7.7	4	4.8	10
Silver	8.5	10	1.9	14	(13.5)	14	(15.5)	14
Housing	8.2	11	7.8	10	4.1	5	7.2	8
Stocks	8.2	12	12.0	3	16.5	2	34.8	2
U.S. Farmland	7.4	13	4.1	12	(6.2)	12	(12.2)	13
CPI	6.9	14	6.8	11	4.0	6	1.5	11
Foreign Exchange	4.2	15	2.4	13	1.8	9	35.0	1

*SOURCE: Southeby's.

Inflation Scorecard (number of assets that outperformed inflation)

Tangibles:	10 out of 10	7 out of 10	2 out of 10	6 out of 10
Collectibles	4 out of 4	4 out of 4	1 out of 4	3 out of 4
Commodities	4 out of 4	2 out of 4	0 out of 4	2 out of 4
Real Estate	2 out of 2	1 out of 2	1 out of 2	1 out of 2
Financials	3 out of 4	3 out of 4	3 out of 4	4 out of 4

Note: All returns are for the period ended June 1, 1986—based on latest available data.
SOURCE: Salomon Brothers, Inc., 1986.

Looking at the beta of these assets—the measure of their sensitivity to the stock market as a whole—gold consistently rates a beta of less than 1. As discussed below, this can also be expressed as a "standard deviation." A beta of 1 would indicate that an asset tends to fluctuate along the same lines as the stock market as a whole. In Exhibit 5-2, the betas for gold, Treasury bills, housing, long-term bonds, and silver are compared for the period from 1968 to 1983. In other words, these investments are compared to the stock market as a whole. Exhibit 5-3 compares T-bills, gold, and silver in relation to a more typical diversified portfolio consisting of equal portions of stocks, bonds, and

---

EXHIBIT 5-2 Betas Relative to the Stock Market

	1968–1983	*1968–1972*	*1973–1977*	*1978–1983*
T-Bills	−.004	−.004	−.01	− .01
Housing	.05	−.06	−.01	.18
Gold	.16	.04	−.15	.58
L-T Bonds	.25	.22	.13	.40
Silver	.48	.37	.03	1.06

SOURCE: L. S. Ritter and T. J. Urich, "The Role of Gold in Consumer Investment Portfolios," *Monograph Series in Finance and Economics,* Salomon Brothers Center for the Studies of Financial Institutions, New York University, 1984.

EXHIBIT 5-3 Betas Relative to Stocks, Bonds, and Housing

	1968–1983	*1968–1972*	*1973–1977*	*1978–1983*
Bills	−.01	−.01	−.01	− .01
Gold	.41	.19	−.22	.80
Silver	.69	.20	−.06	1.25

SOURCE: L. S. Ritter and T. J. Urich, "The Role of Gold in Consumer Investment Portfolios," *Monograph Series in Finance and Economics,* Salomon Brothers Center for the Studies of Financial Institutions, New York University, 1984.

housing investments. The gold beta in both of these tables is less than 1, indicating that it is actually less risky to invest in gold than it is to put your money in any of these alternative instruments, as hard as this may be for some readers to believe.

For you as an investor, this means that you should be placing a part of your assets into gold in an effort to "smooth out" wide fluctuations. Although you might earn more money over a period of time by placing your assets in the stock market, for example, you could just as easily lose more money if everything were placed in that one investment vehicle.

As you read Exhibit 5-4 from the right, it shows what happens if you take a portfolio that consists entirely of stocks and replace part of it with gold. Reading down the table shows what happens when the stock portion is replaced first with T-bills and then with gold. The second number in each grouping, the one that is listed below the percentage of return, is the

EXHIBIT 5-4   Portfolio Alternatives among Stocks, Bills, and Gold

		25 Percent Gold	50 Percent Gold	75 Percent Gold	100 Percent Gold
100% Stocks	8.12% 55.76	10.11% 49.72	12.09% 56.33	14.08% 72.19	16.06% 92.67
25% Bills	7.96% 41.78	9.95% 37.85	11.93% 49.57	13.92% 69.43	
50% Bills	7.80% 27.82	9.79% 28.02	11.77% 46.20		
75% Bills	7.64% 13.96	9.63% 23.03			
100% Bills	7.48% 2.91				

SOURCE: L. S. Ritter and T. J. Urich, "The Role of Gold in Consumer Investment Portfolios," *Monograph Series in Finance and Economics*, Salomon Brothers Center for the Studies of Financial Institutions, New York University, 1984.

standard deviation. A higher standard deviation indicates a higher risk. But Exhibit 5-4 is not a realistic portfolio, since most of us own a combination of assets—some stocks, our house or other real estate, and some bonds, although the bonds may be a "hidden" asset because they are held by a pension fund in which we participate. Exhibit 5-5 shows what happens when both gold and Treasury bills are introduced into a portfolio consisting of equal measures of stocks, bonds, and housing. It demonstrates the impact on the standard deviation and also on the return from the investments.

As I have stated, you must consider a variety of factors before deciding just how much of your portfolio to allocate to gold. You may wish to ponder your view of the world situation and weigh the likely impact of various factors such as inflation, tension, and interest rates. You may also wish to track gold's performance relative to other assets over time. And, of course, your own investment objectives also will come into play. Because these are so subjective, there is no way I know of to quantify this in a chart. However, the exhibits listed in this chapter, especially Exhibit 5-5, should at least help you draw some sort of picture of how certain variables can affect your investment.

EXHIBIT 5-5 Portfolio Alternatives among Stocks-Bonds-Housing (S-B-H), Bills, and Gold

		5 Percent Gold	10 Percent Gold	15 Percent Gold	20 Percent Gold	25 Percent Gold	30 Percent Gold	35 Percent Gold	40 Percent Gold
100% S-B-H	7.12% 29.85	7.57% 29.33	8.01% 29.56	8.46% 30.51	8.91% 32.11	9.35% 34.29	9.80% 36.93	10.25% 39.95	10.70% 43.26
5% Bills	7.14% 28.35	7.58% 27.85	8.03% 28.13	8.48% 29.17	8.92% 30.89	9.37% 33.18	9.82% 35.94	10.27% 39.06	10.71% 42.47
10% Bills	7.15% 26.85	7.60% 26.37	8.05% 26.71	8.50% 27.85	8.94% 29.69	9.39% 32.10	9.84% 34.98	10.28% 38.22	10.73% 41.73
15% Bills	7.17% 25.35	7.62% 24.89	8.07% 25.31	8.51% 26.55	8.96% 28.51	9.41% 31.06	9.86% 34.07	10.30% 37.41	10.75% 41.02
20% Bills	7.19% 23.86	7.64% 23.42	8.08% 23.91	8.53% 25.27	8.98% 27.37	9.43% 30.06	9.87% 33.19	10.32% 36.66	10.77% 40.36
25% Bills	7.21% 22.36	7.66% 21.95	8.10% 22.53	8.55% 24.02	9.00% 26.27	9.44% 29.10	9.89% 32.37	10.34% 35.94	10.79% 39.75
30% Bills	7.23% 20.87	7.67% 20.49	8.12% 21.17	8.57% 22.80	9.02% 25.21	9.46% 28.20	9.91% 31.59	10.36% 35.28	10.80% 39.18
35% Bills	7.25% 19.38	7.69% 19.04	8.14% 19.83	8.59% 21.62	9.03% 24.20	9.48% 27.34	9.93% 30.87	10.38% 34.67	10.82% 38.67
40% Bills	7.26% 17.89	7.71% 17.59	8.16% 18.51	8.60% 20.48	9.05% 23.24	9.50% 26.54	9.95% 30.32	10.39% 34.12	10.84% 38.21

SOURCE: L. S. Ritter and T. J. Urich, "The Role of Gold in Consumer Investment Portfolios," *Monograph Series in Finance and Economics*, Salomon Brothers Center for the Studies of Financial Institutions, New York University, 1984.

Bullion Coins

"Tho wisdom cannot be gotten for gold,
Still less can be gotten without it."

Samuel Butler the Younger,
Note-Books

Fabricated gold takes many forms. Coinage is one of the oldest, dating back to at least the sixth century B.C. Even today, it remains a convenient way to own gold for those investors who wish to take possession of their asset. For those, however, who prefer to have their gold stored in an institution, a certificate program or storage account are equally attractive alternate investment vehicles, broadly speaking.

Some gold coins are said to be "numismatic," while others are described as "bullion coins." Numismatic coins are those with collector appeal and a premium that reflects their status as collectibles. The U.S. double eagle is perhaps the most familiar example. Bullion coins, by contrast, are normally bought and sold for just a modest markup over their intrinsic gold value.

This book does not attempt to discuss rare coins, medals, or medallions; it concentrates instead on reviewing gold bullion coins—for these, in my opinion, are a pure play and far better suited to meeting the objectives of mainstream gold investors.

The value of a bullion coin, unlike that of a rare coin, medal, or medallion, is based primarily on how much precious metal it contains and how much that metal is worth at a given moment. When you buy a gold bullion coin, the gold itself accounts for the lion's share of the cost: You pay the spot price at the time of the transaction plus a small added premium to cover such services as production and distribution.

Unlike their numismatic cousins, gold bullion coins are

traded much the same as gold bullion bars. Typically, the more widely circulated gold bullion coins—the Krugerrand and the Maple Leaf, for example, and the new U.S. gold pieces— generally sell at wholesale for a premium of up to 3 percent or so over the current spot price of gold. The standard point of reference for determining gold's spot price is the second London gold fix for the day. At retail, the premium usually ranges from 2 percent to 8 percent above spot. The prices of some of these coins are listed in the financial pages of many daily newspapers. But many papers carry the wholesale "offer" or "ask" price for each coin, that is, the price at which a dealer will sell the coin to a retail coin shop or broker, which varies roughly between 1 percent and 3 percent above spot gold. As a rule, however, investors' purchase price will be a few percentage points higher—in line with standard retail markups for each coin.

Before buying a bullion coin, the investor should make sure that the retailer, bank, or broker with whom you will be doing business maintains a two-way market and stands ready to repurchase the coin at a later date. A reputable coin merchant will usually do so. When a retailer buys a coin back, the price he quotes is known as the "bid." The difference between his buying and selling—or "bid" and "ask"—prices is called the "spread." This is much like the spread that a broker might quote on other investment vehicles such as stocks, bonds, or options.

Now, the investor, of course, is concerned not only with how much it will cost to buy a gold bullion coin today but also with how much the coin will return in the future, when he chooses to sell it. Therefore, the spread is a basic consideration in deciding where to buy gold bullion coins in the first place. Typically, the spread between bid and ask is smaller for gold bullion coins than it is for other "hard" or "tangible" assets currently available to investors. In recent years, it has been as little as $1 for a one-ounce coin.

A GROWING POPULARITY

Until a few years ago, gold bullion coins were the province of the relatively affluent. At that time, they were available only in the one-ounce size and some dealers routinely rejected smaller orders—those involving fewer than 10 pieces. Since then, many millions of Americans have awakened to gold's potential. And those who produce and distribute gold coins have sought to broaden the market by making them available in smaller, more affordable sizes and quantities. The Krugerrand, Maple Leaf, and Panda, for example, can be purchased now not only in the standard one-ounce version but also in fractional sizes of 1/2, 1/4, and 1/10 (and in the case of the Panda, 1/20) of an ounce. The U.S. Congress followed this lead in December 1985, when it authorized the striking of the first-ever U.S. gold bullion coins, for under that law, they are being struck in the fractional sizes, too. The small coins' affordability puts them within the financial reach of every working American, even people of modest means. It also makes them very attractive as gifts.

So, if you are a small or average investor, bullion coins may be the investment for you to buy, particularly if you want to take delivery of your gold and store it in your safe deposit box. In general, I would say this holds true if you earn less than $100,000 per year, want to invest directly in physical gold, and have a long-term orientation toward investments. Obviously, though, this is just a guideline; it is not a hard and fast rule.

Liquidity—the advantage that is lacking with numismatic coins—is the greatest single asset of bullion coins. Being well known and accepted, the popular bullion coins are widely available at stock brokerage houses, banks, and coin shops. In fact, they can be bought (or sold) in virtually every city of any size in the United States or in just about every country around the world at their current bullion value.

THE DISTRIBUTION CHAIN

Gold bullion coins are made and marketed through a well-organized distribution chain. Think of it as a pyramid. At the top are the issuing countries that fabricate the coins—Canada, South Africa, and the United States, for example. At the base are the coin shops and other retail outlets where they are sold.

Even though they are not made to be circulated as money, some bullion coins carry face values—nominal amounts, well below the value of the metal they contain—and are treated as legal tender by the governments that issue them. The Maple Leaf is a case in point: The Canadian government has assigned it a face value of $50 and made it legal tender in that amount. The new U.S. gold coin has a face value as well: $50 for the one ounce coin, $25 for the half ounce, $10 for the quarter ounce, and $5 for the ¹/₁₀ ounce version. Although it has no face value, the Krugerrand, too, enjoys legal-tender status as official coin of South Africa. So does Britain's Sovereign, a small gold bullion coin that, like the Krugerrand, has no statement of value.

The Austrian 100-Corona, Hungarian 100-Korona, and Mexican 50-Peso gold pieces are considered government "restrikes"—remakes of earlier coins, bearing the original dates—and these are not legal tender. Perhaps I should explain what "legal tender" means. It does not mean the coins are in general circulation or that people routinely use them to pay their bills. It simply means the coins are backed by the issuing country. For you as an investor, there may be an advantage to buying legal-tender gold bullion coins rather than restrikes. Legal-tender coins are considered currency and are not subject to sales tax in many states. Even at the moderate rate of only 5 percent, the sales tax on a $400 coin would be $20. That is not an insignificant sum, and remember, it will not be refunded when the coin is resold to a dealer.

Moving down from the top of the pyramid, the next level in the bullion-coin distribution chain, after the issuing countries, consists of primary dealers. Most of the countries have chosen a handful of companies to act as principal agents in distributing their coins. In the U.S. market, firms such as Mocatta Metals, Republic National Bank, and J. Aron/Goldman Sachs act in this capacity. In effect, they are wholesalers: They sell the coins to companies on the next lower tier in the pyramid as well as to major institutional investors.

The primary distributors all maintain active trading desks. The issuing countries require them to make a two-way market in their coins—always standing ready not only to sell them but also to buy them back at a fair price, regardless of market activity at any particular time. This is not to say that if you had two Krugerrands or Maple Leafs and wanted $1,000 apiece for them, you would get that kind of price from a primary dealer.

Actually, a primary dealer would not do business with you at all. It would, however, buy several coins from those on lower levels in the pyramid, paying the going price based on the market value of gold itself.

Next in line are the secondary distributors—the precious-metal retailers, national brokerage houses, money-center banks (in cities such as New York, Chicago, and San Francisco), large coin dealerships, and regional wholesalers. These firms purchase bullion coins from the primary distributors in commercial quantities. Precious-metal retailers sell primarily to individual investors, although they also sell to retail outlets such as neighborhood coin shops. National brokerage houses and money-center banks sell chiefly to individual clients and smaller institutional buyers.

The retail store stands on the lowest tier of the coin distribution system. This may be a "mom-and-pop" operation or it may be part of a chain with many outlets. Stores such as these often charge higher premiums; by the time they get the coins, they have already passed through several other layers, and premiums have been added at every step of the way. Nonetheless, these stores are a vital part of the system, simply because their presence makes the coins more accessible to buyers and, at the other end, more liquid for sellers.

Remember, bullion coins are an investment, and you should expect service, reliability, and buy-back assurance from the retailer who sells them to you, just as you would from your stockbroker or commodity futures broker. And, like any other investment, if you deal with a reputable broker, bank, or coin shop, you need not be concerned with the authenticity of your purchase. A professional coin merchant can easily spot a counterfeit coin. Indeed, one of the attractions of gold bullion coins as an investment is the difficulty in fabricating acceptable fakes. The degree of fine detail, the measurements—both thickness and diameter—the color, and, of course, the weight, when taken together, make it virtually impossible for a professional to be fooled by a counterfeit coin. So, deal with a professional you trust. In addition, some depositories that store coins and bullion on behalf of investors will authenticate every coin and bullion bar before accepting it for storage. I must say that counterfeit coins have not been a problem in this country.

SELECTING A COIN

There are roughly a dozen gold bullion coins on the market, each with slightly different characteristics. Generally speaking, the small investor should concentrate on those with the widest distribution: The Krugerrand, the Maple Leaf, the Mexican 50-Peso piece—and now the U.S. entry, which figures to be not only the new kid on the block but also the biggest kid in the whole neighborhood.

Liquidity should be your first consideration in choosing a bullion coin. With their far-reaching networks and large shares, the Krugerrand and Maple Leaf have been the most liquid coins up to now. It is too soon to say how the new U.S. coin will be accepted; much will depend on its premium and how well it is marketed and promoted. Still, it seems logical that Uncle Sam's power and prestige should make this an instant superstar—especially considering the fact that it is legal tender.

Not just coincidentally, the new U.S. bullion coin has the same specifications as the Krugerrand. Sponsors of the bill that authorized the coin made it clear that they envisioned it to be a competitor for major coins such as the Krugerrand, and definitely "an American coin for Americans," as one advocate put it. Both contain exactly an ounce of gold, but the gold is alloyed with copper to give it greater hardness. In each case, the total weight is 1.0909 ounces and the gold is 22-karat, or 91.67 percent fine. The Maple Leaf, by contrast, is 24-karat gold, 99.99 percent fine. Some find this purity appealing, and the Royal Canadian Mint makes much of it in ads promoting the coin.

From an investment standpoint, and in spite of the legislative ban directed against new Krugerrand imports in the United States, the Maple Leaf and Krugerrand are equally attractive, I would say. While they differ in weight and fineness, these coins contain the same amount of gold. And, while political problems may have depressed the Krugerrand's price, its deep market roots and wide-branching network of distributors and dealers should enable it to weather the storm. Indeed, it may be a bargain at current levels.

AUSTRIAN, HUNGARIAN, AND MEXICAN COINS

The Austrian 100-Corona and Hungarian 100-Korona gold pieces carry lower premiums than the Krugerrand and Maple Leaf. At the retail level, they can be obtained for only about 3 to 5 percent over the spot price of gold. Thus, at the outset, you get more gold for your money. This is offset, however, when you go to sell the coins—for their premium value is lower at that end, as well. One major drawback of these two coins is the fact that they are not legal tender. Another is their weight: each contains only 0.9802 ounce of gold. Many buyers prefer bullion coins that weigh exactly an ounce, for that makes it easier to calculate their value at any given time—price per ounce being the standard method for quoting the value of gold itself. The gold in the Austrian and Hungarian coins is 21.6 karat, or 90 percent fine.

Mexico's 50-Peso gold piece is somewhat more liquid than the 100-Corona and 100-Korona coins but not as liquid as the Maple Leaf or Krugerrand. Whereas the two European coins are slightly shy of an ounce, the 50-Peso coin, or "Peso," as it is often called for short, weighs in decidedly on the heavy side. It contains 1.2057 ounces of gold. And, since it is alloyed, its total weight comes to a hefty 1.3396 ounces. Again, the irregular size is a turnoff for many investors—and, I must admit, I can see the reason why. Unless you have a calculator at your fingertips, or a mind that operates like a calculator, it is just too cumbersome to figure the price of a coin when its weight includes a decimal point followed by a series of extra numbers. Still, in my opinion, the Peso is among the most attractive bullion coins on the market, and I mean that in terms of both design and investment potential. Because it has drawn a lower level of interest in the marketplace, the Peso has generally traded at relatively lower prices, and given buyers more gold per dollar, than some competitors.

The Mexican government recognized the problems posed by the peso's odd weight, and in 1981 it reacted by introducing a new bullion coin called the Onza. Like the more popular coins, this Onza contains exactly an ounce of gold. But, while it overcomes investors' mathematical objections, the Onza has some problems of its own. Critics have complained that it is not as well struck as the 50-Peso piece, and they have also found fault with the fact that it offers limited marketability.

The Peso, the Maple Leaf, and the 100-Corona and 100-Korona pieces all are more yellowish, while the Krugerrand has a very slight tint of red. This may be of interest to artists and aesthetes—but you, as an investor, should not give much thought to the color of your investment. Rather, you should concentrate on getting the coin with the greatest liquidity, resalability, and potential for return.

Exhibit 6–1 lists the major gold bullion coins, along with the premiums they command and their distinctive characteristics.

U.S. GOLD

The U.S. government was slow to become involved with selling gold bullion in coin or medal form. Deep-seated distrust of gold ownership lingered at official levels even after Americans regained the right to buy, sell, and own gold bullion on December 31, 1974. Thus, for years thereafter, the American public got its introduction to gold ownership, and its basic education on the subject, from foreign coins, chiefly the Krugerrand.

Nearly four years passed before Uncle Sam stuck his toe in this particular pond. And, even then, he was tentative. The first U.S. gold bullion pieces, authorized by Congress in 1978, were medals, rather than coins. Specifically, Congress authorized a series of 21.6-karat (90 percent fine) one-ounce and half-ounce commemorative pieces called "American Arts Gold Medallions," which carried the portraits of people who were famous in the arts—Mark Twain, Louis Armstrong, and Frank Lloyd Wright, for example. These first appeared in 1980 and were issued annually from then through 1984. The series was envisioned as a U.S. alternative to the Krugerrand, the Maple Leaf, and other bullion gold coins from foreign lands. However, it never created much enthusiasm in the marketplace.

Initially, the "medallions" suffered from marketing problems. Would-be buyers had to order them by mail and wait for the government to deliver them—also by mail. This process took more than a month and put the U.S. pieces at a very distinct disadvantage, since other foreign pieces could be pur-

EXHIBIT 6-1 The Popular Bullion Coins

Coin	Country of Origin	Price (U.S. $)	Premium over Gold (percent)	Fineness	Karats	Gold Weight (toz§)	Total Weight (ounces)	Diameter	Type of Coin
American Eagle	U.S.	442.00*	+4.00	.900	22K	1.00	1.901	32.7mm	Legal Tender
Krugerrand	S.A.	387.75*	−0.06	.9167	22.0K	1.00	1.0909	32.6mm	Legal Tender
Maple Leaf	Canada	400.50†	+3.22	.999	24.0K	1.00	1.000	30.0mm	Legal Tender
50-Peso	Mexico	481.65†	+24.14	.900	21.6K	1.206	1.47	37.0mm	Restrike
Onza	Mexico	400.50†	+3.22	.900	21.6K	1.00	1.111	34.5mm	Legal Tender
100-Corona	Austria	379.40†	−2.22	.900	21.6K	0.98	1.0891	37.0mm	Restrike
100-Korona	Hungary	369.00‡	−2.04	.900	21.6K	0.98	1.0891	37.0mm	Restrike
Sovereign‖	U.K.	98.00‡	—	.916	22.0K	0.2354	.2568	22.0mm	Legal Tender

*Manfra, Tordella & Brookes, Inc. wholesale price as of October 16, 1986. Spot gold on October 16th was $425.00.
†Mocatta Metals Corporation wholesale prices as of August 13, 1986. Spot gold on August 13 was $388.00.
‡Manfra, Tordella, and Brookes, Inc., wholesale price as of August 19, 1986. Spot gold on August 19 was $376.70.
§Toz denotes weight in troy ounces.
‖The Sovereign is a fractional denomination.
SOURCE: Gold Information Center—Investment Service; Manfra, Tordella, and Brookes, Inc., Mocatta Metals Corporation.

chased over the counter for immediate possession. In 1982, the U.S. Treasury attempted to revive it by contracting with a major bullion dealer, J. Aron and Company, to bring its marketing know-how to the venture. Among other things, Aron set up an extensive distribution network and carried out a major marketing campaign billing the medals as "U.S. Gold." This and modifications in the gold pieces' appearance sought to make them seem more coinlike. But, even then, the "medallions" were not legal tender, and that hurt their sales and their resale potential, as well.

Although they are competitive in price with bullion coins, the U.S. Gold pieces have continued to languish. Today, their marketing and distribution system faces an uncertain future, and this puts these pieces at a major disadvantage in head-to-head market combat with the other established leaders in the field.

The first real U.S. gold bullion coin was authorized by Congress in December 1985, for market introduction in the fall of 1986. Like the Krugerrand, it has a fineness of 91.67 percent. Like the Maple Leaf, it has a face value of $50 and is treated as legal tender in that amount. And, like other competitors, it comes in a standard 1-ounce size plus three subsidiary sizes of $1/2$, $1/4$, and $1/10$ of an ounce. Perhaps in an effort to give the new coin a special appeal, the U.S. Treasury has chosen to use part of the design from the Saint-Gaudens double eagle on the face of the bullion piece.

OTHER BULLION COINS

There are other gold bullion coins on the market. Those most worthy of note are the Panda, which is minted by the People's Republic of China, and the Chervonetz, which is issued by the Soviet Union. To date, neither of these has had the distribution or marketing support needed to achieve a liquid market. For this reason, they are not suitable vehicles for the serious investor. But during the second half of 1986, many other countries have jumped on the bandwagon and announced plans to issue bullion coins—among them are Australia, Luxembourg, and Brazil, to name a few.

TAX CONSIDERATIONS

Bullion coins, despite their legal-tender status, are considered real property in a legal sense and thus are subject to federal capital gains or loss treatment when they are sold. State and local sales taxes also must be considered. As I pointed out earlier in this chapter, legal-tender coins are exempt from sales taxes in some states, such as Florida and California. Even if your state imposes sales tax on bullion coin purchases, you can legitimately not pay this tax by having your coins shipped to a state, such as Delaware, and then stored in a bank vault in that state. As long as your gold coins remain there, your home state (or province if you are Canadian) will not tax them. At most banks and vault facilities set up to hold precious metals, storage fees are about 0.5 percent of the metal's value per year—and that sum includes insurance at the current market value. Most reputable retail bullion dealers are familiar with how to arrange storage.

Portability is one of the major reasons why bullion coins have been popular around the world. But, unless you are planning to flee across a border, you might want to consider keeping your bullion coins in a safe deposit box. This is a secure location, and it is easily accessible whenever your bank is open. Contrary to popular belief, however, the contents of a safe deposit box are *not insured*. All the bank is doing is renting you space under lock and key in its vault. A simple, inexpensive rider on a homeowner's or tenant's policy will cover the contents of your safe deposit box.

SUMMARY

For the investor, gold bullion coins are an easy way to include gold in an investment portfolio. The things you should consider when deciding on a coin are the *premium*—the additional cost of the coin over the price of gold bullion itself; the *spread*, or difference between the bid and ask prices of the coin; its *liquidity*—how popular and easily recognizable, and therefore easy to buy and sell, the coin may be; *aesthetics*, if attractiveness is one of your priorities; and *country of origin*, if this is of interest to you.

Gold Bullion

While gold coins have traditionally been the province of the small-scale buyer and large bullion bars the haven of the rich, well-heeled investor, a variety of new and innovative gold products now offer the consumer a wide range of bullion investments, hybrids, and proxies.

Paralleling this product expansion during the past five years has been the establishment of new types of marketing outlets on Wall Street and beyond. The entry of more banks and brokerage firms as intermediaries offering these innovative vehicles (often patterned after instruments initially developed for other financial markets) have placed gold high on the list of worthy assets, right up there with stocks, bonds, and money markets. Besides bars and wafers, the array of gold alternatives includes certificates of deposit, passbook or accumulation accounts, storage programs, collateralized bank finance, and, although in a separate category, leverage accounts. These are listed in Exhibit 7-1.

The new paper instruments can be transacted with greater efficiency and yield larger profit margins to retailers than the sale of physical gold and, in many cases, they are better suited to investor's needs because they facilitate easy purchase and resale and often carry lower transaction costs for buyers.

For those conservative investors interested in buying physical gold, bullion is available in wafers and small ingots as light

EXHIBIT 7–1 Table of Gold Investments (There are many ways to buy gold.)

Type of Investment	Types of Institution	Some Product Features
Gold Bullion	Major financial institutions, banks, brokerage firms, precious metals houses, and coin retailers	Physical ownership or storage opportunity
Gold Coins	Major financial institutions, banks, brokerage firms, precious metals houses, and coin retailers	Physical ownership or storage opportunity
Gold Certificates/ Statement Accounts	Citibank Rhode Island Hospital Mocatta Metals Corporation Shearson Lehman Brothers E. F. Hutton Security Pacific National Bank	Certificates registering ownership in bullion, provide storage on a segregated (allocated) basis or unallocated basis upon request. Physical ownership available for some programs.
Gold Passbook Account/ Accumulation Account	Merrill Lynch Shearson Lehman Brothers Security Pacific National Bank	Initial minimum purchase of $100 to $1,000 with additional purchases of $50 to $100; some storage available
Collateralized Bank Finance	Bank of Delaware Wilmington Trust Safra Bank, L. A.	Initial deposit of 20% of total gold loan with bank financing for other 80%. Regular payments.
Leverage Contracts	Leverage contract merchants such as Monex	Initial down payment of 20% of transaction. Subsequently, interest-bearing payments which are usually tied to a percentage point above prime rate.

SOURCE: Gold Information Center—Investment Service, 1986.

as 10 grams (less than one third of a troy ounce) all the way up to bars weighing hundreds of ounces.

As a general rule, buying gold bullion is not economical for the typical American investor in sizes below the 10-ounce bar. If you want smaller quantities, you would be better off buying bullion coins, or what I call "paper gold." But if bigger bullion does fit your budget and your philosophy, you will find there are economies of scale in buying larger bars. In contrast to coins, for example, the only premiums you normally have to pay for bullion bars are brand-name charges—fees for a specific refiner's gold, which represent the cost of fabricating smaller bars. If you buy a 100-ounce bar or the standard-size 400-ounce "good delivery" bar, the chances are good that you will not have to pay any premium at all above the price of the bullion itself—although, as with any investment, you may have to pay a commission to the broker or dealer. This should amount to no more than 1 percent. With smaller bars, of course, you will pay both the commission and the premium. On a 10-ounce bar, the premium may be 50 cents per ounce. On a 1-ounce wafer, it may be as much as $5. Thus, while these two items vary greatly in size, the aggregate premium on both is about the same.

As with the purchase of stocks, a commission is something every gold investor faces. Simply stated, it is what you pay the person who arranges your purchase. Commissions on bullion vary widely. Depending on the size of your purchase, your broker-dealer's competitiveness, and your personal relationship with the firm, it can range from as little as one half of 1 percent of the total cost for large transactions to more than 15 percent—a rate that I consider exorbitantly high. As a rule, you should avoid any firm that charges more than 5 percent, since many reputable retail bullion dealers routinely charge a maximum of 3 percent. Do not confuse commissions with premiums or fabrication fees. These are charges assessed for making gold bars in the size the customer wants, and you may have to pay them even though the bars you buy are mass produced rather than being fabricated just for you.

Gold has to assume some form; consequently, no fee is charged for making a bar in the standard 100-ounce or 400-ounce sizes. For smaller bars, however, there usually will be such a charge. The smaller the bar, the higher per ounce the fee is likely to be. Fabrication charges run from as little as $0.50 per ounce to as much as $5.00 per ounce. Unlike commissions, these charges are usually refunded when you sell your bullion. You may not get back exactly the same amount if you use a different broker, but the buyer will refund at least a portion of your fabrication fees.

BRANDS

Like most products, gold comes in different brands. The product is pretty much the same: To qualify as gold, the metal must meet the chemical definition; thus, there is little or no physical difference between one refiner's gold and another's, as there would be between different brands of toothpaste. However, some refiners are better known than others and their products are recognized the world over. You should buy only gold that is fabricated by a major refiner—one whose large 100-ounce bars have a "good delivery" rating on the Commodity Exchange in New York or other exchanges. And each bar should be stamped with the name of the producer as well as a number certifying that it has been registered.

SPREADS

Most retailers of gold investment products will not only sell you bars and coins but also buy them back from you if and when you decide to liquidate your holdings. As you would expect, a retail gold dealer sells bars and coins at a slightly higher price— the "ask" or "offering" price—than he will "bid" if you wish to sell them back. The difference between a dealer's bid and ask prices is called the "spread." In choosing a place to buy gold, whether it be a local coin shop, your broker, or your bank, make sure that the retailer maintains a two-way market—that is, stands ready to repurchase your bars or coins. And make sure that his spread is reasonable and competitive.

Many bullion dealers, including some banks and brokerage firms, simply base their buying and selling prices on one of the London gold price fixes of the day or on the current spot price of the metal on a futures exchange. If the London afternoon fixing price were $340 an ounce, for example, your broker might be a willing seller at $341 and might buy back the metal at $339. In the vernacular of the trade, he would be quoting a $2 spread. Keep in mind that on top of this price, there also might be a fabrication charge and a commission. A retail firm that buys and sells gold may maintain its own inventory or purchase metal as required from a wholesaler. Larger firms that make a market in gold frequently earn a large share of their profit through the bid-and-ask differentials, leaving commissions to cover administrative expenses as well as commissions to individual brokers.

STORAGE CONSIDERATIONS

There are a few simple rules for investors to follow to assure that the gold they buy will be properly stored. If you purchase your gold from the well-known Wall Street firms or the big-name banks—Merrill Lynch, Dean Witter, E. F. Hutton, Citibank, Security Pacific, to name a few—you effectively have an endorsement of quality and assurance that your gold is being handled responsibly, whether it is in a segregated or nonsegregated account. You should inquire whether you have a direct claim on commingled gold prior to other creditors should the broker become bankrupt. If you do not, find another broker. If, however, you choose not to deal with the big players and wish to rely on a local broker or precious metals dealer to arrange storage for you, it is preferable that you have your gold segregated—that is, identified as your metal and not commingled with the company's bullion or the gold belonging to other customers. The less reputable bullion dealers who went bankrupt in recent years had not segregated their clients' gold; consequently, the bullion controlled by these firms became part of their corporate assets and thus was claimed by creditors when the companies failed.

Many investors who purchase gold bullion or coins wish to take delivery of the metal and store it in their own safe deposit box or under the proverbial mattress, as foolish as that may be. They want the security of having their gold close at hand, and they are also concerned about the risks, real and perceived, of storing it somewhere else.

Unfortunately, in many U.S. states (as in many foreign

countries), investors who take delivery of their gold are subject to sales taxes as I discussed in the previous chapter. Others arrange for storage, on their own or through a broker, at one of the major Delaware banks that offer bullion storage facilities. This can be advantageous in more ways than one: You can avoid sales tax up front—and, down the road, when you want to resell your metal, you probably will not have to pay any assay charges as long as your gold never left the bank depository. Typically, annual storage and insurance fees for leaving your gold in a major bank depository should total about one quarter to one half of 1 percent of the gold's value. Since July 1983, U.S. bullion dealers and retail coin shops have been required to report to the Internal Revenue Service all sales of bullion and bullion coins *by investors*. This is in line with an IRS attempt to discourage income tax evasion. Please note, however, that sales by dealers and retailers *to investors* need not be reported to the IRS.

There is another advantage to storing bullion with a major bank depository. The major depositories will not accept bullion (or coins, as I mentioned in the prior chapter) without assurance of its authenticity both in terms of content as well as brand name. So, you will not have to worry about bogus bars if you store your metal or take delivery from a depository at some later date. If you are concerned about the authenticity of your purchase, you might consider the storage or "paper" gold alternatives to physical delivery.

PAPER GOLD

Buying gold bullion may seem like a simple, straightforward sort of process. But just as there have been many new "products" in the equities and futures markets, there are also many ways to purchase bullion, as can be seen in Exhibit 7-1.

Many mainstream investors shy away from buying physical gold. For them, one of the best alternatives is to buy gold certificates of deposit. These are offered by a number of major banks and stock brokerage firms. A certificate is a convenient way to own gold without the added concerns for delivery, storage, sales tax, resale, assays, and other details that go with the buying of the metal.

Since you are not receiving segregated bullion, you should buy certificates from nationally recognized firms. Commissions can range from as much as 6 percent of the total value of a certificate down to 1.5 percent or lower. Many sellers also will charge you an annual or quarterly storage fee. This can be either a flat amount or a sum based on the current market value of the metal that's involved. In some programs the holder of a certificate can request delivery of the gold at any time. However, you then may have to pay a delivery charge, as well as a fabrication fee. There also may be no assurance that you will receive a particular brand of gold—though most firms that sell certificates purchase only gold which is deliverable against a futures contract. Be sure that the gold represented by your certificate meets these standards. In other programs it may not be possible to take delivery, but the investor can liquidate his position for the current value of the certificate at any time.

ACCUMULATION ACCOUNTS

Another popular alternative to buying physical gold—one which is a cross between bullion and gold certificates—is an accumulation account with a bank or broker. This type of account is similar to a payroll savings withholding plan. In an accumulation account you agree with the broker or dealer to pay a set amount periodically at a given time during the month—perhaps on the last business day. The broker invests your money, purchasing as much bullion as he can, and you are apprised of the actual physical amount of your acquisition at the end of the month, or on your particular "buying day."

Accumulation plans serve as a convenient way to "dollar-average" your purchases. This means that when the price of gold is low, you will get a larger quantity—while at high prices, the quantity will be proportionately less. Accumulation plans are a good method through which to acquire gold for the risk-averse mainstream investor and for the consumer who is interested in increasing his gold savings over a period of time. This strategy has enabled many investors to reap the benefits of lower unit costs for their holdings; and because it takes the guesswork and speculation out of buying bullion, it is an easy way to maintain a portion of assets in gold. Generally, an

---

EXHIBIT 7-2 Accumulating Wealth—A Systematic Gold Program (total ounces of gold accumulated by investing an average of $1,000 each quarter for the ten-year period, 1976–1986)

Year	Quarter 1	Quarter 2	Quarter 3	Quarter 4	Yearly Total	Cumulative Total
1976	8	8	9	7	32	
1977	7	7	6	6	26	58
1978	6	5	5	4	20	78
1979	4	4	3	2	13	91
1980	2	2	2	2	8	99
1981	2	2	2	3	9	108
1982	3	3	3	2	11	119
1983	2	2	3	3	10	129
1984	3	3	3	3	12	141
1985	3	3	3	3	12	153
1986	3	3	2		8	161

Gold Accumulation Program 1976–1986

Present Portfolio Value (9/22/86)	$70,115.50
Cumulative Investment	$44,133.25
Gain	$25,982.25
Total Return	58.87%

SOURCE: Gold Information Center—Investment Service, 1986.

---

accumulation plan requires an initial deposit. In some plans, this can be as low as $50 to $100; in others, it can be $500 or even $1,000. This is then followed by smaller subsequent outlays.

The cost averaging example in Exhibit 7–2 illustrates my point. This shows that over a 10-year period (1976–86), an investor who would have set aside $1,000 every quarter to purchase gold through an accumulation plan would have realized over 59 percent as a return on his investment. That is to say that, at the end of that period, the total portfolio value of the gold would be worth $70,115.50 (with gold purchases of 161 ounces) against an investment outlay of $44,133.25.

COLLATERALIZED OR BANK-FINANCED GOLD

Because regulations of the Federal Reserve Board and Securities and Exchange Commission prohibit brokerage firms from selling precious metals on margin, you cannot buy gold on credit through a stock or commodity brokerage house. You can, however, take advantage of an emerging method of gold investment—collateralized loans—which allows investors to arrange for purchase of gold, in whatever form, through a bank loan. This basically works on the same principle as a real estate mortgage loan. The investor agrees with a dealer to buy a specific amount of gold at a specific price and puts a down payment of as little as 20 percent while the bank finances the balance of 80 percent. The investor then makes interest-only payments on the amount financed by the bank until such time as he chooses to pay off the loan or sell his gold.

As one of the conditions for this type of loan, the bank has possession of the gold; and, if the price of the metal at any point in time falls to approximately the amount of the loan, the bank requests an additional margin deposit from the investor (to maintain the original 80 percent position). In the event that the investor cannot come up with this payment, the bank has the right to sell the gold to pay off the loan. In that instance, of course, any excess balance from the sale would be returned to the investor. This is a shrewd purchase strategy for the fairly aggressive investor or for someone who (because he expects the future price of gold to rise) wishes to purchase large amounts of the metal and lock in at today's price for a large quantity of gold. Among the banks already dealing in collateralized loans for gold investment are the Bank of Delaware, the Wilmington Trust, and the Safra Bank in Los Angeles.

LEVERAGE CONTRACTS

A leverage contract allows an investor to acquire a multiple of his actual cash investment. It is somewhat similar to a futures contract because it is a legal obligation to deliver (or take delivery) of a fixed quantity of a given commodity at a set price and at some specified future time. But, if you buy a gold futures contract, you do not actually own any gold, although you will benefit or suffer from any changes in the metal's price. With a leverage contract, by contrast, you do own the metal—and you can take delivery of it when the purchase price is paid in full.

Leverage contracts allow you to "buy" gold or other precious metals with a down payment of as little as 20 percent. The firm offering the contract will finance the balance—normally at a rate that is tied to the prime interest rate. (Typically, it will be anywhere from one half of 1 percent to a full percentage point above the prime rate). Firms of this type will advertise that you can "control" $5,000 worth of metal for as little as $1,000. This is the leverage they are touting. But leverage contracts, unlike futures contracts, are not traded on any exchange and are subject to only a minimal amount of regulatory oversight by the U.S. government. The Commodity Futures Trading Commission (CFTC) has jurisdiction over leverage contracts, but its powers have been severely curbed by Congress. The CFTC attempted to place leverage contract dealers under the same registration and capitalization requirements as futures brokers but ran into heavy lobbying from the leverage industry.

While leveraging may appear to be a good investment, it is not an advisable strategy for most investors. Leverage firms usually fail to explain that as an investor, you can be subjected to margin calls which may exceed your initial down payment. Failure to meet these calls can result in the "forced liquidation" of your account. A leverage firm may tell you that your metal is segregated and not a part of its assets—but because it loaned you the money, the firm will have a "first lien" against your metal. Most leverage contracts are "open ended"—that is, they have no due date, and the seller is content to let you maintain an open balance as long as you are paying the interest. But, in some programs, should the seller find himself in need of immediate cash, he can insist you pay the balance at once or face liquidation of your metal, regardless of the current market price. Under most such contracts, you will not be paying anything toward the credit balance as you would be with a normal installment loan. Rather, you will be paying just the interest. If you stop to think about it, the gold you buy under a leverage contract will never be your metal free and clear, since the seller will always have a lien against it unless you pay the credit balance in full. Those who sell leverage contracts are required by the CFTC to maintain a two-way market and thus must stand ready to buy back their gold. However, if such a firm should go out of business, you will find yourself owing money to whoever picks up the lien against your contract, and that party may not be interested in continuing the contract.

So, before you decide to pursue a leverage contract, you should consider the alternate strategies that offer similar benefits without the associated risks of the leverage technique.

In conclusion, gold investing is no longer the province of the doomsayer or the gold bug. The remarkable growth in the infrastructure of the gold market as well as the dramatic increase in the choice of products that have become available have placed gold within the reach of every investor. The next chapter will review additional investment opportunities and discuss the background of gold-mining equities.

CHAPTER EIGHT

Gold-Mining Equities

*"A gold mine is a hole in the ground
with a liar standing next to it."*

Mark Twain

Buying mining equities is buying gold in the ground. It combines gold ownership with many of the advantages and disadvantages of investing in securities. For this reason, you should define your investment goals before you buy gold equities or shares in a gold-stock mutual fund. Are you investing for long-term protection against inflation? Are you speculating on a short-term gold-market rally? Perhaps you see the gold-mining industry as just another part of the stock market and believe we are entering a phase of the business and stock-market cycle when this sector will outperform others. Examine your investment objectives carefully before deciding which gold-mining equities, if any, are best for you.

Mark Twain's warning is as valid today as it was a hundred years ago, and there are still plenty of promoters hyping "holes in the ground." But there are also many fine investments and reputable miners. Thus, while "caveat emptor" ("buyer beware") is surely sound advice for someone investing in gold, the prudent investor can do extremely well.

Before investing in mining stocks, you must analyze a series of factors, including gold's price outlook and the ledger sheets and prospects of specific mines. You also should consider minimizing some of the risks by diversifying your mining-share portfolio or investing through a gold-oriented mutual fund.

Many gold-mining companies pay their shareholders regular dividends and so can be a steady source of income. Gold-mining companies also provide a leveraged investment. In other words, your equity value usually rises or falls by a higher percentage than the price of gold. But gold-share investors are taking chances, as well. They not only risk a fall in the price of gold but also accept the hazards that go with mining. A foreign mine, for instance, may expose your investment to political problems and currency fluctuations. In addition, there are risks related to a mine's financial situation—its capitalization, cash flow, and the like; its labor relations; its geology; and even the real possibility of floods, fires, and other calamities.

Various factors, objective as well as subjective, govern the price of stock in a company such as General Motors: How well the auto industry in general has been faring, GM sales figures, management efficiency, the price of the stock compared to company earnings, and the price of GM stock compared to that of other auto manufacturers. These and other factors determine GM stock's investment potential. One thing most GM investors *do not* look at, though, is the price of a Chevrolet or a Pontiac, or any other GM car or truck.

Gold-mining equities are different. With them, you must consider all the factors you would with other investments, plus the present and prospective price of the company's product: the price of gold.

THE IMPORTANCE OF OPERATING COSTS

One of the first things most professional analysts and traders look at is a mine's production costs. The cost of producing gold can be as low as $100 an ounce or less, as it is for some of the highest quality South African producers, or as high as $305 an ounce, as it is at the venerable Homestake mine in the United States. It can even be so high as to make a mine unprofitable at current gold prices.

Investing in a low-cost producer is a conservative approach, but a high-cost producer can give you substantial leverage (in terms of both risk and opportunity) if the price of gold should rise or fall. For example, let us compare the Campbell Red Lake and Dome mines. At Campbell Red Lake, operating costs are about $100 an ounce, leaving a net profit of $200 an ounce when gold is at $300. If the price of gold were to rise from $300 to $330 (an increase of 10 percent), the mine's profits also would rise $30, from $200 to $230. That is an increase of 15 percent. But now let us look at Dome, a higher cost producer, and see what happens there in the same scenario. The Dome mine has an operating cost of almost $260 an ounce, so its net profits are $40 an ounce when the price of gold is $300. But if gold were to rise the same 10 percent to $330, Dome's profits would climb from $40 to $70—a 75 percent increase. So, with an identical 10 percent rise in the price of gold, Campbell Red Lake's profits would show a gain of only 15 percent, while Dome's profits would soar by 75 percent. And, to a large extent, the price of each company's shares would reflect the change in each mine's profitability.

One strategy for the aggressive, savvy gold-share investor requires an understanding of each company's relative performance at different points in the gold-price cycle. As gold begins a cyclical advance from its trough, you buy higher quality mines. As the price advance continues, you switch into lower quality mining companies. Then, near the peak, if you wish to retain some gold-share investments, you switch back to the lowest cost producers (or bullion itself), which will be less vulnerable in percentage terms during a bear-market phase.

THE TYPES OF GOLD MINES

For gold-bearing rock to be considered gold ore and counted as "reserves" by a mining company, it has to contain enough gold to permit the yellow metal's extraction at a profit. "Profit" is the operative word—and given the way the price of gold fluctuates, what is waste rock one day may be ore the next, with a rise in the price.

The key to profitable extraction is to keep costs down, so a mine can ride out any reasonable troughs in the price of gold. Of the two basic types of gold mine—open-pit (surface) and underground—open-pit operations are far cheaper. When ore is located close enough to the surface, the overlying soil and waste rock, if any, can be removed and the ore can then be drilled and blasted into convenient-size pieces. These will then

The Making of Gold

We generally think of gold as coming straight out of the ground, but the yellow metal is actually a refined product—the end result of several enriching and purifying processes.

Initially, the gold is found in mined ore. But unless that ore comes from a "placer" deposit—one that exists in a stream bed, where the metal is relatively free from impurities—it has to be separated from its host ore.

When Americans think of gold miners, they tend to picture grizzled old prospectors riding mules, wielding picks, and panning mountain streams for gold nuggets. It is true that this method can lead to the discovery and recovery of gold. But it lacks the economies of scale that make a modern mine financially viable.

Rather than plodding through mountain streams, the modern U.S. gold miner is more likely to be found operating huge earth-moving equipment and stripping away ore in which there may be only microscopic amounts of metal. Or, if he works in an underground mine, he probably spends his workday detonating explosives to shatter massive amounts of ore, then hoisting them to the surface. Either way, the next step is equally unromantic. Once the ore is removed from the mine, it is crushed, ground, and mixed in a water slurry and roasted in large, pressurized oxidation vessels. This cooking yields a pulp that is then treated with lime and a cyanide solution to "leach" out the gold. Finally, the gold is extracted from the leached solution, refined, and cast into "dross" bars. These may have a gold content as low as 60 to 70 percent or as high as 90 percent.

"Good-delivery" bars—bars that may be delivered to satisfy contracts on the futures exchange—must have a purity of 99.5 percent. To reach that level, the gold in the dross bars has to be further refined, either through a fire-refining process or through the more efficient electrolytic refining—the method that is used to produce gold of 99.9 percent fineness.

be hauled to a mill, where the ore will be crushed, ground, and treated to remove the gold or the gold will be removed through a heap-leaching process. An open-pit mine looks like a stone quarry, a gravel pit, or even a highway rock cut.

Deeply buried ore requires an underground mine. If the ore is inside a mountain, it may be possible to drive a horizontal tunnel into the mountain's side to gain access. If the gold is buried too deeply to remove the overlying rock, a shaft can be sunk next to the ore and tunnels driven off the shaft into the ore.

It is easier, and therefore less expensive, to push a load along a level plane than it is to lift it vertically. The distance from a surface mine to its associated mill is largely horizontal, and thus the ore can be moved by truck, conveyor belt, or even railroad, depending upon the circumstances. But ore from an underground mine must be either hoisted up the shaft or trucked up a steep spiral incline. There are variations, but the vertical component is what makes it relatively expensive to move such ore, along with the fact that all the tunnels and passageways have to be made large enough to accommodate the mining equipment. These accessways must be carefully designed and reinforced to keep them from collapsing under the weight of the overlying rock—and this adds further to the cost. Underground miners require more skill, and are subject to greater discomfort and danger, than those engaged in open-pit mining.

Most South African gold comes from underground mines. These mines have the deepest shafts in the world, with depths ranging from 5,500 feet to over 12,400 feet (more than two miles) below the surface. By contrast, many of the newer mines in North America are open-pit operations.

To justify their higher costs, operators of underground mines require either rock that contains more gold or gold that is somehow easier to extract. Getting the gold out of the ground is only part of the story: After that, the gold must be removed from the rock.

Time and again, a body of gold-bearing rock whose existence was widely known has overnight been upgraded to ore, making it profitable to mine, because a new process has made it possible to recover the gold at a reasonable cost. One of the more recent, and more important, of these processes is heap leaching.

Heap leaching is an inexpensive means of extracting very fine-grained gold from low-grade ore. Unfortunately, this method will work only for certain types of low-grade ore and usually will recover only 60 to 70 percent of the gold in the rock, compared to the 90 to 99 percent that a traditional, more capital-intensive mill can remove. Traditional mills crush and grind the ore to a fine powder before removing the precious metal. The grinding is the most expensive part of the process—and for rock containing only $3/100$ of an ounce of gold per ton, and that in the form of microscopic particles, the cost cannot be justified. But, with the heap-leach process, the same ore can be crushed to only half-inch fragments (some mines, in fact, do not even crush it at all) and "heaped" on what looks like an asphalt parking lot in flat-topped piles 10 to 20 feet or more in height, containing from 5,000 to 2 million tons. The piles are sprayed with a cyanide solution that dissolves the gold out of the rock—the "leach" part of heap leaching.

The "parking lot" is an impervious leach pad designed to collect the leaching fluid after it has percolated through the ore. The now gold-rich fluid flows through a series of channels to a holding tank and then is pumped to a gold recovery plant. The leaching fluid sprayed on the heap is a mix of about one pound of sodium cyanide and one or two pounds of lime per 250 gallons of water, and is applied to the top of the heap by a sprinkler system—one not too different from the kind suburbanites use on their front lawns. The lime prevents the formation of deadly cyanide gas. Rock that contains sulfur-rich or carbon-rich material often may not be suitable for heap-leach processing.

After the solution has percolated through the heap, the gold is removed through a process involving activated carbon granules in a series of tanks. The gold adheres to the surface of these granules, and the granules are then stripped of the gold chemically and the gold is removed from the fluid electrolytically. An alternate method, known by the name Merrill-Crowe, uses zinc dust to precipitate the gold from the leaching solution. The end product shipped from a mine can be anything from gold-rich carbon granules all the way up to high-purity gold bars, depending upon such factors as the size of the mine and the level of the company's security.

Heap leaching of precious metals came into its own in the 1970s at the Cortez gold mine in Nevada. It has since become fairly widespread. If the rock is suitable for heap leaching, the method is inexpensive and can be set up quickly (one company had a heap-leach operation running within four months)—and the rapid recovery of gold generates funds that can be used to finance mine expansion or a more sophisticated recovery system. Heap leaching requires a much lower level of capital investment to establish production and a much smaller labor force to sustain it, and these are important considerations. Using this process, it is possible to put a 5-million-ton-a-year operation on stream for about $10 million.

Heap leaching is particularly popular in the southwestern United States, where the ore deposits lend themselves to this technology. Among the important heap-leach operations are Amselco-Nerco's Alligator Ridge and Echo Bay's Round Mountain, both in Nevada; Consolidated Goldfield's Ortiz mine in New Mexico; Pegasus Gold Corporation's Zortman/Landusky mine in Montana; Wharf Resources' Annie Creek mine near Rapid City, South Dakota; Sonora Gold Corporation's Jamestown, California, mine; and Galactic Resources Limited's Summitville property at Del Norte, Colorado.

To summarize the advantages of heap leaching:

1. Low capital cost is the principal plus.
2. It permits extraction of gold from very low-grade ore.
3. Because large quantities of ore are moved only short distances, labor requirements are low. And because the ore is not ground, direct operating costs are low—$4.50 to $6.00 per ton of ore processed, or $100.00 to $300.00 per ounce of gold recovered.

ORE RESERVES AND GRADE

After the cost of production, the next thing you should look at is a company's ore reserves. Ore is rock that a company can mine at a profit, and ore reserves are simply the amount of ore on its property. Gold often runs in veins beneath the earth's surface, but in many of the newer open-pit mines, the gold is distributed—frequently in microscopic particles—throughout a large volume of rock. Ore grades must be considered, as well. Essentially, "grade" refers to how much gold each ton of rock contains. Ore grades are an important factor in determining the cost of a mining operation. As I have noted, the best South African mines have about one quarter of an ounce of gold per ton of ore. Ore reserves may be "proven" or "probable." Proven reserves are outlined very carefully by closely spaced drilling and sampling, often along a tunnel that is dug for just this purpose. Probable reserves are less rigorously defined, perhaps through relatively shallow (though closely spaced) drilling from the surface of the property.

Proven ore reserves are much more expensive to determine than probable reserves. Many mining companies will prove out only two or three years of reserves, even though the ore body may have enough gold for many more years of profitable mining. In most cases, the probable reserves will give the company—and the investor—a more than adequate picture of the mine's actual long-term potential.

Generally, the newer mines just coming on stream will have a relatively short life span—in some cases, less than 10 years. Some of the older South African mines *appear* to be nearly exhausted. In these cases, though, the ore-reserve data supplied by a company may not be a good indicator of a mine's life expectancy, since new reserves often are proven each year as old reserves are depleted.

Despite all this, published reserve figures remain, in many cases, an accurate reflection of a company's unit growth. In these terms, gold production has become one of the most rapidly growing industries in North America. A number of well-capitalized producers have added substantially to their reserves—among them Lac Minerals, Echo Bay Mines, and Newmont. By contrast, older companies such as Dome Mines, Campbell Red Lake, and Homestake are regarded now as underperformers because their reserves have gone up by less than triple since 1978.

The following table compares recent growth in reserves.

EXHIBIT 8–1 North American Mines—
Industry Production and Financial Statistics
Reserve Growth of Major North American Gold Producers
(in millions of ounces)

Company	1980	1985E	Percentage Growth	Rank
Newmont Mining*	2.7	17.0	530	1
Lac Minerals	2.4	11.2	373	2
Homestake Mining	3.7	8.9	140	3
Consolidated Goldfields USA*	0.5	6.4	1,182	4
Echo Bay*	0.8	5.5	588	5
International Corona, Teck, Noranda, Goliath, G. Sceptre	0	4.0	NM	6
Freeport Gold, FMC, and Bull Run*	2.7	4.0	47	7
Campbell Red Lake†	1.4	2.8	103	8
Battle Mountain Gold*	0.5	2.3	404	9
Barrick Resources and Partners*	0.3	2.0	575	10
Pegasus and U.S. Minerals Exploration*	0.7	2.2	218	11
Breakwater, Asamera, and Partners*	0	1.9	NM	12
Placer Development	0.3	1.4	466	13
Lacana, Rayrock, and Partners	0.4	1.1	209	14
Galactic Resources	0	1.0	NM	15
Dome Mines‡	0.6	0.6	−9	16
Subtotal: 16 Major Producers and Partners	16.9	72.4	328	

Note: Includes U.S. and Canadian mines only.
*Indicates major additions to ore reserves in 1985 and 1986.
†Excludes Kiena.
‡Excludes Falcenbridge.
SOURCE: Oppenheimer & Co., Inc. Company Reports, 1986.

ANALYZING IT ALL

Once you finish compiling information on the properties and operating efficiencies of a mining company, you have the basic tools needed to analyze whether a particular firm will be a good investment. (Operating efficiencies are reflected in the company's operating costs.) You can obtain information on an individual mine or mining firm by asking for the company's annual and quarterly reports. (For more details, you might look at its 10-K and 10-Q reports. These are filed with the Securities and Exchange Commission and are available from a company's

---

South African Gold-Mining Industry— Dividend Payments

The South African gold-mining companies traditionally pay dividends twice a year, profits permitting, of course. Those gold-mining companies with June or December fiscal year-ends would normally announce their half-yearly dividends in June/ July and December/January each year with record date being a Friday two or three weeks later. Payment usually takes place some six weeks after the record date. The half-yearly dividends from those companies with March or September year-ends are normally declared in March/April and September/October with similar periods in respect of record and payment dates.

For shareholders not resident in South Africa, there is a 15 percent withholding tax which is deducted at source. Payment of the dividend to nonresidents of South Africa is made in dollars or sterling. The conversion to these currencies is calculated at rates prevailing at the time of payment.

---

shareholder relations department if its stock is traded on a U.S. exchange.) Exhibit 8–2A and Exhibit 8–2B give some of the important statistics for several North American and South African mining companies.

Are you looking for income? South African mines are required by law to pay out a certain percentage of their earnings in dividends to shareholders, and they typically are high-yielding investments, with dividend returns sometimes in the double-digit percentage range. U.S. and Canadian firms have no such requirements and often are miserly in their dividend declarations, preferring instead to reinvest the capital in the company and new mining ventures. Dividends—and the regularity with which they are paid—are matters of public record, so it is not too difficult to obtain this information. The more money a company retains for future development, the easier it will be

EXHIBIT 8-2A South African Gold-Mining Industry—Production and Financial Statistics

Production Statistics	Mar. 86 Quarter	Dec. 85 Quarter	Sep. 85 Quarter	June 85 Quarter	Mar. 85 Quarter	Percent Change Past Year
Tons Milled (millions)	31.90	32.10	32.40	30.80	N/A	4.9
Gold Produced (metric tons)	155.40	161.40	164.70	159.20	N/A	− 6.3
Gold Price Received:						
Rand per ounce	765.00	834.00	694.00	628.00	N/A	+27.1
Dollars per ounce	344.00	313.00	321.00	320.00	N/A	+16.2
Costs:						
Rand per ton milled	63.71	60.77	58.92	56.70	N/A	+17.8
Dollars per ounce produced	182.00	141.00	166.00	174.00	N/A	+19.7
Distributable Earnings (rand millions)	536.00	766.00	551.00	530.00	N/A	+ 3.1

Financial Statistics (Quarterly Industry Profit Figures)	Mar. 86 Quarter	Dec. 85 Quarter	Sep. 85 Quarter	June 85 Quarter	Mar. 85 Quarter	
Dollars per Ounce:						
Gold Price	344	313	321	320	296	
Cost of Production	182	141	166	174	152	
Profit	162	172	155	146	144	
Rand Millions:						
Total Revenue	3,909	4,428	3,779	3,434	3,428	
Total Costs	2,023	1,950	1,907	1,746	1,645	
Pre-Tax Profits	1,888	2,478	1,872	1,688	1,783	
Tax and Lease	836	1,113	795	686	865	
After-Tax Profits	1,050	1,365	1,077	1,002	918	
Capital Expenditure	514	599	526	471	398	
Available for Shareholders	536	766	551	530	520	

EXHIBIT 8–2A (continued)

Mining Company/Mine	Symbol	Range (U.S. dollars, 12/85–3/86)	Breakeven (dollars per ounce) Mar. 86	Tonnage (thousands) Mar. 86	Grade (g/t) Mar. 86	Cost/Ton (rand) Mar. 86
Blyvooruitzicht	BLYVY	3.81–8.94	203	498	6.20	90.04
Bracken	BRCEY	1.00–5.00	217	237	3.40	52.75
Buffelsfontein	BFELY	18.25–47.38	193	704	8.56	117.67
Deelkraal	DLKLY	1.40–3.05	204	375	5.10	74.06
Doornfontein	DOORY	6.25–20.50	230	366	6.07	99.66
Driefontein	DRFNY	12.13–29.38	114	1,425	10.41	82.07
Durban Deep	DUROY	4.75–16.00	320	583	3.83	73.85
Ergo	ERGOY	3.38–6.00	246	5,275	0.43	7.49
ERPM	ERNDY	3.75–9.63	386	656	3.54	97.63
Elandsrand	ELRDY	4.00–15.17	168	462	5.90	70.65
Freegold	FSCNY	10.50–12.88	211	5,293	5.07	76.58
Grootvlei	GROVY	3.13–10.50	246	440	3.37	59.15
Harmony	HARMY	6.88–17.00	255	2,017	3.56	64.89
Hartebeestfontein	HBEEY	2.75–6.75	133	790	9.50	90.39
Kinross	KNRSY	8.75–24.00	129	535	6.16	61.28
Kloof	KLOFY	4.95–8.88	106	540	13.00	98.76
Leslie*	LSLEY	5.00–16.25	252	346	2.60	46.72
Libanon	LIGOY	10.50–26.50	191	435	5.30	72.13
Loraine	LORAY	2.63–5.75	248	390	5.40	95.72
Randfontein†	RNDEY	6.20–9.55	140	161	4.00	47.87
St. Helena	SGOLY	8.88–19.88	185	580	4.90	64.84
Southvaal	SVALY	22.00–52.00	115	1,096	9.09	74.61
Stilfontein	STILY	4.75–10.13	258	417	5.44	100.25
Unisel	UNSLY	5.38–11.13	111	335	7.11	56.55
Vaal Reefs†	VAALY	4.63–10.75	140	2,908	7.23	72.49
Venterspost	VENTY	4.38–11.25	322	390	3.37	77.48
Western Areas	WAGMY	2.00–5.50	233	959	4.20	84.04
Western Deep	WDEPY	23.50–49.25	143	1,270	7.49	76.48
West Rand Consolidated	WESKY	2.00–10.25	305	510	1.96	42.75
Winkelbaak	WINKY	12.50–40.00	142	567	5.65	57.14

*1 ADR = 5 shares.
†10 ADRs = 1 share.
SOURCE: Reprinted from "South African Gold Mines" by permission of Merrill Lynch, Pierce, Fenner & Smith Incorporated. Copyright 1986 Merrill Lynch, Pierce, Fenner & Smith Incorporated. December 1986.

for the company to survive and thrive over the long run. If your budget does not require a steady flow of dividend income (as it might if you are retired, for example), you should consider total returns over time—that is, capital gains plus reinvested dividends—rather than the current dividend income alone. On this basis, many North American mines have outperformed some of their South African cousins in recent years, largely because of the growth in the number of ounces produced at relatively low cost by these North American companies and perhaps also because of some investors' anxiety regarding South Africa's long-term prospects.

BEWARE OF PENNY STOCKS

If you like to speculate, perhaps you might be interested in "penny stocks." In general terms, a penny stock is one that sells for under $5 per share and is not expected to pay a dividend in the near future. Some gold-mining stocks are categorized as penny stocks. A penny gold-mining stock might be a share in anything from a small, family-run operation to a multimillion-dollar firm. But, as a rule, the companies that issue such stock are relatively small and should not be considered for investment unless you have a strong indication that the price of gold will increase dramatically in the near future—and that the mine itself has real profit potential and is not Mark Twain's "hole in the ground." The penny-stock market thrives on hype and promotion. The price of a company's shares will sometimes rise and fall with the public relations efforts of its management and key "inside" shareholders. Many stockbrokers will not handle penny stocks because the commissions are small. If you find an interesting penny stock, you can buy shares through a discount brokerage house. You will not need a national "full-service" broker with an extensive research department, since it is not likely to have a securities analyst who specializes in penny-stock firms. Most of the brokerages that do specialize in these stocks are located in places like Spokane, Washington, and Denver, Colorado—the sites of two regional stock exchanges that list and trade many of these equities. If you decide to speculate in this sector of the gold-share market, you should consider subscribing to some of the newsletters and investment services that focus on such companies.

UNDERSTANDING PRESENT AND RELATIVE VALUES

The current price of a gold-mining share, like the price of any other equity, should be related to the level of return the investing public expects from that particular stock. In investment theorists' jargon, this is the current or present value of the expected future stream of earnings. Buyers of gold-mining equities are concerned about whether the going price per share reflects the present value of the equity—in other words, whether it reflects the value of the company's gold properties and its potential for paying dividends, both of which are related to the present and expected future price of gold. Some professional analysts use complicated computer models of a mining company to estimate present value, plugging in such variables as production costs, mine life, ore reserves, and ore grades, along with assumptions about future gold prices and interest rates. The resulting estimates of present value then may be compared to actual share prices to help the investor determine the relative over- or undervaluation of mining company equities.

One common standard for evaluating the relative value of a mining stock is its price-to-earnings (P/E) ratio. A P/E ratio is simply the price per share divided by the company's earnings per share. This statistic is listed in many newspapers' stock market tables. A low P/E number may be an indication that the stock is a "good buy," while a higher P/E ratio can be a signal that the stock is overpriced. Obviously, an investor cannot simply shun all stocks that have a high P/E number and buy anything with a low number; to do so would ignore the reasons for the individual numbers. In looking at gold equity P/E ratios, you should be comparing them with those of other mining firms, not with the figures for computer manufacturers or oil-drilling equipment firms—and within the gold-mining sector, you should be comparing the price-to-earnings ratios of companies that are fairly similar. Do not compare South African with North American mines, or open-pit with deep-shaft mines, or long-life, high-grade mines with short-life, low-grade operations. A look at a company's P/E ratio will give you a first indication of whether its stock is over- or undervalued.

Another technique used by some professional analysts is to determine how much a company produces annually per $1,000 of shareholder equity investment, and how large its reserves are per $1,000 equity. The second number will tell you how much gold you are "buying" for your investment, while the first is an indication of how efficiently the company is producing it. To calculate the production per $1,000, first multiply the number of shares issued times the price per share, then divide the annual production by this figure. To calculate the reserves per $1,000, first take the size of the reserves and multiply it by the ore grade. This represents the actual amount of gold in the reserves. Then multiply the number of shares by the price per share and divide this figure into the amount of gold in the reserves. Exhibit 8–2B shows these statistics for 20 major North American mining companies.

The various tables that comprise Exhibit 8–2B provide key financial information on 20 North American mining companies. This data was taken from financial analysts' research and includes not only the P/E ratio but also cash flow per share, return on equity, and several other financial characteristics.

Australian gold producers are growing rapidly in importance, though not yet at the capitalization level of the major North American mines. Only eight Australian producers have reached the level of $70 million capitalization; by contrast, more than 20 North American precious-metals mines have exceeded the $100 million level. Allowing for the various political, currency, and other risks involved, Australian mines tend to be valued at 30 to 50 percent of comparable North American mines.

GOLD PRODUCERS

In addition to considering a mining company's operating costs and ore reserves, you also should examine its infrastructure, that is, its method of producing gold. Does it have its own refining operation? This could be a plus if it is a low-cost, efficient refinery. But if it is an old, inefficient plant, it could be a

EXHIBIT 8–2B North American Mines—Industry Production and Financial Statistics
Traditional Mine Valuation Measures for Major Gold Mines

Company	Cash Flow 1985E	Per Share 1986E	Book 1985E	Value 1986E	ROE 1986E	Dividend Yield (percent) (Jan. 86)	Breakeven Metal Price (U.S. Dollars)
Homestake Mining	0.40	1.20	11.54	11.97	5.4	0.8	300
Lao Minerals	1.35	2.50	7.52	8.30	12.6	0.9	225
Newport Mining	3.75	6.50	48.75	51.50	7.5	1.9	225
Dome Mines	0.47	0.71	1.57	1.88	23.1	0.8	300
Echo Bay Mines	0.65	1.00	3.22	4.16	15.7	0.6	240
Campbell Red Lake	0.70	0.94	2.65	2.95	21.4	1.4	200
Placer Development	0.85	1.45	10.50	11.13	7.9	1.2	250
Battle Mountain	0.55	0.83	1.24	1.74	40.4	0.7	220
Freeport Gold	0.25	0.55	1.60	1.90	17.1	0.0	275
American Barrick	0.60	1.00	4.00	4.38	9.1	0.0	250
Pegasus Gold	0.00	0.54	3.93	4.33	9.7	0.0	275
Intn'l Corona Res.	-0.20	0.10	1.50	1.43	-5.1	0.0	200
Galactic Resources	0.00	0.75	1.10	1.50	30.8	0.0	250
Agnico Eagle	0.55	0.67	2.92	3.22	14.7	0.8	225
Asamera	0.60	0.80	3.04	3.23	9.6	1.4	275
Breakwater Res.	0.04	0.70	1.60	2.05	24.7	0.0	200
Lacana Mining	0.75	1.03	5.43	5.65	6.0	1.4	225
U.S. Minerals Exploration	0.00	0.00	0.11	0.11	0.0	0.0	250
Rayrock Yel. Res.	0.55	0.51	3.34	3.64	10.6	1.2	225
Malarctic Hygrade	0.50	0.75	2.35	2.48	27.0	4.7	200

E = estimated.

SOURCE: Oppenheimer & Co., Inc., Company Reports, January 1986.

EXHIBIT 8-2B North American Mines—Industry Production and Financial Statistics Summary Stock Information for Major Gold Mines

Company	Price (1/30/86)	F.D. Shares Outstanding	Market Cap (millions of dollars)	Ticker Symbol	Dividend (Jan. 86)	1988E Annual Production (ounces of gold, in thousands)
Homestake Mining	26.00	49.4	1,283.6	HM	0.20	685
Lao Minerals	25.00	28.2	705.0	LAC	0.22	594
Newport Mining	52.00	30.3	1,575.6	NEM	1.00	550
Dome Mines	10.88	80.6	876.9	DM	0.09	400
Echo Bay Mines	15.63	41.4	647.1	ECO	0.09	340
Campbell Red Lake	21.88	48.0	1,050.2	CRK	0.30	315
Placer Development	18.00	49.8	896.6	PLC	0.22	290
Battle Mountain	15.25	44.0	671.0	BMGC	0.10	265
Freeport Gold	11.50	40.0	460.0	FAU	0.00	250
American Barrick	7.63	21.0	160.2	ABXFF	0.00	243
Pegasus Gold	7.88	8.9	70.3	PGULF	0.00	150
Intn'l Corona Res.	11.16	15.0	167.4	ICR.TO	0.00	120
Galactic Resources	7.38	20.0	147.6	GALCF	0.00	110
Agnico Eagle	18.75	14.2	265.7	AEAGF	0.15	95
Asamera	8.00	37.0	296.0	ASM	0.11	70
Breakwater Res.	5.13	18.7	96.0	BWRLF	0.00	67
Lacana Mining	7.63	11.3	86.4	LCNAF	0.11	60
U.S. Minerals Expl.	0.56	60.6	33.9	USMX	0.00	50
Rayrock Yel. Res.	5.67	10.0	56.7	RAY.TO	0.07	33
Malarctic Hygrade	11.13	3.5	38.9	MHG	0.52	20

E = estimates.

SOURCE: Oppenheimer & Co., Inc. Estimates. Company Reports, 1986.

EXHIBIT 8–3 Major Australian Gold Producers—Industry Production and Financial Statistics

Company	Major Investors	Equity (percent)	Estimated 1985 Production (thousands of ounces)	Estimated 1985 Production Costs (Australian dollars per ounce)	State
Kidston	Placer Development	70.0	280,000	195	Queensland
	Elders Resources	15.0			
	General Public	15.0			
Mt. Charlotte/Fimiston	Homestake Mining	48.0	234,000	294	Western Australia
	Kalgoorlie Gold Mines	24.0			
	Poseidon	24.0			
	Western Mining (indirect)	10.2			
Telfer	Newmont Mining	70.0	130,000	280	Western Australia
	BHP	30.0			
Kambalda	Western Mining Corporation	100.0	130,000	245	Western Australia
Norseman	Cental Norseman	100.0	107,000	220	Western Australia
	Western Mining (indirect)	—			
Tennant Creek	Peko Wallsend	100.0	59,000	260	Northern Territory
Fimiston	North Kalgurli	100.0	62,000	380	Western Australia
Sons of Gwalia	Sons of Gwalia	100.0	48,500	200	Western Australia

SOURCE: Oppenheimer & Co., Inc. Estimates. January 1986 Report.

burdensome expense. You should take careful note of the quality and age of any existing equipment, as well as the degree of likelihood that it may have to be replaced in the near future. If the company is planning to develop new properties, will it be using an underground mining operation requiring substantial capital investment or an open-pit operation with low start-up costs? Will it have to invest heavily in new milling or concentrating equipment in the near future? Much of this information is available from a company's quarterly and annual reports.

NORTH AMERICAN OR FOREIGN?

Just as gold is an international commodity, so gold mining is an international industry. Some foreign gold-mining firms are listed on U.S. and Canadian stock exchanges. Benguet Consolidated, the largest Philippine operation, is listed on the New York Stock Exchange, for example. So are Dome Mines and Campbell Red Lake, both of which are Canadian—while Echo Bay and Placer Development, also Canadian, are listed on the American Stock Exchange.

South African mining shares are not listed on U.S. exchanges—with the exception of shares in ASA, a closed-end investment company whose stock is traded on the New York Exchange. Nevertheless, it is easy for Americans to invest in these companies if they so wish. Instead of trying to buy the shares directly through a South African broker on the Johannesburg Stock Exchange, they can use an alternative vehicle developed to facilitate investments in foreign shares by U.S. residents. This vehicle is known by the name "American Depository Rights," or ADRs, for short. Many foreign equities not listed on a domestic exchange may be purchased indirectly in this form in over-the-counter markets. ADRs are issued by U.S. banks that hold shares in the foreign companies on behalf of the ultimate investors. They are listed and sold in U.S. currency, so there are no exchange-rate problems when buying or selling these instruments. If you purchase ADRs in a given mining company, you will not be listed on the firm's books as a shareholder, just as you are not listed on the corporate books if your stock is held in a street name. ADRs are very liquid investments and can be traded on over-the-counter markets during U.S. business hours without the bother of overseas communications. The financial institution that issues an ADR will charge you a slight premium that you will have to pay in addition to any commissions your stockbroker charges you. But this small fee is worth paying, for such a transaction eliminates the complications that can arise from trading a stock listed only on a foreign exchange. Moreover, the issuing institution collects the dividends on your behalf and converts them into U.S. dollars before paying them to you. Usually, it deducts a small fee for this service.

THE RAND-DOLLAR RELATIONSHIP

The relationship between the South African rand and the U.S. dollar is an important consideration for someone interested in the equities of mining companies in that country. And the strength or weakness of the rand is closely tied to the price of gold itself, since the yellow metal is the country's principal export and the source of much of its foreign-exchange revenue. In recent years, the relationship between the value of the rand and the price of gold has shielded the South African mines during periods of gold price weakness by protecting their rand-denominated profit margins. During 1984 and early 1985, for example, the rand fell faster vis-à-vis the dollar than did gold. The result was a rising rand gold price at a time of falling U.S. dollar gold prices. High-cost mines that were unprofitable or only marginally profitable became healthier financially as their profit margins widened—and, for the South African industry as a whole, dividend payments rose. Although the South African shares dropped in value along with the U.S. dollar price of gold, their falls were cushioned by the improving margins at the mines and rising dividend yields. Of course, this mechanism could move in reverse if appreciation of the rand were to outpace a gold price recovery.

Weakness in the rand during the mid-1980s has been largely a consequence of South Africa's political and social problems. Lack of confidence in the country's future prospects has boosted the price of gold, as denominated in the local currency, even though the dollar price in international markets has been subdued.

Just as the weakness of the rand helped South Africa's mines, the recent strength of the U.S. dollar against other currencies, most notably the Canadian dollar, also helped to shield gold-mining operations elsewhere. This was true as long as the price of gold, stated in U.S. dollars, fell more slowly than the value of that currency against the dollar. Weakness in the Canadian dollar, for example, has increased the price Canadian mines have received for their gold.

One result of these currency trends is that profit margins have widened at many mines in South Africa and other weak-currency countries. Almost paradoxically, this has taken place at a time when the U.S. dollar price of gold has been restrained.

BY-PRODUCTS AND COPRODUCTS

Among the variables you should look at in evaluating a mining equity is just what products are being mined. A pure gold mine is rare. Homestake's mine, for example, is located in Leadville, South Dakota—and, as the name of the town implies, lead is a by-product of the mine. Many gold mines produce small amounts of by-product silver, which may provide extra profit. In South Africa, a number of the gold mines also produce uranium ore. Generally, if the value of the mineralization of a given ore body lies primarily in one product, then other metals recovered there are known as by-products. If the value of the other minerals is roughly equal to that of the gold, then they are known as coproducts.

In assessing a mine's viability, it is important to know how much of its earnings come from by-products or coproducts. Although the prices of gold and other metals do not move in lockstep, patterns do occur—and often if one is depressed, the prices of the others will also be down. Nonetheless, these other minerals can make the difference between a profitable mining operation and an unprofitable one.

MUTUAL FUNDS

If you cannot decide on a single company in which to invest or cannot afford to invest in more than one firm (as you definitely should, in order to maintain a diversified portfolio), then you should be considering gold-mining mutual funds. A mutual fund pools many people's money and invests it in the financial instruments outlined in the fund's prospectus.

Basically, there are two kinds of mutual funds: open-end and closed-end. Open-end funds are ones in which the number of shares outstanding rises or falls as investor participation expands or shrinks. As an investor in an open-ended fund, you can buy or sell shares at any time at a price equal to the per-share value of the fund's portfolio. This kind of fund often is managed by a major brokerage house. But, just as often, the managers are professionals who specialize in this particular industry.

A closed-end fund, such as ASA Ltd., is one that has an initial offering period during which a set number of shares in the fund are sold. After the end of that period, the managers take the pooled cash and invest it. While it is possible to buy the shares of a closed-end fund after the initial offering, your investment will not go into the fund itself but rather will be paid to whoever sells the shares. Unlike an open-end fund, where the price per share is tied to the value of the portfolio, the price paid for shares in a closed-end fund after the initial offering will depend upon the supply and demand for these shares among investors in the secondary market. Closed-end mutual funds work like equities in a company. When those equities are first sold, during a period known as an "initial offering," the company takes the investors' money and applies it to its own needs. Any time those shares are bought or sold after the initial offering, the money is exchanged among the individual shareholders, not with the company itself.

An open-end mutual fund, on the other hand, has no real counterpart among investment instruments in the equities market. Because closed-end funds are traded constantly, they usually are listed on a stock exchange, although they may be traded on the over-the-counter market. No matter where they are traded, they must be registered with the Securities and Exchange Commission if they are offered in the United States, as are shares in open-end mutual funds sold in this country.

Exhibit 8–4 shows a list of open-end mutual funds available in the United States.

There are two kinds of open-end funds: load and no-load. A

EXHIBIT 8–4   Gold-Oriented Mutual Funds

Fund	Assets 6/30/86	Load	Invests in South Africa
Colonial Advanced Strategies	19.5	SC	No*
Fidelity Select American Gold	7.6	LO-R	No
Fidelity Select Precious Metals	102.8	LO-R	Yes
Financial Portfolio—Gold	2.2	NO	Yes
Franklin Gold Fund	93.1	LO	Yes
Freedom Gold and Government Trust	41.6	SC	Yes
Golconda Investors, Ltd.	20.6	NO	Yes
Hutton Investment Series—Precious Metals	25.9	NO	Yes
IDS Precious Metals	11.4	SC	Yes
International Investors, Inc.	692.8	SC	Yes
Keystone Precious Metals	55.0	R	Yes
Lexington Gold Fund	15.5	NO	Yes
Midas Gold Shares and Bullion	2.7	SC	Yes
Oppenheimer Gold and Special Metals	29.1	SC	Yes
Strategic Investments	65.6	SC	Yes
United Gold and Government	5.5	SC	Yes
United Services Gold Shares	214.8	NO	Yes
United Services Prospectors†	61.0	NO	No
United Services New Prospector	27.3	NO	No
USAA Gold	17.5	NO	Yes
Van Eck Gold/Resources	8.6	SC	No
Vanguard Special—Gold	26.3	NO	Yes

SC: Sales charge; the fund is a load fund up to 8½ percent load.
LO: Low-load fund; the fund charges a load up to 4½ percent.
NO: No-Load fund; has no sales charge.
R: Fund charges ½ of 1 percent on sales and redemptions.
*Not a fundamental policy; may be changed without shareholder approval.
†Fund closed to new investors.
SOURCE: American Precious Metals Advisors/Gold Information Center—Investment Service.

load fund is one in which you as an investor pay a commission when you buy shares in the fund. A no-load fund is one in which no commission is charged when you buy, but in some cases one may be charged when you sell your shares in the fund.

In both open-end and closed-end funds, the manager will charge a fee for administering the fund—a fee that normally is paid out of the portfolio's dividend earnings. In considering a fund, you will naturally want to determine whether this fee is reasonable. You should make this determination based upon the record of the fund's management. That record plus the expected earnings of the fund are the two most important considerations in choosing a fund. If it is an open-end fund or an initial offering of a closed-end fund, your broker will be able to provide you with a prospectus which will detail the management's record and experience as well as the anticipated earnings. If it is an open-end fund or you are buying shares of a closed-end fund after the initial offering, your broker should also be able to give you information on the management as well as the record of the fund since its establishment.

EQUITIES SUMMARIZED

Before you invest in equities, there are several points to keep in mind.

First, you must determine the operating costs of the mining property. This figure can be obtained by reviewing a company's annual 10-K filing with the Securities and Exchange Commission if it is a U.S. firm, or it can be obtained through your stockbroker's research department if it is a foreign company. There are many publications that regularly review the operating costs of every gold mine. Appendix D, Information Sources about Gold and Gold Investments, lists several sources that will help you analyze individual properties.

Next, determine the mine's ore grade and life expectancy. You should look at the company's physical plant. How is the ore processed? Will maintaining the mine and plant infrastructure require any unusual expenses in the near future?

If it is a foreign company, you should look at the political and social environment to determine the stability of the host country. You also should look at the country's currency situation.

In evaluating an individual company, its price-to-earnings ratio can be helpful in determining whether a share is over- or underpriced.

As an overriding concern, you must analyze the price of gold bullion. Can it be expected to rise or fall? No matter how efficient a company is, or how rich its ore body, it will not make money if the price of gold is below its operating costs; on the other hand, every company will make more money when the price of gold rises. Remember, the price of equities of a low-grade company will not rise as quickly as those of a high-grade company at the beginning of any rally in bullion prices but will rise proportionally faster the longer a rally continues.

To calculate how much gold, in ounces, you are buying when you invest in a given mine, you should figure the number of ounces in the firm's reserves per $1,000 of shareholder capitalization. Likewise, to determine how efficiently a firm is using your shareholder investment, calculate the number of ounces it produces per $1,000 of shareholder equity.

If you are unable to decide on a particular company or cannot afford to diversify by buying shares in more than one company, consider a mutual fund. Remember, there are basically two types of funds: open-end and closed-end. Within the open-end category, there are load and no-load funds. A closed-end fund is one where you purchase shares from another investor (unless you buy during the initial offering period). An open-end fund is one where you buy from the manager of the fund. A no-load open-end fund is one where you pay no commission when you buy but in some cases pay one when you sell. Factors to consider in both types of funds are the expected yields and the experience of the manager.

Your own objectives will determine what mining companies you should look at. If you want stability, one of the older North American firms should be your investment vehicle. If you want income, the South African mines are among the richest and most efficient in the world—and, with an average of 95 percent of earnings paid out to shareholders, they could interest you. A fall in South African share prices represents an adjustment for heightened risk. If you want speculation and the possibility of high growth, you might be interested in penny-stock firms—those with a per-share price of under $5.

Finally, you should consider a company's by-product and coproduct output. If it mines uranium as well as gold, what is the outlook for the nuclear energy industry (not just in the United States, but worldwide)? If its coproduct is lead or copper, how have base metal prices been holding up?

CHAPTER NINE

Futures—Their Origins, Purposes, and Workings

"A commodity (futures contract) is something the seller
   doesn't own, never did own, and never wants to own.
"And the buyer doesn't want, doesn't need,
   and never will own."

An anonymous skeptic

This and the following chapter are about gold futures exchanges—what they are, how they work, and how they can be useful to you, regardless of whether you are a short-term trader, a speculator, or even a long-term investor in gold bullion.

Those who consider themselves "conservative" investors may cringe at the thought of gold futures, but the futures markets hold opportunities for some investors, perhaps even those who consider themselves as conservatives in the investment arena. Of course, as noted in Chapter 4, Technical Analysis—A Primer, the futures markets may offer traders and investors in other gold instruments some important clues to trends in the metal's price and opportunities to make money and protect their investments.

This chapter is intended for the novice in futures, the seasoned trader, or the person who may be familiar with the stock market but not with the commodity futures exchange. The following chapter, Futures—The Techniques, will explain how you can use the futures markets as prudently as possible. It will give you advice that should be helpful, even if in principle you are not interested in short-term trading or speculating but simply are seeking an economical way to acquire or hedge your gold bullion investments.

At this juncture, I would be remiss if I did not indicate that, as a matter of practical experience, 90–95 percent of investors who have speculated on the commodities futures exchanges have lost their investment.

A great many people in the investment world know little about commodities beyond what they learned from reading about the adventures of the Hunt brothers in the silver market, watching the movie *Trading Places*, or listening to a friend or relative who lost his shirt trading pork bellies or, less likely, made a bundle in soybeans. Mention the words "commodities futures market" to most people, and they think immediately of high-risk gambling.

Although commodity exchanges—or futures exchanges, which is what we are talking about—may have the image of a gamble, they were established to serve legitimate business needs, which they do. Instead of trading actual physical items such as gold bars, buyers and sellers on futures exchanges trade *contracts* to "make" or "take" delivery of such items on some specific future date. A gold futures contract calls for the delivery of a specified quantity of gold, such as a 100-troy-ounce bar of a specified purity (for example, 99.5 percent), at a specified price at a specified time in the future.

The actual gold bar may never change hands; fewer than 5 percent of all contracts entered into on the various gold futures exchanges ever result in actual delivery. And even when there *is* a delivery, the gold itself often does not move. Instead, its ownership changes through transfer of a *depository receipt*. This is a receipt issued by the exchange's official depository that states the quantity of gold it represents, the fineness, the hallmark of the gold bar, and the location of the bar in the depository. The amount of gold in exchange-approved depositories is enough to back at least part of the open interest (the number of unfulfilled contracts) for each delivery month listed on the particular exchange. It does not cover the total amount of gold represented by the open interest. There is no need for that, since not every holder of a contract to buy gold will want to take possession. Even if everyone did want to do so, the holders of the contracts to sell the gold would be legally bound by those contracts to make delivery. To date, there has never been a default by one of these holders, known as "shorts," in commodity lingo, on an obligation to make delivery on a U.S. or Canadian gold futures exchange contract (although there have been defaults against some of the agricultural futures exchange contracts).

Instead of resulting in the taking or making of delivery, most gold futures contracts are closed out before their expiration date. Usually, they are satisfied when the holder of a contract to *buy* the goods sells that contract before the specified delivery date—or when, on the other side, the holder of a contract to *sell* gold "offsets" that contract by buying it back before its specified delivery date.

Although most gold futures traders never take or make delivery, and rarely intend to, delivery of gold through an exchange may be your best method not only for taking possession but also for storing your metal over a long period of time. The next chapter will explain how and why.

Apart from their usefulness to an investor or speculator, gold futures exchanges serve several very important and legitimate business and economic purposes:

- **Hedging** for both buyers and sellers of gold and transferring of risk from the gold producer or end-user to speculators who have the willingness and financial ability to assume this risk. By using the futures market, a gold miner, for example, can "sell" his output in advance of actually mining the metal or having it refined; or a gold jewelry manufacturer can "buy" gold in advance of actually needing it, without the expense of having to pay for and store his entire future gold needs immediately.
- **Providing a system for delivery** of gold, as well as locations where the metal may be stored in safe, insured vaults.
- **Identifying prices** through an open-outcry bidding system which attaches a current market value to the metal— a price that often serves as a benchmark for physical gold transactions off the exchange.
- **Enhancing market liquidity** by increasing the number of participants. Because speculators who normally might not participate in the gold markets do so through the

futures exchanges, there are more potential buyers and sellers and more business is transacted.

- **Providing investment opportunities** that offer substantial rewards for those who use this market judiciously. Even the U.S. government recognized this point in 1979, when the Department of Labor stated that a "prudent man" could invest in futures and allowed union pension funds to hedge their portfolios with futures.

THE ORIGINS OF FUTURES IN THE UNITED STATES

In the United States of the early 1800s, it was common for farmers to bring their goods to regional markets at a given time each year following harvests or in anticipation of the slaughter of livestock. Because so many farmers descended on the market at the same time, there frequently were conditions of oversupply; as a consequence, prices were pushed down, to the detriment of the individual farmer. At other times, by contrast, drought or other adverse weather produced shortages, forcing buyers to pay more for what little supply was available.

In order to avoid this near-chaotic pricing system and allow the participants to estimate how much they were going to earn, or how much they could expect to pay, farmers and their customers began to make contracts for delivery ahead of time—a practice that originated in Chicago soon after that city's founding in 1833. This was a form of hedging, very much like the system whereby the modern commodity exchange allows participants to buy or sell their wares in advance of production or use. It was not until the U.S. Civil War that these forward contracts, known as "to-arrive" contracts, became codified and standardized on the Chicago Board of Trade (CBT).

The concept of trading futures later was adopted in New York, and the New York Metals Exchange gradually evolved into the Commodity Exchange (Comex), now the leading gold futures exchange in the world. Initially, metals such as tin, silver, and copper were traded along with nonmetal commodities such as rubber, silk, and hides, offering producers and industrial buyers a chance to hedge their business commitments and, in the bargain, giving investors and speculators a new arena in which to make money.

Just as the trading of physical gold by private individuals was banned in the United States in 1933, there likewise was a proscription against trading gold futures. Even before 1933, no gold futures had been traded in U.S. markets, largely because the buying and selling of gold was dominated by England and the London bullion market. It was not until 1975 that gold futures trading began in this country, with the Comex soon assuming leadership. Exhibit 9-1 shows how gold futures trading has grown and how the New York Commodity Exchange has gained preeminence in the field.

The trading of gold futures began in Winnipeg, Manitoba, where contracts calling for the delivery of as few as 20 ounces of gold are still available. Since its introduction, gold futures trading has spread beyond New York, Winnipeg, and Chicago to exchanges in Singapore, Hong Kong, Sydney, Tokyo, and London, as well as a new exchange in Hamilton, Bermuda, opened in late 1984, that uses computers instead of open-outcry bidding.

There are variations in the ways the exchanges operate—the most obvious being differences in the sizes of the contracts being traded. But there also are a number of similarities. One common thread among most of them is a requirement that gold must be delivered in the form of bars with a purity of not less than 99.5 percent. For a list of the major gold futures exchanges in the world, plus salient facts about each, see Exhibit 9-2.

The Sydney Futures Exchange (Simex) and the Comex have established electronic trading linkage for gold futures, based on the 100-ounce Comex contract. Under this agreement, it is now possible to institute a gold futures position in New York and liquidate it in Sydney, or vice versa. Trading in Sydney begins at 4 P.M., New York time, and continues until midnight. After the Simex closes, there will be a "lag" until the Comex market opens at 9 A.M. This elongated "trading day" will end with the Comex close at 2:30 P.M. All contracts traded under this proposed linkage will be cleared—that is, handled—by Comex. A broker in the United States will be able to place an order for

EXHIBIT 9–1 Gold Futures Contract Trading Volume and Value on the U.S. Exchanges
(Annual data in troy ounces and millions of U.S. dollars)

	New York Commodity Exchange Volume	International Monetary Market Volume	Chicago Board of Trade Volume	Mid America Commodity Exchange Volume	Total Volume	Total Value
1975	39,351,700	40,696,800	5,240,225	662,804	85,951,529	13,686.70
1976	47,936,300	34,092,100	1,055,163	248,166	83,331,729	10,036.17
1977	98,155,100	90,818,000	1,326,477	255,593	190,555,170	2,811.12
1978	374,237,800	281,287,000	5,446,531	4,355,007	665,326,338	127,719.62
1979	654,189,300	355,896,000	10,989,704	20,036,686	1,041,111,690	313,130.49
1980	800,141,000	254,341,900	6,893,623	44,749,400	1,106,125,923	650,312.07
1981	1,037,370,600	251,843,500	1,474,800	46,946,000	1,337,634,900	593,335.09
1982	1,212,398,700	153,346,600	1,951,500	38,349,900	1,406,046,700	520,184.30
1983	1,038,280,500	99,413,200	10,641,355	34,904,400	1,183,239,455	486,930.90
1984	911,550,400	884,100	9,732,654	6,097,500	928,264,654	339,789.02
1985	777,383,400	700	5,418,312	3,154,300	785,956,712	252,043.01

Note:

IMM terminated trading gold futures contracts effective July 1985.

CBT in 1979 changed from 3 kilo trading unit to 100 oz.; in 1983 changed from 100 oz. trading unit to 1 kilo.

MACE in 1979 changed from a 3 kilo trading unit to 33.2 oz.

MACE in June 1986 discontinued trading on Chicago gold contracts but continued trade on New York gold contracts.

SOURCES: New York Commodity Exchange, International Monetary Market, Chicago Board of Trade, Mid America Commodity Exchange.

EXHIBIT 9–2 Commodity Futures Exchanges Offering Gold Contracts

---

Exchange	Size (in troy ounces)	Trading Months	Quoted In
Chicago Board of Trade (CBT)	32.15 (1 Kilobar)	Spot, Feb., Apr., June, Aug., Oct., Dec.	U.S.$
Commodity Exchange (Comex)	100	Spot, and 2 months immediately following, Feb., Apr., June, Aug., Oct., Dec. (23 months)	U.S.$
Mid America Commodity Exchange (MACE)	33.2	Spot, Feb., Apr., June, Aug., Oct., Dec.	U.S.$
Hong Kong Commodity Exchange	100	Feb., Apr., June, Aug., Oct., Dec.	U.S.$
International Futures Exchange (INTEX)*	100	Feb., Apr., June	U.S.$
London Gold Futures Market	100	Spot plus 6 months	U.S.$
Singapore	100 (futures) 3 Kilobars (spot)	Spot, next 5 months	U.S.$
Sydney Futures Exchange	50		Aust$
Tokyo Gold Exchange	1 Kilogram	6 months from spot, Aug., Oct., Dec.	Yen
Winnipeg	20	Mar., June, Sept., Dec. (2 years)	U.S.$

---

*Trading done via computer linkage between INTEX and brokerage firms, largely in United States and Canada.

SOURCES: American Precious Metals Advisors; Gold Information Center—Investment Service

execution in Sydney, but the margin requirements and commissions involved will all be paid to the U.S. firm. Likewise, a trader in Australia will maintain an account with a broker in that country, paying all fees to that broker.

There is gold futures trading somewhere in the world nearly

every minute of the day. But, until now, the lack of reciprocity between exchanges has made it difficult, if not impossible, for an investor in this country to trade simultaneously on more than one exchange because of the time, currency, and communications problems. Since the Sydney–New York hookup is such a new development, this book will concentrate primarily on the Comex, because it is by far the largest, most active, and most liquid gold futures exchange. (In 1984, the Comex accounted for more than 90 percent of all gold futures contracts traded in the United States.)

THE WORKINGS OF AN EXCHANGE

Gold futures exchanges serve primarily two groups of participants: the hedgers and the speculators. A hedger is a trader who either mines the physical gold, owns it, or plans to buy it in the future for use in manufacturing such items as jewelry or electronic components. A major bank or dealer with large gold holdings may be a hedger, using futures contracts as "insurance" against a possible loss in the value of those holdings.

A mine owner who expects to sell gold in the future might sell futures contracts in order to lock in his selling price today rather than risk a drop in price that would make it unprofitable to continue mining and force him to shut down the mine and lay off employees. A jewelry manufacturer, on the other hand, expects to buy gold in the future. Consequently, he would buy futures contracts and thus lock in the price of future purchases. Or he might hedge his inventory risk by selling futures as protection against a drop in the value of his holdings.

Unlike the hedger, a speculator is someone who has no commercial interest in buying or selling physical gold. Instead, the speculator has an opinion on the direction of gold prices and tries to profit from any changes. If, as a speculator, you believed the price of gold would rise, then you would buy futures contracts in hopes of selling later at a higher price. If you believed the price would drop, then you would sell futures contracts in hopes of buying them back later at a lower price.

Hedgers and speculators both play vital roles in gold futures trading—hedgers by producing, merchandising, and consuming physical gold, and speculators by assuming the price risk of buying and selling which commercial hedgers are striving to avoid. This transfer of risk from one group to the other is the principal economic benefit of the futures markets.

CONTANGO

If you look at a table of gold futures market prices in a daily newspaper like *The Wall Street Journal,* you will notice that prices for the future months are consecutively higher than those for the current or spot month. This spread between the lower spot and higher futures is known as *contango*—a London Metal Exchange term which simply means that prices for deferred delivery of a metal are higher than those for prompt, or nearby, delivery.

Contango reflects the costs of financing, insuring, and storing gold bullion from now until the time when the metal will be delivered—costs that are borne by the holder of the gold.

Let us suppose, for example, that the costs of financing, insuring, and storing a quantity of gold for one year came to 10 percent of its value. The price of gold for delivery in 12 months would then have to equal the spot-month market price plus 10 percent. The bulk of the surcharge, perhaps 9.5 percent, would be the cost of financing, with storage and insurance accounting for the rest. Finance charges fluctuate with changes in interest rates, while storage costs remain relatively stable. If the spot price today were $300 per ounce, the futures market price for delivery one year from today would be $330, assuming a 10 percent surcharge for financing, insurance, and storage.

If the price of gold were to fall below $330 for delivery in 12 months—say, to $320—bullion dealers with large inventories of gold would sell physical metal for $300 per ounce and buy futures contracts for $320. At the same time, the dealers would invest the cash they received for selling the gold ($300 per ounce) at 9.5 percent interest (the rate they would have charged to finance the gold bullion for 12 months). In one year's time, their cash position would grow to $328.50 for each ounce sold ($300.00 plus 9.5 percent interest), leaving them with an $8.50 profit on the $320.00 cost of the futures contract. And they would not have to pay for insurance and storage.

In the agricultural and industrial metal markets, the price for the spot month occasionally will be *higher* than that of futures—a situation which is referred to as "backwardation" or an "inverted market." Backwardation occurs in the gold markets only for fleeting moments. To an analyst, backwardation indicates there is a tightness of supply for prompt delivery. But there is never concern about this in the gold bullion market, since the major international bullion houses and banks always have adequate gold to satisfy world investor and industrial demands.

The bullion dealers and banks have large enough supplies, and access to sufficient capital, to enable them to sell physical gold and buy futures at any time, should the spot and futures prices diverge from the appropriate contango relationship. But, since the movement away from normal contango is usually just a matter of cents instead of dollars, massive amounts of gold would have to be traded before such a move could be profitable. Very few private investors have the necessary thousands of ounces of metal or millions of dollars at their disposal. Even so, this type of arbitrage activity is significant enough to assure that the gold market never moves into a situation of backwardation.

SHORTS AND LONGS

Unlike stock markets, where "going short" involves the sale of a borrowed security and may be done only if the previous price change in the equity was an increase or an "uptick," commodities may be "shorted" any time the market is open, regardless of previous price activity. In fact, every gold futures trade involves someone going short and someone going long. The item being traded is really just a contract, with the short side being a promise to deliver at some future date and the long side being a promise to accept that delivery. As a consequence, in a futures market—unlike an equity market—there is a winner for every loser. In the jargon of a mathematician, the futures market is a "zero-sum" game, since all long and short positions are equal and opposite. However, in certain instances, buyers and sellers both could lose money, after taking commission fees into account.

It is possible to calculate the total value of equities traded on a given stock market. By taking the price of every share, multiplying that price by the number of shares outstanding for each company listed, then adding all these figures together, you can arrive at the total capitalization of all the stocks traded on a given market.

There are some days on the stock market when losers outnumber gainers, so the market value of all listed equities will fall. Or, if gainers outnumber losers, the stock market's total value will increase. But on futures exchanges, for every loser—everyone who had the price go against a position—there will be someone who gained by the same amount.

THE CLEARINGHOUSE

Overseeing the whole operation of a commodity futures exchange is the *clearinghouse*—an agency connected to the exchange through which all commodity contracts are processed. The clearinghouse may be a separate corporation in which clearing members are partners, as is the case with gold futures exchanges, or it may be part of the exchange. Either way, the clearinghouse is responsible for matching up the participating firms in each transaction. The firms are responsible for keeping track of their (that is, their customers') trades. The clearinghouse then tells the member firms at the end of each trading day what their net margin requirements are, based on all the long and short positions each firm's clients held at the end of that day. Eventually, it either matches offsetting orders from each firm or handles notices of intention to make delivery on behalf of the holders of short positions from each firm. These notices are given to those firms which, according to clearinghouse records, have held long positions for the greatest amount of time. The member firms, in turn, pass on the notices to the customers with the oldest long contracts.

It is the responsibility of the clearinghouse to guarantee every contract traded on a given exchange. Thus, it is the clearinghouse that gives commodity futures exchanges their integrity.

While the clearinghouse is made up of exchange members, not every member is a *clearing member*. In order to be a clearing member—one that helps guarantee the contracts—a firm must furnish evidence of extensive financial assets.

At first, it may appear to you that the clearinghouse has a stake in the gold futures market. But, in actuality, it has no financial interest in the gold that is traded. Likewise, the exchanges themselves have no financial tie to the gold being traded: It is owned by the exchange members or their customers. The exchanges and their members have a stake in only the volume of contracts traded, since each trade involves a small fee paid to the exchange. (This exchange fee is included in the fees your broker will charge you.)

CHOOSING YOUR BROKER— DISCOUNT OR FULL-SERVICE?

Since 1978, brokerage firms have been free to set their own commission rates—a function that previously had been dictated by the exchanges. The result of this deregulation has been the advent of "discount brokers"—brokers whose main task is simply to take and execute orders without giving any trading advice or opinions on market direction to their customers.

The advice offered by a futures commission merchant can be misleading or self-serving, so paying for this advice by going to a "full-service" broker may be doubly costly. If the broker knew which way the market was headed, would he share his insights with you? Probably not. In all likelihood, he would be rich and retired rather than sitting at a desk and processing your orders. A full-service broker may charge more than $100 for a gold futures transaction if he handles both the purchase and sale of a single contract, giving him what is known as a *round-turn* commission. On the other hand, a discount broker might charge as little as $20 for the same transaction.

The major difference between a discount broker and a full-service house is the discounter's lack of certain additional services—chiefly analytical advice and research facilities. Discount brokers will simply take your order and relay it to the trading floor. But, in reality, that is all the full-service broker does in most instances anyway. One other drawback of discount houses is that they may not be able to handle both stock and commodity business.

While discount brokers generally do not offer market advice, they *can* give you *information,* such as where the market is at any given moment and what the trading range has been for that particular day. Some might even have access to important wire-service stories about the market from sources such as Reuters, Commodity News Services, Dow Jones, or Commodity World News. Whatever kind of broker you decide to use, make certain in advance that the firm is properly capitalized.

By purchasing this book, you have taken the first step toward becoming your own analyst—and if you make it your business to keep informed on the gold market and events that might affect it, and understand the technical picture of the futures market, you are probably as well prepared as most brokerage house research analysts. If you feel comfortable making your own decisions, by all means use a discount broker.

THE TRADING PROCESS

Whether you are a gold hedger or a speculator, you have to begin with the same first step: You must open an account with a commodity brokerage house—known legally as a "futures commission merchant" (FCM)—where a broker, known legally as a registered commodity representative (RCR), will be assigned to work with you. FCMs and RCRs are registered with the Commodity Futures Trading Commission (CFTC) as well as with some of the exchanges.

Next, you must deposit a margin in order to initiate a transaction. Unlike a margin deposited with a stockbroker, which constitutes a down payment on equities, the margin deposited with a commodity broker is considered a good-faith guarantee that the investor is financially able to make or take eventual delivery of the commodity.

Another important difference between equity and commodity margins is their size. Under Federal Reserve Board regulations, a margin on an equity must be at least 50 percent of the total cost of the shares being purchased. Typically, the margin on a gold futures contract is only about 10 percent of its total value. The stockbroker lends the customer (for a finance charge) the balance between the margin payment and the total cost of the shares, which the brokerage house then will purchase on its customer's behalf. In a gold futures transaction, there is neither lending nor borrowing of money by either the broker or his customers.

Commodity futures margin requirements are established by the individual exchanges, and two rates are set to distinguish between hedgers and speculators. This exchange requirement is known as "minimum margin." Brokerage houses usually will require more than the exchange minimum from their customers. Because a hedge customer has the gold or other commodity in his possession, or has a commitment to buy the commodity in the future, the margin required for hedge customers—under the rules of both the exchange and the brokerage house—is generally lower than that required of speculators. The reasoning behind this disparity is that the hedger, being in the business of buying or selling gold, is better able financially to assume the risks involved in futures trading and also will, at some point, have the physical metal—which then may be legally attached in case of default. The speculator, since he usually has no intention of ever making or taking delivery of the gold, has no physical asset in most cases.

The first deposit required by either the exchange or the brokerage firm is known as the *initial margin*. This becomes a customer's capital position. Each day, this position is adjusted according to the market performance of gold. In other words, if you—the customer—buy a contract, also known as *going long*, the difference between the price you paid and the *settlement price* on a given day would be added to, or subtracted from, your capital or equity position (not to be confused with a stock market equity). If you sell a contract, known as *going short*, and the gold market price drops, this result would be added to your capital equity.

The settlement price is often mistakenly called the "closing price"—an equities market term referring to the last trade of the day. The settlement price is actually a price set by an exchange's "settlement committee," and is the one listed as the "official" final price of the day. It might coincide with the price of the day's final trade; or, on the other hand, it might be an average of the trades at the end of the day. It might even be just a price arrived at by the committee based on the current contango, in a case where no contracts were traded that day in a given delivery month. Every contract month listed on a gold futures exchange will have a settlement price at the end of each trading day.

In addition to initial margins, which must be posted before a position may be placed on a commodity exchange, there also is a second figure known as a *maintenance margin.* Let us suppose your initial margin on a Comex gold contract, whether long or short, was $2,000. The maintenance margin would be a figure below $2,000—say, $1,500. If the market moved against you to the point where your capital position was reduced to less than the $1,500 maintenance-margin level, you would be required to either liquidate your contract or deposit additional money sufficient to bring your capital balance up to the original $2,000 level. Such a requirement is known as a "margin call." Long- and short-position traders must make the same margin deposits, because their market price risks are the same.

FCMs must post sufficient portions of their clients' margin money with the exchanges to cover the minimum margin requirements for all their customers' net positions (that is, the long positions minus the short ones). If an FCM's capital position were to drop below that total margin requirement, the firm would receive a "variation margin call" from the exchange and would be required to post that money within one hour. You, the customer, have it a little easier: You have 24 hours after the market's close in which to deposit additional cash in your margin account. The reason FCMs generally require more than the exchange minimum margins from their clients is to give them enough leeway to cover variation margin calls as well as to allow customers the "luxury" of having 24 hours to meet calls, instead of the one hour within which the FCM must act. The one-hour rule is the reason U.S. exchanges require FCM members to have an office within one mile of the exchange floor. Those FCMs that are not members must use a member FCM to "clear"—or handle—all transactions. Such member FCMs are known as "clearing members."

If you live a long way from your FCM or use a branch of your FCM that is located a considerable distance away, you may be forced to transfer funds from your bank to the FCM's bank via the Federal Reserve System, otherwise known as "wiring Fed funds."

Because the futures exchanges have assumed such a major role in the pricing of gold and their influence has extended so far beyond Chicago, New York, or Winnipeg, they cannot be ignored by anyone seriously interested in transacting in gold. While you still may scorn futures because of their reputation as high-risk arenas—and the risks are certainly high for the speculator—you cannot disregard these important markets. The next chapter will list some of the techniques for trading futures.

CHAPTER TEN

Futures—The Techniques

Few investment arenas offer as great a level of potential rewards—or losses—as the futures markets.

Take, for example, the simple transaction of purchasing one gold contract calling for delivery in three months. If you bought the gold for $350 per ounce and within a month the price rose to $400 (a scenario that actually occurred during the 1982 gold-market recovery), your profit would be $50 per ounce multiplied by the number of ounces in the contract. In the case of a typical Comex contract, that would be 100 ounces, or $5,000. In the course of one month, the return on the $350 investment would have been more than 14 percent. And that was in just one month! Annualized, the rate of return would have been 168 percent.

Of course, if you had gone short, or sold for future delivery, the price of gold would have gone against your investment for a loss of $5,000. Assuming the initial margin deposit on this trade was $2,500 and the maintenance margin requirement was $1,750, there obviously would have been several margin calls.

The rewards of trading gold futures contracts are potentially large, but the risks are equally large. These are leveraged investments, which means that your cash or capital investment is only a fraction of the value of the gold you control. For example, your initial margin of $2,500 exposes you to potential gains or losses on 100 ounces of gold (the contract traded on the Comex) with a market value of $35,000, based on a market price of $350 per ounce. If gold prices went up by $30 per ounce, or 8.6 percent, your $2,500 investment would rise by $3,000, or 120 percent.

TAKING DELIVERY

Investing with the hope of short-term profit is one reason you might want to use the gold futures markets. They also provide an excellent way to acquire physical gold for those who can afford the minimum quantity specified in the contract—100 ounces on the Comex, but as little as 20 ounces on the Winnipeg Exchange or 32.15 ounces on the Chicago Board of Trade.

A retail bullion dealer will charge you a commission ranging from as little as one half of 1 percent to as much as 8 percent of the total value of your purchase. In many cases, you will also have to pay assorted other charges, such as a fabrication fee for making a gold bar the desired size, a storage charge, an insurance premium, shipping costs for transporting the gold from the refiner or dealer to wherever you want it stored, and possibly sales tax, depending on the state where delivery is being accepted. When you want to sell the gold, you will be charged a commission again. Only the fabrication fee will be remitted.

Anyone who is involved in these markets should realize that the commissions on futures market transactions generally take the form of flat fees per contract—regardless of the dollar value of a given contract. They can range from as little as $20 at a discount brokerage firm to more than $100 at a full-service house.

If you were to buy 100 ounces of gold from a retail bullion dealer at $350 per ounce, the total cost of your purchase would be $35,000. If the commission rate for a sale of that size was 1 percent, the commission would be $350. And you would still have to pay the additional fees.

By taking delivery through futures, you not only get to pay lower commissions but also can avoid some of the extra fees if you are willing to accept a commodity contract instead of the actual metal. Obviously, this assumes a certain trust in the commodity exchanges—but, on the whole, the record of these exchanges is good.

If you are willing to put some faith in the exchange, then by going long in the farthest-out delivery month—which, in the case of the Comex, is 23 months in the future—you can buy 100 ounces of gold and have it stored for you for almost two years. As explained in the previous chapter, the price you pay for a futures contract has the storage and insurance costs built into the contango.

"CASHLESS" GOLD

If you are interested in buying a contract-size quantity of gold but do not want to be bothered with margin calls, the answer is to post the entire value of the contract as a minimum margin. If gold were at $350, this would amount to an investment of $35,000. But you would not have to pay it in cash. Treasury bills are accepted as margin deposits for futures contracts for up to 90 percent of their maturity value. By depositing $35,000 in T-bills, you would be earning interest on your "gold"—interest which should offset the higher cost of the gold futures contract.

When it comes time to sell your gold, you will find there is another advantage to purchasing futures contracts rather than buying physical gold outright for the very large investor. If you had bought or taken possession of your 100 ounces, the dealer buying your gold later may have insisted that your bullion be assayed to determine its purity. This is especially likely if you have been holding the metal in your own storage facility, such as a safe deposit box. But gold held in a commodity exchange account need not be assayed since it never left the site of the depository.

When your gold futures contract nears maturity, you can "roll over" the long position just before you are scheduled to take delivery—so instead of allowing a holder of a short position to make delivery, you simply instruct your broker, in effect, to sell that long and buy another contract calling for more distant delivery of gold. Although this appears to involve two separate transactions, you would have to pay only one commission. On commodity futures exchanges, commissions are charged on a "round-trip" basis—which means the amount you paid initially, when you went long, covered not only the commission to buy but also the commission to sell. In other words, you have effectively already paid the selling commission.

THE MINUSES

Buying gold on the futures markets has some drawbacks. The first and most obvious is the large amount of metal you must buy. The minimum amount you could acquire would be 20 ounces—and to get that small an amount, you would have to use the Winnipeg Exchange. If you are looking to buy only 5 or 10 ounces, it simply cannot be done this way.

A second drawback stems from the tax consequences. Under newly enacted United States Internal Revenue Service regulations, which became effective on January 1, 1987, the Internal Revenue Service requires that all commodity futures positions be "marked to market" the tax year—in other words, it totes up all profits and losses on futures positions still outstanding and then taxes the profits, regardless of whether actual profits or losses have been realized. (If you had a loss on your futures transactions during the year, even if it was only a "paper" loss, you can deduct it on that year's tax return.) If you took delivery of your gold against a futures contract, your trades would no longer be considered futures transactions but simply investment purchases. It is best to check with your tax accountant to see how these provisions apply to you. Under the old tax code, the maximum tax rate on futures positions was 32 percent, since every futures transaction was treated as being 40 percent short term and 60 percent long term, regardless of how long the position was held.

A third disadvantage for some people is uncertainty over where the gold will be stored, if you wish to take delivery of the actual bullion upon maturity of your long contract. The holder of a short position has the discretion to dictate the exact time and *place* of delivery. If you are dealing with a Comex contract, this does not present much of a problem, since all Comex-approved depositories are located in New York. But, if you buy from the International Monetary Market division of the Chicago Mercantile Exchange, authorized vaults for delivery from that exchange could be in either New York or Chicago.

This is really a problem only for people who actually want to take possession of the gold, hold it in their hands, and store it some place under their control. Most investors will store their gold in a bank vault. If this is true of you—and I hope it is—you should not be concerned at all whether that vault is in Chicago, New York, Cleveland, San Francisco, or any other city in the country, as long as it is insured and it is a safe, recognized bank or vault facility.

STOPPING LOSSES

Earlier in this chapter, I noted the profit potential of futures as well as the high risks—but simple knowledge of how a market works is only the first step toward using it. Statistically, 90–95 percent of all futures trades lose money—not a good average. But while it would appear that the deck is stacked against the futures trader, it really is stacked only against the trader who lacks simple discipline.

Many of the techniques of successful gold futures trading involve the use of technical analysis. Fundamental analysis will tell you *why* you want to trade gold futures, but technical analysis will tell you *when*—and that timing can be crucial.

The first step in successful futures trading is deciding how much money you are willing to lose on each trade. This sounds like a negative approach, but in reality it is a constructive one. The futures trader who really loses is the one who has not set a limit on his trading and is not willing to admit that he or she made a mistake. The futures trader who profits may make many such mistakes, but will limit losses on each to a minimum. It takes just one good trade now and then to offset limited losses, as long as the profits on that one good trade are big enough. As a rule, you should invest no more than 10 percent of the discretionary funds you have set aside for trading gold futures in any one speculative futures contract.

In order to set limits, the trader must use *stops*—predetermined points at which a position is liquidated before losses mount. On the more positive side, stops may also be used to take profits. But let us look first at the stop-loss technique.

Say you establish a long position of one December Comex

gold contract, buying at $400, and are willing to risk—that is, lose—$1,000. At the same time your broker places the order to buy at $400, you also should have him enter a stop order to sell at $390. (The $10-per-ounce loss multiplied by the 100 ounces in the contract would produce a total loss of $1,000.) This will be triggered if the market goes against you. Whatever you do, *leave the sell order in place,* even if you think the drop in price is only temporary. Discipline is one of the prime attributes of a successful trader.

AT-THE-MARKET ORDERS

Assuming the initial order was placed when the market was trading at or very close to $400, it would be considered a "market order." If you are a technical trader, you will insist that your order be placed at an exact point, as determined by your charts. Most fundamental traders are not so stubborn as to try to pick an exact entry point. If the market is close to the point where they want to buy or sell, they will often place orders "at the market." This means that the floor trader will execute the order as quickly as possible, without worrying about slight differences away from the intended point of entry.

RESTING ORDERS

Unlike a market order, which is meant for immediate execution, a *stop* order is a resting order that will not be executed unless the market is bid or trades at that price. Should that happen, the stop order immediately would become a market order.

A stop order can be either an order to buy or an order to sell. It also can be used to initiate a new position or liquidate an old one. A stop order to buy is initiated *above* the present market, while one to sell is placed *below* the market. (Otherwise, it is known as a *market-if-touched* or a *limit* order, as described below.)

If you are initiating a new position, you are hoping that the market will move in that direction so you can enter it. If you are liquidating a position with a stop-loss order, you are hoping that the market will *not* move that way, since that would mean a loss—but still, the order would help to minimize that loss.

Once the designated price point in a stop order is reached, transforming it into a market order, the floor broker will execute it as quickly as he can. In a fast-moving market, it is possible that the order finally may be executed considerably away from the stop point.

LIMIT ORDERS

Sometimes you may want to buy or sell only at a specified price. To do this, you would place a *limit* order with your broker. Limit orders are like stop orders in that they instruct the floor broker at what specific point to enter the market. But unlike stop orders, which actually may be executed above or below the stop point once that point is touched, limits may be exercised only at the limit *or better*. With a limit order to buy, any price below the limit would be better for the trader; with a sell order, any price above the limit would be better.

Remember, there is no guarantee that a limit order will be executed, nor is there any legal obligation on the part of the floor broker to execute such an order. Sometimes the market will dip down to a limit where one trade will be executed, then immediately turn around and head higher. Since the floor broker cannot buy at the higher level, he cannot execute the trade.

STOP-LIMIT ORDERS

Stop orders and limit orders may be combined in a *stop-limit* order. This kind of order becomes active when the market reaches the stop point, but the floor broker is limited. A stop-limit order is used to set a maximum price, if you are buying, or a minimum price if you are selling. Say you want to buy gold, which currently is trading at $375, but do not want to pay more than $378. Your order to your broker would be to "buy at $375 with a stop limit at $378." If the market "runs away" from you and rises to $380, your order will not be executed because of the limit. Stop-limit orders are used when you are fairly certain how high or low the market may go.

MARKET-IF-TOUCHED

There will be times when your technical analysis indicates a good point at which to enter the market, but the market simply is not at that point. Then you will want to use a *market-if-touched (MIT)* order. An MIT order is a resting order which becomes a market order when the chosen price is "touched."

MIT buy orders are placed when the desired point is below the current market, while MIT sell orders are placed when that point is higher than the current market. Like a limit order, an MIT order is not executed until the market reaches a given point—but unlike a limit order, an MIT order becomes a market order, and must be executed by the floor broker, even if the market moves away from the desired entry point.

To take an example, suppose February Comex gold futures are trading at $390 and your technical analysis tells you the market may drop to a floor of $383 but then rebound sharply. You could simply place an order to buy at the market, but then you would have a "paper loss" of $700 before the rebound. That paper loss could be turned into a real profit if you waited for the market to meet your expectations and bought at $383. Of course, you might not be quick enough to "catch" the market exactly at that point, but your MIT order would become a market order there, so you might end up buying at slightly above that level or slightly below. Professional commodity traders have two sayings that may be worth remembering in such a situation: *"Don't chase the market"* and *"Let the market come to you."*

ORDER TIME SPAN

Generally speaking, when your broker receives an order, it is good for the whole trading day. If the order is not executed prior to the end of the day, it will expire—forgotten when the market opens the next day. Occasionally, as a trader, you may want to initiate a position, but at a point well away from the current market price.

Instead of calling your broker daily, you might place an expanded time frame on an order. Under the rules of most gold futures exchanges, floor brokers will not hold an order for longer than one week—say, from Monday until Friday's market close or the close of the last trading day of the week, if Friday is a holiday.

While floor brokers will hold orders only "good the week," your account executive can be given a blanket order to buy or sell at a given price and be told to continue entering the order week after week until it is executed. Generally speaking, such a blanket order would be ill-advised, since market fundamentals may change rapidly. If you do not have the time to call your broker regularly, you should not be trading gold futures.

FILL OR KILL

Most orders remain good for the day entered, but sometimes a trader wants to enter the market at a particular level or not at all. A *fill or kill* order is either executed immediately by the floor broker, at the specified price or better, or not executed at all. Fill or kill orders also are known as "immediate-or-cancel" or "quick" orders. You should enter a fill or kill order when, after technical analysis, you want to buy gold futures at a specific price and specific time. A simple limit order would satisfy your price requirements but not your time needs.

ONE CANCELS THE OTHER

Suppose you have a feeling that the market is potentially volatile, ready to move one way or another—perhaps because it is hovering near some significant chart point, or a piece of news is expected that may greatly influence the market. The results of an election would be one example of such news. Another would be important economic statistics, such as the weekly money-supply figures from the Federal Reserve Board. You may want to enter the market, but you may not be sure whether to enter from the long or short side, since the market appears poised to head sharply in either direction.

You can place two orders—one to buy at a certain level and the other to sell at another level. Should the buy order be executed (or "filled"), then the sell order would be canceled (or "killed"), or vice versa.

MARKET ON OPEN OR MARKET ON CLOSE

If you believe a piece of overnight news or trading activity may influence the price of gold, possibly even causing it to quickly become "locked limit" on the futures exchanges, you might consider entering an order to buy or sell *market on open*. The floor broker would be limited to executing this within the opening period set by the exchanges. ("Locked limit" is a term describing a market that has been traded up or down by its allowable daily limit. No further trading will take place that day unless someone bids above the limit, if it is limit down, or offers below the limit, if it is limit up.)

Each exchange has a period, normally about five minutes long, which is designated officially as the opening. A market-on-open order may not be the first trade of the day, but it will be filled within this time span, if possible. If the market opens up or down by the daily price limit—that is, "locked"—then the trade might not be executed.

Sometimes the course of trading activity during a day will appear to be exaggerated, with a buying or selling surge causing the market to become either overbought or oversold. You might be justified in assuming that the market will correct in the next session, and therefore in wanting to catch the end of the momentum by taking a position opposite the trend of the day. Generally speaking—and this is partly due to the number of computers dictating the same trade at the same time—when a technical price point is touched, an overwhelming number of orders will be in place at that point. As a result, the market will exceed what your analysis said should be expected. However, it often takes until the end of the trading day or the start of the next session before the market "returns to its senses."

Just as an order can be entered for market on open, orders can also be placed for *market on close*. The closing period, like the opening, is a time officially set by the exchange and normally lasts about five minutes.

Although an exchange closes at a specified time, there is a brief period known as the "runoff" when the clerks catch up with the floor brokers. As a result, anyone watching a screen or price ticker will notice prices changing even though it is after the closing bell and orders can no longer be executed. This "runoff" period is the reason why the final trade of the day may not be the basis for the settlement price on which margins are calculated. The settlement price is arrived at by a committee of exchange members who decide what the official price for any given month should be, based on trading activity that day in all the months, as well as where the contango is. It is called the settlement price because this is the price at which those holding contracts to buy or sell physical gold bullion settle those agreements.

STRADDLES AND SPREAD ORDERS

Since gold contracts for many delivery months are traded on an exchange, it is possible for you to be long one month and short another—a situation known as a *straddle* or *spread*. If the price of gold were to move, the value of the straddle would change very little, since the loss in one "leg" would be largely offset by a gain in the other. Because of this reduced price risk, margin requirements usually are lower for straddles. Traders often use straddles as a short-term tactic to take advantage of an aberration in the contango.

Just as margin requirements are lower for holders of straddles than for those with outright gold-market positions, someone holding physical gold in an exchange-approved depository would pay a lower margin on a short position since the bullion would be available to fulfill the contract.

Similarly, intercommodity or intermarket spreads can be established to take advantage of a temporary aberration between the different markets or commodities. A long gold, short silver position would be an intercommodity spread. A long December Comex gold, short April CBT gold position would be an intermarket spread. A long December Comex, short April Comex position would be an example of an intramarket spread.

Spread orders are given to an account executive as one order, even though they involve two transactions. Because there is a lower price risk, intramarket spreads require lower margins than outright positions. But your broker will charge you two commissions.

As a rule, when "unwinding" a spread, or liquidating the positions, both should be liquidated at the same time. However, it often happens that one leg is very profitable and seems likely to continue being so—in which case you may want to liquidate only the unprofitable side. But remember, if you have posted a lower spread margin, you will have to deposit more money if only one leg is left at the end of a trading day.

SWITCH ORDERS

A *switch* order, as the name implies, is simply an order switching a position from one month to another. Switch orders often are used to continue a market position while avoiding a delivery notice.

Switches may also be used to exit losing positions in a lock-limit market. Although the use of stops will normally keep you from getting caught in a locked market, that predicament still can happen to even the most cautious trader. Under exchange rules, there are no limits in the spot or current month, and trading will continue in that contract—even though the others may be locked. If you find yourself in a locked futures position, you should try to switch into a spot contract, which then can be liquidated.

DAY TRADING VERSUS POSITIONS

Commodity futures markets, especially active ones, can be fast-moving. A profit or loss amounting to thousands of dollars is possible within a very short time span. For the trader with access to "real-time" market information—that is, a computer screen or wire-service ticker giving trade-by-trade information—*day trading* in commodities is possible and can be highly profitable.

Because the market exposure in day trading covers a relatively short period of time, the margin requirements normally are lower than for trades held "overnight"—also known as *position* trades. Many brokers charge day traders lower commissions because they usually trade more often than people taking positions.

While it may be profitable, day trading should be done by professionals who devote their full time to the market.

Floor brokers trading their own accounts are often day traders. Because they pay lower commission fees, floor brokers are satisfied with lower profits. (Their commissions are paid to the exchange rather than to an account executive; everyone else pays the exchange commission as a part of the commission paid to a brokerage firm.) It is not uncommon for a floor broker to exit the market with a gain of only a dollar or less. Such activity, whether on the part of a floor broker or an outside speculator, is known as "scalping" the market.

SHORTS

In the previous chapter, we talked about a mine owner selling gold futures. But anyone can, in principle, sell futures. Although you may be a fundamental believer in higher gold prices, there are times when it seems a market will not rise—due to technical conditions—or it may be because, based on the fundamentals, the time is not quite right.

You can profit from both sides of the futures markets. But as I noted in the last chapter, futures exchanges are net-zero markets—meaning that for every dollar made, a dollar is lost.

PYRAMIDING

Just as futures trading can offer high profits, it also can offer tremendous leverage—an opportunity to reinvest profits back into the same instrument without any additional cash outlay.

Increasing the size of a position by using previous profits is known as *pyramiding*. The temptation to take all profits and plow them back into the market is strong for the gold futures trader. My advice: RESIST IT! Only a portion of the profits should go back into the market. The remainder should be placed in an interest-bearing vehicle, such as a money-market account.

As a gold investor using the futures market, you always should have an objective—a desired rate of return. Once you reach that objective, you should take your profits out of the market. If there is money left over, that is what you might consider for pyramiding—building more leverage into your position. A cautious approach such as this can make the difference between a consistently profitable gold futures market investor and one who occasionally strikes it big but often loses all his profits.

If you bought a gold futures contract at $350 per ounce, placing $2,500 into your account as margin, and the price of gold rose to $400, you would have realized a profit of $5,000. In short, you would have doubled your money. Instead of taking your $5,000 and doubling your position or even tripling it, take your profit out of the market. If you are still bullish, maintain your position by leaving the initial $2,500 margin on deposit with your broker.

Taking the example above, say you had been greedy—and instead of taking your profits out of the market, you had added two more positions, using the $5,000 paper profit to cover the two $2,500 margins. It would be perfectly possible for the market to retreat all the way back to $380, leaving you with a substantial loss.

MOVING STOPS

If the market is going your way and you have placed stops to protect yourself against losses, now is the time to move them to protect your profits—especially if you have been pyramiding your position.

Assume you are long gold at $400 and have a stop at $390. The price of your future is now $425. If you left the stop in place at $390, your $25 profit could evaporate if the market were to take a sharp turn—so move the stop up to $410, thus ensuring at least a $10 profit.

But do not move the stops so close to the market that you will be stopped out in a temporary swing. Say, in the case above, you moved the stop to $423 and the market dipped $4, then rebounded. The stop at $423 would have been triggered, taking you out of the market and leaving you on the sidelines as prices continued to climb.

One technique that helps determine where to place stops is to use a technical chart, drawing a channel by connecting the highs and lows of a particular market move. If you are holding a long position, your stops should be placed just below the lower line of the channel. If you sold gold futures short, your stops should be just above the higher channel line. As time progresses, you can see exactly how to move your stops so they will not be "triggered" unless the market moves sharply against you.

When the market moves in your favor, as long as there are no changes in the fundamentals, a position should be left in place until the desired profits are reached.

A trend is a friend. Do not argue against it, even if you can see no apparent fundamental reason for it.

DO YOU HAVE TO BE IN?

There are times when the gold market appears to be doing nothing, that is, it trades in a narrow range. The price may change by less than $1 a day or even $1 a week. Unless you are a trader with a seat on the exchange and are willing to scalp for small profits, this may be a good time to find something else to do with your money.

There is no law that says a gold futures speculator always has to be in the market. A wise gold trader will stay out and wait for this congestion of prices to break up. The wait may be only a matter of days, or it could last for a whole season, or even much longer. Summers are often times when the gold markets "go to sleep." It is as if all the traders have gone on vacation—and probably they have.

There are times when technical analysis becomes more important, because there may be no change in the fundamentals. If you have decided to invest in the futures markets, *you must keep charts.* The charts will tell you when there has been a change in the market environment and you should be reassessing your fundamentals.

RISK VERSUS REWARD

Perhaps the first question you should ask yourself before trading gold futures is: "What's in it for me?" If you are considering a particular investment, look at your price charts. If it involves buying a futures contract, how low can the price go? Are you willing to lose that much money before you begin making profits? How high can the price go? Is that high enough to cover the costs of commissions to your broker as well as any interest income that may have been lost because your money was tied up in futures margins?

This analysis is known as weighing the *risks* ("How much can I lose?") against the *rewards* ("How much can I gain?"). It should be done anytime you make any kind of gold investment, whether it's buying physical metal, futures, options, or equities. In each investment arena, you can at least use technical analysis to calculate a risk/reward ratio. You know, for example, the price of gold will not drop below $100 per ounce. And, on the other side, it is highly unlikely the price will rise to $5,000 within the near future. Each investor may have his own ideas about the reasonable limits on the downside and upside— which will define risk and reward.

Figuring risk/reward may be a technical project—but, like the analysis in this book, it still must contain an element of common sense.

HEDGING

As I pointed out in the previous chapter, futures markets originated as a vehicle for farmers to hedge against bad crop years. The gold futures markets continue to serve similar commercial hedging needs.

You do not have to be a jewelry manufacturer or a mine owner to use these markets for hedging—although these two elements of the gold industry typically are major participants in futures. You might be a private individual who already owns some gold and feels the need for protection against a possible drop in its value, just as you might be using the gold itself to hedge against a drop in the value of other elements in your portfolio.

First, let us take a look at the private individual hedger. If you are holding 200 ounces of gold bullion or bullion coins, for example, and the average cost of your investment was $370 per ounce, the futures markets can allow you to preserve that value in case of a sharp drop in the price of gold. Once again, I will assume that you have done at least some preliminary fundamental and technical analysis of the market. If your analysis indicates that the gold price may drop soon, you can sell gold futures contracts equal to a portion (or all) of your individual holdings. If your fears are realized and the price actually drops, you will show a profit on your short futures position equal to the loss in the value of your portfolio. The advantage of the futures market is that it allows you to "sell" your gold—make a contract to deliver gold in the future—without actually having to part with your metal. As I have pointed out, fewer than 5 percent of gold futures contracts are satisfied through actual delivery of the metal—and you, as a hedger, would join the majority in this case and not make delivery against your short positions. (If you wanted to make delivery, it would be easier to sell your gold through more traditional channels, such as a retail bullion dealer or coin shop, rather than use the futures markets.)

Of course, if your analysis does not point to a pending drop in the price of gold, you would do best to stay away from the futures markets, since selling short would only result in losses.

For commercial users of gold, the futures markets are useful for either sell-hedging (such as the case above, where futures were used to protect the value of the gold already held), or buy-hedging. If you are a consumer of gold, either for jewelry or industrial purposes, you know you will be buying gold in the future, and these markets can help you take some of the guesswork out of how much you will have to pay for your metal.

Take, for example, the case of a jewelry manufacturer who plans to use a set amount of gold in the coming year and wants to publish a catalog of his wares, complete with prices. In order to assure himself that the prices will be in line with what he has to pay for the gold, the manufacturer could buy enough gold on the spot market to fill all his needs for the coming year. Alternatively, the prudent manufacturer could buy futures contracts calling for delivery of however much gold he will need. Doing this will enable him to establish the cost of his inventory in advance.

Should the price of gold rise during the year, the jewelry manufacturer would show a profit on his futures market positions roughly equal to the amount of additional cash he will have to pay to acquire the gold needed for manufacturing. Should the price drop, his loss on the futures positions would be offset by his savings in the cash or physical gold market.

A producer of gold is someone who plans to sell it in the future. A producer would do the opposite of the consumer in the above example. A gold miner, for example, would sell or go short on a futures market. Suppose you are a miner who anticipates producing 100,000 ounces of gold in the coming year, with annual production costs of $290 per ounce. The spot market is now at $340—a level you regard as dangerously close to the combined total of your production costs plus the return you hope to earn. Lower gold prices could result in losses for your mine, possibly forcing you to suspend operations and lay off employees. To hedge against such a possibility, you can sell 100-ounce Comex contracts—as many as you feel necessary. If the price of a futures contract is $410 per ounce, you can sell that contract and guarantee yourself that return. Although the spot price of gold may have dropped to $300 by the time your contract matures, meaning that you have a $110 gain on your short futures position, that gain will have been erased by a loss in your physical transactions if, in the meantime, you have sold your production on the open market.

There is one thing that you must keep clearly in mind: Hedging is not trading for speculative gain. One problem many hedgers have is that they try to "play the market"—and, in doing so, they become speculators. Corporate treasurers, purchasing agents, and financial officers who try to play the market may find themselves out of a job.

When hedging through futures, do not forget to take into account the costs of using these markets. Just as the private investor has to deposit margin money and pay commissions, so, too, does the hedger. Since hedgers are assumed to be lower risk traders than speculators, hedge margins generally are lower than those for speculators—but generally, the hedger assumes a larger number of contracts than the average individual speculator. Margin money, of course, is money that could be put to other uses. While hedging makes good business sense, it also makes good sense to pay all margin deposits in the form of T-bills.

Just because a hedger is protecting a potential cash position, that does not mean he has to be married to a futures contract, any more than a speculator should be. Hedging is no excuse for poor trading. But, as the Comex is fond of pointing out in its marketing literature, hedging is a form of insurance against the commercial risks every producer or user of gold must assume. The commission costs and loss of access to money tied up in margins should be viewed in the same light as the premiums paid on an insurance policy. To repeat what the Comex stresses in its literature, hedging may seem like speculating, since it shares the same marketplace—but not to hedge is really to speculate that the price of gold will not fluctuate in the coming months. And that is an unlikely prospect.

One caveat: *There is no such thing as the perfect hedge.* No matter what, there always will be slight differences between the futures and cash markets. But hedging reduces large differences to slight ones which are acceptable and do not threaten the profitability of a business.

SUMMARY OF TYPES OF GOLD FUTURES ORDERS

Market Order. Executed immediately on receipt by floor broker, regardless of price.

Stop Order. A resting order which is executed only if the market is bid or trades at a specific price. Stop orders to buy are placed *above* the market; stop orders to sell are placed *below.*

Limit Order. Places a floor or ceiling on the price at which floor broker may execute.

Market-if-Touched. Becomes a market order when selected price is "touched." MIT orders to buy are placed *below* the current market; those to sell are placed *above.*

Time Orders. Specify a time span in which trade may be executed.

Fill or Kill. Must be done immediately or is canceled.

One Cancels Other. Two orders doing opposite things. If one is executed, the other is canceled.

Market on Open. Must be executed within the opening period.

Market on Close. Must be executed within the closing period.

Spread Order. Establishes long position in one month and short position in another (also known as a "straddle").

Switch Order. Exchanges a long or short position in one month for the same position in another contract month.

_____

CHAPTER ELEVEN

Options—Their Origins, Workings, and Purposes

*"Foul cankering rust the hidden treasure frets,
But gold that's put to work more gold begets."*

                                          George Herbert

So far, we have talked about gold bullion, coins, gold-mining equities, and gold futures contracts. Options to buy or sell these various assets are yet another vehicle for the investor, speculator, or hedger—a vehicle that is, in a sense, a hybrid with its own distinct advantages and disadvantages. This chapter will explain why options exist, who should use them, and how, while Chapter 12, Options—The Techniques, will show specific trading examples in options.

An option is the right, although not the obligation, to buy or sell a specific item—such as 100 ounces of gold or 100 shares of Homestake Mines—within a specific time frame at a specified price. Until recently, most option trading was in equities, but the trend toward financial innovation has led to the adoption of this instrument in other investment markets, as well.

Years ago, options had their roots in the real estate arena, where, in return for a cash payment (known as the premium), a developer received the right from a property owner to buy land at a specific price (the strike price) within a specified time (the maturity). If the developer decided not to buy, the only money he lost was the premium, or the cost of acquiring the option. The grantor of the unexercised option benefited, too—for while he did not sell his property, he did derive some income (in the form of the premium) while the developer was reaching a decision on the purchase. If another potential buyer had come along while the option was still in force, the property owner could not have sold the land, because the option was binding.

GOLD OPTIONS

Like the real estate option, gold options have a strike price at which an option may be exercised, a maturity on which the option expires, and a premium—the price the buyer pays to obtain the option. Basically, the investor in gold can acquire three types of options: options on gold bullion, options on gold-mining equities, and options on Commodity Exchange gold futures contracts.

Options come in two varieties: *puts* and *calls*. A put option gives the holder—the person who bought it—the right to sell the bullion, equities, or futures contract to the seller (also known as the grantor or writer) of the put at a given price within a given time period. The grantor of such an option must buy the specified quantity of bullion, equity shares, or futures contracts at the strike price if the holder of the option decides to exercise it.

A call option gives the holder the right to buy the underlying asset from the grantor. The grantor must sell it at the option's strike price, regardless of where the market price may be for the underlying asset at the time the option is exercised.

Options are known by the name of their underlying asset, the maturity month of the option, and their strike price. For example, an option to buy a February Comex gold futures contract at $400 per ounce would be known as a February 400 call, while an option to sell 100 shares of Campbell Red Lake stock at $20 per share between now and April would be known as a Campbell Red Lake April 20 put.

Depending upon the relationship between the strike price and the price of the underlying asset, options are also identified as being either *in the money, at the money,* or *out of the money.* A call option is said to be in the money when the strike price is lower than the underlying asset price. Both puts and calls are said to be at the money when the strike price is either the same as, or very close to, the price of the underlying asset. A call option is out of the money when the strike price is higher than the underlying asset, while a put is out of the money when the strike is lower than the underlying asset.

For the investor, there are three uses for options: as a *hedge* to protect the assets in your portfolio against adverse price moves or to lock in a price before buying or selling; as a *trading vehicle* in and of themselves; or to *generate income* for the writer.

As a hedger, you would buy a put option to guarantee a predetermined return on your asset—that is, an established price at which you could sell your bullion, futures position, or mining equity. Or you would buy a call option to guarantee that you would be able to buy the gold-related asset at a set price and no higher.

If you are using options as a trading vehicle, you are looking for a price change in the underlying asset that would enable you to sell your options for a higher premium (that is, price) than you paid for them. In the case of mining equities, for example, if you purchase a call, then an increase in the price of the underlying equity will result in an increase in the premium of the call; if you purchase a put, then a decrease in the price of equity will result in an increase in the premium for your put. In either case, instead of exercising the option, you simply would sell it, much the same as you would sell an equity or a bar of gold, if the price were to rise to your trading objective.

You can generate income through options by writing puts or calls and earning the premium paid by the buyer. Often a hedger will use the options market not just for hedging but also to generate income by writing an option on a gold inventory and using the premium to cover part or perhaps even all of the carrying costs—the insurance, financing, and storage fees— associated with holding that inventory.

Looking at options as the writer or grantor, you would sell a call option because you believed the price of the underlying gold asset would not rise to the strike price, and thus the option would expire unexercised, in which case you would have earned the premium that was paid for the call you sold. Should the price rise to the strike level and your asset be "called" away from you, you would earn both the premium plus any profits you might have realized from appreciation of the asset above the price you paid for it initially.

This is assuming that you owned the asset in the first place.

Writing options when you own the underlying asset is known as writing *covered* options. If you do not own the asset, you have written a *naked* option. In general, *I would advise strongly against writing naked options.* Doing so is extremely risky and can be quite costly to you should the market move to the point where the option is exercised and you are forced to buy the underlying asset in order to fulfill your obligation to deliver to the option's owner.

The writer of a put option does not think the price of the gold-backed asset will drop to the strike level, and thus believes that the option will expire unexercised while he receives the premium income. At the same time, the writer of a put option must be prepared to purchase the asset at the strike price—and ideally should be someone who would like to buy gold bullion, equities, or futures at that level because he or she believes it to be a good price. A put option also could be written by the holder of a short futures position—someone who has contracted to sell gold in the future. In such a case, if the option is exercised and the gold is "put" to the writer, the gold that he buys will be offset automatically by his short future position. In other words, the writer would already hold a contract to sell the gold. A put may be a covered option only if the writer has an obligation to sell the gold or gold asset.

DETERMINING PREMIUMS

If you are new to gold options, the level of the premiums may puzzle you at first. You may understand how the price of gold itself is set—either through one of the London fixes or through the open bidding on a futures exchange, for example—and you probably understand how the price of a gold-mining equity is related to earnings expectations as well as to the value of a company's mining properties. But, on first glance, option premiums are not so clear-cut.

These premiums are determined by a number of factors:

- The time left before maturity—what is known as an option's *time value*. The closer an option is to its maturity, the less the time value and, therefore, the lower the premium.

- How much the option is in or out of the money—a characteristic known as its *intrinsic value*. Obviously, the more an option is out of the money, the less it is worth; conversely, the farther it is in the money, the more it is worth.
- The volatility of the underlying asset's price. The greater an asset's price volatility, the higher the probability that the option will move from out of the money to in the money, and this is reflected in its premiums.
- In the case of Comex options, the cost of carrying the underlying asset, since this is also a consideration in the pricing of a futures contract and these are options on those contracts.

Just as the contango on a gold futures exchange is determined in part by the carrying costs for the gold itself, so the premium on an option also will reflect these charges. If the costs of storing, insuring, and financing gold are 10 percent per year and gold is selling for $400 per ounce, then it would cost $4,000 per year, or just over $333 per month, to store 100 ounces. That comes to $3.33 per ounce. This price, as I say, is reflected in the premium of an option—in theory. But, of course, theory may not always be translated into practice when the market is not willing to pay the price, and that is a consideration if you are planning to write options to cover the cost of carrying your physical gold.

In the case of equity options, the premium also will reflect expectations of dividends that may be paid. Every company that pays dividends on its shares—and most companies whose equities are optionable do declare quarterly dividends—will have what is known as an "ex-dividend" date. This is the day on which holders of shares are entitled to the dividend payment. How close the maturity of an option is to the ex-dividend date is one consideration in determining the premium of an equity option. Another is the size of the dividend itself.

BULLION OPTIONS

Options on gold bullion are offered in the United States by Mocatta Metals, Inc., in New York City, a bullion house that acts as the originator or grantor of your right to buy from it, or sell to it, 100 ounces of gold bullion per option at a specified price within some specific future time period.

These are called "dealer options" because the grantor, Mocatta, is a bullion dealer. They are marketed through many commodity and stock brokerage firms and are not traded on an exchange. Consequently, the premiums are established not by a free market but by the issuing dealer. However, the premiums still should reflect the prices of options that are traded on an exchange, such as the Comex.

Because dealer options are not traded on an open exchange, and quotations of their prices are not published in any general-circulation U.S. periodical, they are not the best vehicles for the average private investor.

In addition to these dealer options, bullion options also are traded on exchanges in Amsterdam, Montreal, and Vancouver. Because they are exchange-traded, their prices are determined in a free and open marketplace. That is an important consideration—although there is still the problem of a lack of readily available price quotes in U.S. newspapers. Exchange-traded options offer an important advantage over dealer options: The dealer-option market effectively depends on the continued operation of one or more dealers, while exchange-traded options are typically handled by a broader base of companies and backed by the exchanges on which they are traded.

The American Stock Exchange in New York began trading gold bullion options in April 1985. The Amex option is based on the price of 100 ounces of bullion. Unlike the Comex futures option, which is settled by the transfer of futures contracts, the Amex option is settled in cash. This means you cannot exercise an Amex call option and receive 100 ounces of gold: Instead, you will receive the current cash value of 100 ounces.

EQUITY OPTIONS

Options on gold-mining equities are traded on several exchanges. For example, options on Homestake Mines, a large U.S. gold producer, are traded on the Chicago Board of Options Exchange; options on Campbell Red Lake Mines and Dome Mines, major Canadian producers, are traded on the

Philadelphia Stock Exchange; and options on ASA, Ltd., a closed-end investment fund whose portfolio consists of South African gold-mining companies, are traded on the American Stock Exchange.

Each equity option gives you, the holder, the right to sell or buy (depending on whether it is a put or a call) 100 shares of the stock. Stock options are highly liquid if there is interest in the underlying stock. If you think the underlying equity is under-valued, but you are unwilling to buy the stock at the present time, options are an excellent way to lock in the present price—to hedge against the chance that the price may run so high that you cannot afford it. Or, you can use them simply to speculate on a price rise.

INDEX OPTIONS

You also can buy an option on the Philadelphia Stock Exchange's Gold/Silver Index. This option is similar to equity options, but the value, in cash terms, of the Gold/Silver Index rather than shares in a gold-mining company serves as the underlying asset. The Philadelphia Exchange's Gold/Silver Index is based on the share prices of seven companies: ASA, Ltd., Callahan Mines, Campbell Red Lake, Dome Mines, Hecla Mines, Homestake Mining Company, and Sunshine Mining Company. While holding a put or call in this option will not allow you to buy or sell any individual equity, it can allow you to profit from the fortunes (or misfortunes, if you buy a put) of the precious metals mining industry. Settlement of regular equity options—what you receive if you exercise them—is always in shares of stock (although you can always sell the option directly for cash rather than exercising it). All settlements of Gold/Silver Index options transactions are in cash, as in the case of the American Stock Exchange bullion option.

The Gold/Silver Index is a capitalization-weighted index calculated by determining the current number of outstanding shares for each equity listed, then multiplying that number by the current market price for each share and dividing the product of that multiplication by a base market divisor of 1,250—a figure determined by the exchange based on the values of January 1, 1979, then updated to December 18, 1983, the date trading actually began. Both the number of shares and the base divisor are revised periodically by the exchange, and the current market price is updated daily.

EQUITY OPTIONS MARGINS

The margin—the money you must deposit with a broker—for writing or selling naked equity options (if you do not own the underlying stock), or for writing options on the Gold/Silver Index, is determined by a somewhat complex formula. This figure is determined by taking a minimum of 30 percent of the value of the underlying stock or index share, multiplying this by 100, and adding or subtracting the amount that the option is in or out of the money. A deposit of at least $250 is required. If you are writing—selling—a covered option, the stock you own will serve as a margin deposit. As an alternative, whether you are writing naked or covered options, you may use up to 90 percent of the maturity value of U.S. Treasury bills deposited with your broker. While your broker holds the T-bills, you are entitled to any interest they may pay.

GOLD FUTURES OPTIONS

Options on Comex gold futures contracts have been traded on that exchange since late 1982. When trading started, the exchange advertised them as "gold for the not so bold." While options represent a limited risk for the buyer, they are not appropriate trading vehicles for the timid—although they can be used by even the most timid as hedging vehicles or income-generating devices when the underlying asset, a 100-ounce gold futures contract or that quantity of gold bullion itself, is actually owned by the option writer.

Remember, the holder of a futures contract has a virtually unlimited risk. In other words, the market can go against his position, whether it be long or short, indefinitely. As a result, an investor using the futures markets always faces the possibility of margin calls. The buyer of an option, on the other hand, pays only the premium and faces no maintenance margin calls. Still, many an option player has lost the entire premium.

Gold futures options are available against contracts calling for delivery in the nearest four Comex gold futures contract months. (Keep in mind that Comex delivery months are February, April, June, August, October, and December.) For instance, if it is now the beginning of July, options are being traded on August, October, December, and February contracts. As soon as the August option matures in mid-July, trading begins in options for April of the next calendar year.

In August 1984, when the price of February 1985 gold futures was $376, the premium on a February 400 call was slightly under $7. In other words, if you had bought one of these options, you would have paid a total of $700, since the premium quoted must be multiplied by the 100 ounces in the contract. Before you could just break even, the price of February gold would have had to reach $407 per ounce, at which point you could have exercised the option and paid $400 for the contract, then resold it for the entry price plus the $7 premium you paid for the option itself.

MARGINS ON FUTURES OPTIONS

The buyer of a futures option has no margin requirement, and that is one of the reasons these vehicles are attractive. But the writer of such an option does incur some risk. Should the market move against him, he would have to make margin payments. However, there would be no margin requirement if, as the writer of an option, you held an offsetting futures position. This would be the case if you were the writer of a call and you owned a long futures position in the same delivery month—or if you were the writer of a put and you owned a short futures position in the same delivery month. If you have gold bullion which is stored in a Comex-approved warehouse, or if you have a Comex warrant or warehouse receipt (a certificate issued by the exchange clearinghouse indicating that you hold title to gold stored in a Comex-approved depository), this will be sufficient to cover your margin requirements. But, if you are writing a naked option, then you will be required to deposit whatever margin your broker may require for a futures position, plus or minus the amount that the option is in or out of the money.

As with futures contracts, option margin requirements may be met by depositing Treasury bills with your broker. You may use up to 90 percent of the bills' maturity value to cover margins. While your broker will hold a lien against the T-bills, any interest that accrues will be credited to your brokerage account.

SELECTING A BROKER

Selecting a broker to handle your options transactions can be complicated by the fact that although most options are regulated by U.S. government agencies, the regulations are enforced by two different agencies, depending on whether they are gold futures options or equity options.

Options on gold futures contracts are regulated by the Commodity Futures Trading Commission, which is charged with administering the examinations used to qualify brokers dealing in these instruments. Consequently, before you can trade Comex options, you must establish an account with a commodity broker. The American Stock Exchange gold bullion options also are in the domain of the CFTC, even though they are traded on a stock exchange.

Equity options, on the other hand, come under the jurisdiction of the Securities and Exchange Commission, which administers a separate examination to qualify stockbrokers as well as brokers who handle equity options. While many individual brokers are both stock and commodity registered—that is, they have passed both the CFTC and the SEC examinations—there is no guarantee that someone who calls himself a broker is legally entitled to trade both gold futures options and gold-mining equity options. Even when you do find a broker who can legally handle both, there is no guarantee that he (or she) has had any experience in these relatively new fields. Unless you feel confident using a discount broker—in which case you will be the one calling the shots and will not be looking for advice but merely mechanical competence—you should select a broker who has had experience with the option markets and whose firm is also experienced in these vehicles.

SUMMARY

To recap this introduction to options, call and put options grant the owner the right, but not the obligation, to respectively buy or sell a given quantity of the underlying asset at a specified price within a specified time—and the grantor or writer is obligated to fulfill the other side of the transaction, should the owner of the option decide to exercise it. Gold-related options are available on three types of underlying assets: bullion, gold futures, and shares in gold-mining companies. Bullion options in this country are offered by Mocatta Metals and are available from many brokers; in addition, there are exchange-traded options on the Montreal, Amsterdam, and Vancouver stock exchanges and, since April 1985, on the American Stock Exchange. For the individual investor, the exchange-traded options offer the safest and most efficient vehicle. Equity options are traded against the stock of several mining companies, and the options are listed on the Chicago Board Options Exchange, the American Stock Exchange, or the Philadelphia Stock Exchange. Philadelphia Stock Exchange Gold/Silver Index options are akin to equity options but are based on an index of seven gold- and silver-mining companies. Finally, there are options on Comex gold futures contracts. Which option should you use? That would depend primarily on which gold-related investment vehicle you are interested in.

Options may be used to hedge against changes in the price of gold, as trading vehicles in and of themselves or to generate income for the writer. The next chapter will explain some of the techniques involved in achieving each of these purposes.

CHAPTER TWELVE

Options—The Techniques

Options are still relatively new to the world of gold, and many participants in the gold markets do not yet understand them very well. Most gold investors who do have some familiarity with options have used them as speculative trading instruments—as vehicles for translating a particular view of the market into a potential profit. Others have used options, particularly options on gold-mining equities, as income-generating vehicles by writing covered calls. Some investors are now beginning to use options, particularly on physical gold or gold futures contracts, as hedging instruments—a practice that is familiar to many commercial participants in these markets.

HEDGING WITH OPTIONS

Options may be used by both producers and industrial users of gold as well as by individual and institutional investors, to hedge against adverse price moves or a market where the price of gold "runs away." A hedger using options may be either a buyer or a writer. Exhibit 12-1 shows how you can buy an option to lock in a profit in the gold market, using a gold futures option on the Commodity Exchange. Imagine that you, an investor, are the buyer in this example. In October, you buy 100 ounces of metal at $340 per ounce. (The purchase could be in the form of either bullion or gold futures.) By December, the price of gold has risen to $370 per ounce, and you are showing a

---

EXHIBIT 12–1 Buying a Comex Put Option to Hedge 100-Ounce
Gold Position

	Cash Bullion Price		*Option Premium*
	In December	$360.00	$ 4.50 (April $360 put)
	In March	$380.00	$ 0.00*
Gross Profit		$ 20.00	$(4.50)
Net Profit	$20.00 − $4.50 =	$ 15.50	

The purpose of this exhibit is to show how options may be used to hedge cash bullion or gold futures contract positions. In this case in the text, the holder of the bullion or futures contract already had a $2,000 "paper" profit at the time the option was purchased, so all the buyer wanted to accomplish was to protect that profit against a drop in the price of gold.

*Because the price of gold rose, the premium for the option dropped to zero since the option had no time or intrinsic value by March when it expired.

profit of $3,000. You would like to take advantage of any further price increase, but you also want to protect your profit against a possible drop in the price of gold. To do this, you should buy an April 360 gold put. This will allow you to sell your gold at $360 per ounce, locking in a $20-per-ounce profit, as long as you exercise the option before it expires in the middle of March. Even if the price of gold drops, as it often does at the beginning of the year, your gold position is hedged against any decline below $360.

If the price of gold rises—say, to $380 per ounce—your profit on your actual gold position will increase accordingly, while the premium on your 360 gold put will go down since the market has moved against your option position. If the price of gold continues to rise, the premium value of your put will become insignificant. You should think of the premium as the cost you are paying to insure your position against loss between December and mid-March, when the put option expires. Exhibit 12–1 takes you through the arithmetic of this hedge transaction.

If you hold a gold-mining equity, you should observe the relationship between changes in the price of your shares and changes in the price of gold itself. This will help you decide how many gold futures options you should purchase to hedge each 100 shares you own in the "XYZ Company." You can use equity options if your stock is listed as "optionable"—meaning options on that particular equity are traded on one of the exchanges (not every stock is optionable). Say you own 100 shares of Homestake Mining Company stock which you purchased for $22 per share. It is late October, and the price of your Homestake stock has risen to $26 per share—and it seems to have the potential for even greater gains, since the price of gold itself appears to be low and could rise. You can lock in a $3-per-share gross profit by buying a Homestake 25 put with an April expiration date. That will give you about four months, from October to the middle of March, to exercise the option. Say the premium on your put is $1.20. If, by March, the price of Homestake stock has dropped to $18 per share, you still can sell your 100 shares by exercising your option and "putting" the stock to the writer of the option at the strike price of $25 per share.

Another method of hedging via options is to buy a call option that will enable you to buy (call) a gold futures contract in the future. Exhibit 12-2 shows how such a tactic would work. If you think you may want to invest in gold in the future but are not sure whether you will be able to afford it, you can "lock in" your price through options. You also could do this through buying gold futures—but for one futures contract, you would have to deposit a margin of more than $1,000 with your broker. On the option market, by contrast, your initial cost would be only $300 to buy the one call option shown, and your net cost would be just $180 by the time you sold your long call position.

Exhibit 12-2 illustrates a case where buying a call option led to a loss. But, if the market had gone the other way and the price of gold had risen while the option was in effect, the value of the premium also would have risen—and the holder could have used his profits from trading options to offset the higher cost of gold itself.

USING OPTIONS AS TRADING VEHICLES

The Comex slogan—"Gold for the not so bold"—was an effort to appeal to the speculator in gold who did not want to risk having margin calls. As I pointed out in Chapter 10, Futures—The Techniques, people who speculate in gold futures should be willing to lose the entire sum of money that they have set aside for speculating. Likewise, if you plan to use the option

---

EXHIBIT 12–2   Buying a Comex Call Option

	Comex Gold Futures Contract	Option Premium
	In July $351.40	$3.00 (December $380 call)
	In October $342.20	$0.20
Net Loss	$ 9.20	$2.80

Although there was a loss in the option position as well as a drop in price of the futures contracts, the buyer of this option was seeking protection against the price of gold "running away;" the buyer was hedging a planned purchase against higher, unaffordable prices in the future. By purchasing the call option, the buyer was "insured" of buying gold at no more than $380, the strike price of the call. Should the price of gold have risen above that figure, the buyer could always exercise the option and "call" the gold away from the grantor of the option.

market as a trading vehicle, you should be ready to lose the entire premium you have invested, or nearly the entire premium. But, because the premium on an option contract is much lower than the initial margin on either a gold-mining equity purchase or a gold futures contract, your initial investment in options will be smaller.

Equity options allow you to "play" the market from either side. If you believed the price of a mining stock would advance, you would buy a call. As the price of the underlying equity rose, the price of the premium on your call would rise, too. But, if you believed the price of the equity would drop, you would buy a put instead. As the price of the stock dropped, the premium you paid for your option would increase. Exhibit 12–3 shows this relationship in diagram form. If you simply invested in the stock market, the only way you could profit from a drop in equity prices would be to sell stock short. You would have to borrow shares to do that, and you would have to wait for the price of the stock to rise before you could use the procedure.

In thinking of options as trading vehicles in and of themselves, just keep in mind that the premium is the price of the option—and it changes in relation to the price of the underlying gold investment vehicle.

GENERATING INCOME WITH OPTIONS

So far, we have looked at two different uses for gold options: as a way to hedge gold holdings and as trading vehicles. A third

---

EXHIBIT 12–3 The Relationship between
Option Premiums and the
Underlying Asset Price

Asset Price	Call Premium
Rises	Rises
Drops	Drops

Asset Price	Put Premium
Rises	Drops
Drops	Rises

---

use—generating income—involves the writing or granting of an option. This use of options enables you to take investment instruments that often are viewed as sterile assets—gold bullion and gold futures contracts—and earn income from them.

These assets are viewed as sterile because, unlike money-market accounts or even dividend-paying mining equities, bullion and futures contracts pay no income. The only way that you, as the holder of these assets, can show any profit is by selling them for a higher price than you paid. While you own them, they actually are a drain on your financial position, since the money you used to buy them could have been placed instead in an interest-bearing vehicle. However, by writing an option on such an asset, you immediately receive the premium. Even if you are writing an option on a dividend-paying mining equity, you will be augmenting your income from your stocks while continuing to collect the dividends.

Remember, there are two kinds of option writing—covered and naked. And remember, I urge you strongly not to write a naked option. If you do, you will run the risk of having gold or mining shares you do not own called away from you, forcing you into the market to buy. Or you may end up having gold—or a gold-related asset—put to you, once again forcing you to buy.

Brokers who specialize in the options markets say the only way to really make money is by writing these vehicles—writing covered options, that is. If you decide to do so, remember that you will have to make some kind of margin payment. If you are writing options against gold-mining equities, you should hold an equivalent number of shares of the underlying stock. If you are writing options against gold-mining equities, you should hold an equivalent number of shares of the underlying stock. If you are writing options against gold bullion or futures, you should hold the actual gold or futures position. By holding the gold itself or the shares, you will have met the margin requirement—since the only reason for having such a requirement is to make sure that you, the investor, can afford to cover the option if it should be exercised against you.

You always should strive to write options that are way out of the money, since these are the least likely to be exercised. Often, when a gold futures option or an equity option is first listed, the premium on this out-of-the-money vehicle will be at its highest point, since it has the greatest time value. This is the best time to write an option, even though you are granting the buyer the best chance for the option to become profitable. Exhibit 12-4 shows a Comex April 360 call that was sold (written) at a premium of $8.50. At the time this option was granted, Comex April gold futures were trading at $347.70, and spot Comex gold was trading at $333.80. In order for the buyer of this option to break even, the price of April Comex gold would have to rise to $360.00 (the strike price) plus $8.50 (the premium), or a total of $368.50, plus whatever the buyer paid in commissions and other fees.

In the meantime, you, as the seller of this option, would have received $850 in payment—or about 2.5 percent of the $340-per-ounce strike price of the underlying asset. Granted, a 2.5 percent return on an asset is not overwhelming. But the gold bullion would have yielded no income at all if you had not written the option.

If the gold market moves against your option position, you have two choices: You can either allow the market to move to the point where the option will be exercised—or, as an alternative, you can buy back the option. If the option is exercised, one of two things will happen, depending on whether it is a call option or a put option: Either your gold asset will be called away from you, or you will have the gold put to you. If you made a profit on your initial asset, you could allow the option to be exercised. If, for example, you wrote a call against a gold futures contract that you had purchased at $347.70, as in Exhibit 12-4, and the price rises to $360, the strike price, you

EXHIBIT 12-4 Writing a Covered Call Option Against Cash or Futures

Cash Gold		April Comex Future	April $360 Call Premium
On October 31:	$333.80	$347.70	$8.50
End-March:	$345.50	$348.00	$0.00

Results:			
Paper Profit:	$1,170	Cash Profit:	$ 30
Premium Received:	$ 850	Premium Received:	$850
Total Profit	$2,020	Total Profit	$880

would have a profit of $2,620 per contract on your underlying asset—plus the money you got as a premium. If you buy the option back, chances are the loss in time value will partly overcome any increase in the price of the premium.

SUMMARY

For many, the options markets, like the futures markets, are something of a mystery. Not understanding them, some investors will not even consider them.

But if you are a serious investor or trader, whether in bullion, mining equities, or gold futures contracts, you should take a close look at the options markets as a method of either raising money, protecting value, or cautiously approaching one of the other gold markets.

If you would like a more detailed explanation of option tactics, the Commodity Exchange has prepared several excellent booklets on these strategies, which I refer to at the end of this book.

PART FOUR

Appendixes:
More Information About
Gold and Gold Investments

Some Important Dates in the History of Gold

"Time will run back and fetch the Age of Gold."

John Milton

3000 B.C.: Gold was first discovered in ancient Egypt. Soon, the pharaohs and temple priests started to use it for adornment. However, early Egypt's medium of exchange was not metallic coins but barley.

700 B.C.: The first coins made partly from gold were minted in Lydia, a kingdom in Asia Minor, from a gold and silver alloy called electrum. Later, in the sixth century B.C., Lydia was also the site of the first pure gold coinage in the world.

50 B.C.: During the time of Julius Caesar, the Romans began issuing a gold coin called the aureus.

400 A.D.: As the Romans abandoned the British Isles, they took all the gold and silver with them. This resulted in long-term deflation—a drop in the prices of commodities.

1066: With the Norman conquest, a metallic currency standard was finally reestablished in Britain with the introduction of a system of pounds, shillings, and pence. The pound was literally a pound of sterling silver. This silver standard lasted until 1377, when Britain shifted to a bimetallic standard—one based on both gold and silver.

1284: Venice introduced the gold ducat, which soon became the most popular coin in the world and remained so for more than five centuries.

1343: England issued its first major gold coin, the florin. This was followed shortly by the noble, and later by the angel, crown, and guinea.

1717: The Bank of England put that country on a de facto gold standard through a royal proclamation declaring an ounce of gold to be worth 3 pounds, 17 shillings, and 10.5 pence. Thereafter, Britain's wholesale price index underwent only minor fluctuations until 1930—more than two centuries of price stability for the British economy.

1792: The U.S. Congress adopted a bimetallic standard for the new nation's currency, with gold valued at $19.30 per ounce. This remained essentially unchanged until 1834, when the price was raised to $20.67—a level it held for the next hundred years.

1817: Britain introduced the sovereign, a small gold coin valued at one pound sterling. It went on to become one of the most widely used gold coins in the world and still is being minted today.

1848: A carpenter named John Marshall found flakes of gold while building a sawmill for John Sutter near present-day Sacramento, California. The discovery triggered the California Gold Rush and hastened the settlement of the American West.

1873: The United States effectively ended bimetallism and went on a gold standard when Congress omitted silver from its list of coins and decreed that only gold would be granted free coinage.

1896: William Jennings Bryan delivered his famous "Cross of Gold" speech at the Democratic national convention, urging a return to bimetallism. The speech gained him the party's presidential nomination, but he lost in the general election to William McKinley.

1900: The Gold Standard Act placed the United States officially on the gold standard.

1914: The United States and Britain both abandoned the strict gold standard when the turmoil and economic displacement of World War I made such a system impractical.

1922: An international conference in Genoa, Italy, decided that the exchange values of all European currencies should be based on gold, but allowed smaller countries to substitute either the pound sterling or U.S. dollar as the basis for their currency reserves. The agreement lasted only a few years, until the Great Depression.

1931: Britain abandoned the gold standard completely.

1933: President Franklin D. Roosevelt devalued the dollar and raised the price of gold to $35 per ounce in order to artificially boost commodity prices and revive production. He also barred private U.S. citizens from buying, selling, or holding gold except in the form of jewelry or numismatic coins.

1944: A second international conference on gold was held in Bretton Woods, New Hampshire. The participating nations agreed to adopt the U.S. dollar as their reserve currency and the United States, in turn, agreed to exchange dollars at the official rate of $35 per ounce of gold, which it had established a decade earlier.

1961: The central banks of Belgium, France, Italy, the Netherlands, Switzerland, West Germany, and the United Kingdom agreed to form the London Gold Pool and cooperate with the Federal Reserve Bank of New York to stabilize the price of gold at $35.0875 per ounce. The year before, the price of gold had reached $40 per ounce—a level not seen since the U.S. Civil War.

1967: South Africa produced the first Krugerrand. This one-ounce bullion coin would become a best-seller worldwide.

1968: The United States abandoned the London Gold Pool and the organization was dissolved. It was replaced by a two-tier market in which central banks were required to convert their gold reserves at the official price of $35 per ounce, but individuals could buy gold freely at levels determined by the laws of supply and demand. The spot price ran up to $42 per ounce.

1971: The Smithsonian Agreement raised the official price of gold to $38 per ounce. President Richard Nixon hailed it as "the most significant monetary agreement in the history of the world."

1973: In February, just 14 months after the Smithsonian Agreement, the United States was forced to devalue the dollar a second time by raising the official price of gold to $42.22 per ounce. Dollar-selling continued, and finally all currencies were allowed to "float" freely, without regard to the price of gold. By June, the market price in London had risen to more than $120 per ounce.

1974: President Gerald Ford signed legislation lifting the restrictions on gold ownership that had been imposed on Americans 40 years earlier. Effective December 31, U.S. citizens were free once again to buy, sell, or own the yellow metal.

1975: The U.S. Treasury held a series of auctions at which it accepted bids for gold in the form of 400-ounce bars. In January, 754,000 troy ounces were sold, and another 499,500 were sold in June of that year.

1975: Gold futures trading began in the United States, with the Commodities Exchange, Inc. (Comex) in New York assuming a dominant role.

1975: The Krugerrand was launched onto the U.S. market.

1976: The International Monetary Fund held a series of gold bullion auctions similar to those held by the U.S. Treasury.

1977: Record demand and supplies, greater than any previous years (except 1967 and 1968 when central banks were forced to supply gold to private purchasers at a fixed price of $35 per ounce).

1978: U.S. Treasury commenced regular monthly gold auctions, selling 300,000 ounces per month in May through October. Sales increased in November and December to 750,000 and 1.5 million ounces, respectively.

1978: A weak U.S. dollar propelled interest in gold, aided by such events as the U.S. recognition of Communist China, events in Iran, and Sino-Vietnamese border disturbances.

1979: The one-ounce Maple Leaf was introduced in the United States.

1979: Regular monthly U.S. gold sales continued through November at a monthly rate of 1.5 million ounces through April, 750,000 ounces in May through October, and in its last auction, 1.25 million ounces in November.

1980: The abortive U.S. military attempt to rescue Iranian hostages illustrated that perhaps only truly threatening events (such as the real possibility of a U.S.–Soviet confrontation) are likely to drive up the gold price. On the other hand, the Soviet invasion of Afghanistan and the beginning of the Iran/Iraq war (placing the oil supplies of Japan and the West in possible jeopardy) did manage to set off a flurry of activity in the gold market.

1980: Jimmy Carter was voted out of office and the Democrats' control of Congress was upset. As the new conservative administration of Ronald Reagan announced the plans to curb runaway spending, a cautious but hopeful stability was felt in the gold market throughout the rest of the year.

1980: Gold reached an all-time record price of $850 per ounce on January 21 in London.

1980: The U.S. Treasury began accepting orders for "American Arts Gold Medallions"—one-ounce and half-ounce gold medals honoring Americans who had gained recognition in the arts.

1981: Treasury Secretary Regan announced the formation of a Gold Commission "to assess and make recommendations with regard to the policy of the U.S. government concerning the role of gold in domestic and international monetary systems." The commission's conclusion was that "no change in the present role of gold is currently desirable."

1982: New gold deposits were discovered in North America and Australia, which resulted in further expansion of supply from the producer.

1982: Canada introduced the fractional Maple Leaf coins in sizes of $1/4$ ounce and $1/10$ ounce: these coins were designed to compete with the Krugerrand family which landed on the world market in October of 1980.

1984: The United States Mint produced an eagle, or $10 gold piece, to commemorate the Los Angeles Olympic Games. It was the first gold coin issued by the United States in more than half a century.

1985: Congress authorized another commemorative gold coin—this time a half eagle, or $5 piece—to honor the Statue of Liberty. Later in the year, it also authorized a one-ounce U.S. gold bullion coin plus three subsidiary pieces in sizes of 1/2, 1/4, and 1/10 of an ounce—all with legal-tender status. They were scheduled to reach the market in late 1986.

1986: The international media reported huge purchases by a "mystery" buyer, later revealed to be the Japanese government, in preparation for the minting of a major commemorative coin. This coin honoring the 60th anniversary of Emperor Hirohito's reign was issued in November.

1986: In October, the U.S. government officially issued its first legal-tender gold bullion coins in more than half a century. At the same time, other countries—Australia, Brazil, Luxembourg—have announced plans to launch their own gold bullion coins.

Gold Bullion Prices (1975–1986)

In my years of experience in the gold market, I have frequently received requests from journalists, financial analysts, interested laymen, and others for various gold prices often over a historical time frame. This is a compilation that provides monthly average and month-end gold bullion prices from January 1975 through July 1986.

EXHIBIT B-1   Gold Bullion Prices in U.S. Dollars per Troy Ounce
(Month Average and Month End, London P.M. Fixes) 1975–1986

		Jan.	Feb.	Mar.	Apr.	May	June
1975	Mo. Avg.	176.27	179.56	178.16	169.84	167.39	164.24
	Mo. End	175.80	181.75	177.25	167.00	167.00	166.25
1976	Mo. Avg.	131.49	131.07	132.58	127.94	126.94	125.71
	Mo. End	128.15	132.30	129.60	128.40	125.50	123.80
1977	Mo. Avg.	132.26	136.29	148.22	149.16	146.60	140.77
	Mo. End	132.30	142.75	148.90	147.25	142.95	143.00
1978	Mo. Avg.	173.17	178.15	183.66	175.27	176.30	183.75
	Mo. End	175.75	182.25	181.60	170.85	184.15	183.05
1979	Mo. Avg.	227.27	245.67	242.04	239.16	257.61	279.06
	Mo. End	223.70	251.30	240.10	245.30	247.60	277.50
1980	Mo. Avg.	675.30	665.32	553.58	517.41	513.82	600.71
	Mo. End	653.00	637.00	494.50	518.00	535.50	653.50
1981	Mo. Avg.	557.38	499.76	498.76	495.80	479.69	460.74
	Mo. End	506.50	489.00	513.75	482.75	479.25	426.00
1982	Mo. Avg.	384.38	374.13	330.04	350.34	333.82	314.98
	Mo. End	387.00	362.50	320.00	361.25	325.25	317.50
1983	Mo. Avg.	481.29	491.96	419.70	432.93	438.08	418.84
	Mo. End	499.50	408.50	418.00	429.25	437.50	416.00
1984	Mo. Avg.	370.90	386.33	394.33	381.36	377.40	377.67
	Mo. End	373.75	394.25	388.60	375.80	384.25	373.05
1985	Mo. Avg.	302.74	229.43	304.17	324.74	316.64	316.83
	Mo. End	306.65	287.75	329.25	321.35	314.00	317.75
1986	Mo. Avg.	345.38	338.89	345.71	340.44	342.56	342.57
	Mo. End	350.50	338.15	344.00	345.75	343.20	346.75

SOURCE: Gold Information Center—Investment Service, 1986.

EXHIBIT B–1 *(concluded)*

		July	Aug.	Sept.	Oct.	Nov.	Dec.
1975	Mo. Avg.	165.17	163.00	144.09	142.76	142.42	139.30
	Mo. End	166.70	159.80	141.25	142.90	138.15	140.25
1976	Mo. Avg.	117.76	109.93	114.15	116.14	130.46	133.88
	Mo. End	112.50	104.00	116.00	123.15	130.25	134.50
1977	Mo. Avg.	143.39	144.95	149.52	158.86	162.10	160.45
	Mo. End	144.10	146.00	154.05	161.50	160.05	164.95
1978	Mo. Avg.	188.72	206.30	212.07	227.39	206.07	207.83
	Mo. End	200.25	208.70	217.10	242.60	193.40	226.00
1979	Mo. Avg.	294.73	300.81	355.11	391.65	391.99	459.74
	Mo. End	296.45	315.10	397.25	382.00	415.65	512.00
1980	Mo. Avg.	644.28	627.14	673.62	661.14	623.46	594.92
	Mo. End	614.25	631.25	666.75	629.00	619.75	589.50
1981	Mo. Avg.	409.28	410.15	443.58	437.75	413.36	410.09
	Mo. End	406.00	425.00	428.75	427.00	414.50	400.00
1982	Mo. Avg.	338.97	364.23	435.76	422.15	414.91	444.30
	Mo. End	342.90	411.50	397.00	423.25	436.00	448.00
1983	Mo. Avg.	422.72	416.24	411.80	393.58	381.66	387.56
	Mo. End	422.00	414.25	405.00	382.00	405.00	379.50
1984	Mo. Avg.	347.47	347.70	341.09	340.17	341.18	320.16
	Mo. End	342.35	348.25	345.75	333.50	329.00	309.20
1985	Mo. Avg.	317.38	329.33	324.25	325.93	325.22	320.81
	Mo. End	327.50	333.25	325.75	325.10	325.30	324.85
1986	Mo. Avg.	348.54					
	Mo. End	347.50					

A Glossary of Gold Investment Terms

Actuals. See *Physicals.*

Alloy. A mixture of metals. Because it is an extremely soft metal, gold is often alloyed with small amounts of copper, zinc, nickel, or silver to improve its durability.

American Arts Gold Medallions. See *U.S. Gold.*

American Depository Receipts (ADRs). Certificates entitling the holder to the rights associated with ownership of an equity, including any dividends that might be declared. ADRs are created by major banks against stock in a foreign company, often a gold-mining firm. The issuing bank actually holds the underlying equity. ADRs allow individual investors to participate in foreign stock markets without having to worry about exchange rates or trading hours in distant time zones, since they are priced in U.S. dollars and are traded during regular U.S. business hours.

Apothecaries' Weight. Literally, the weighing system used by pharmacists. Gold and other precious metals traditionally are weighed in troy ounces, which are units of apothecaries' weight. One troy ounce is equal to 31.1035 grams, while a standard or avoirdupois ounce is equal to 28.3495 grams.

Arbitrage. The simultaneous buying and selling of a commodity in two different markets or exchanges to take advantage of a difference in price. Arbitrage may be done between physical and futures markets, between different physical markets (a procedure known as location arbitrage), or between different delivery months in the same futures market (see *Spreads*).

Ask. The price sought by a seller of gold.

Assay. A chemical test of gold to determine its purity. Assays may be accomplished either by taking a small bore sample of the metal or by chemical testing of a bar or ingot.

At the Money. An option-market term describing the point when the strike price and the price of the underlying asset are the same or roughly the same.

Avoirdupois. The standard or "English" weighing system. Gold and other precious metals are weighed in troy ounces, which are units of apothecaries' weight.

Bar Chart. (Also known as a *High-Low-Close*.) A technical-analysis chart which graphs price action in a market by using a vertical line to show the price *Range* for an entire trading period and a short horizontal line to indicate the level of the *Settlement Price*.

Basis. The difference between the price of physical gold and the price of gold futures at the time a futures contract is bought by a hedger.

Basis Risk. The risk assumed by a hedger that the basis might change while he is holding a futures contract.

Bear. Someone who believes the price of gold will go lower.

Bear Market. A market in which the price is dropping.

Beta. A statistical term used to describe the amount of variation between the prices of different financial instruments. If the variation is great, an instrument is said to have a "high beta," while if it is not great, the instrument is said to have a "low beta." Compared with stocks, bonds, and many other financial instruments, gold and gold-related investments are said to have a high beta.

Bid. The price a potential buyer is willing to pay (see *Offer*).

Bretton Woods Conference. An international monetary conference held in 1944 in Bretton Woods, New Hampshire, where the conferees agreed to adopt the U.S. dollar as their reserve currency, or money they must have on hand in official accounts to back up individual national currencies.

Broker. In the gold market, an individual who is paid either a salary by a firm or commissions by clients to arrange for the buying and selling of gold or gold futures contracts. A broker is never the buyer or seller but serves as an intermediary between the two. Sometimes, the firm itself is referred to as the broker.

Bull. Someone who believes the price of gold will rise.

Bullion. Physical gold in bar form or coins (known as *Bullion Coins*) whose price is based on the quantity and quality of the gold plus a small premium to cover fabrication and marketing costs.

Bull Market. A market in which the price is rising.

Buying Hedge. The buying of futures contracts to protect against possible increases in the cost of gold which will be purchased in the future for commercial or industrial use.

By-Product or Coproduct. A by-product is a mineral that is mined along with another mineral (as uranium often is mined with gold) but is secondary in importance in the total mining operation of a firm. A coproduct is a mineral that is found along with others in a mining operation and shares in importance with the others.

Call Option. The right, but not the obligation, to buy gold bullion, mining equities, or futures contracts at a specified price (known as the *Strike* price) within a specified time frame (known as the *Maturity*) in exchange for a listed fee (known as a *Premium*) from an individual (known as the *Writer* or *Grantor* of the option).

Carry. The cost of holding gold or some other commodity over the life of a futures contract. In the gold futures market, there is always "positive carry" because the prices will always be higher in future months than in nearer ones (see *Contango*).

Carrying Charges. The cost of storing gold bullion in a depository, including insurance fees and the interest charges associated with financing. The gold futures market is said to be in "full carry" when the difference between the futures prices and the nearby ones is sufficient to cover all the carrying charges.

Cash and Carry. A technique that combines the physical gold and futures markets by using the futures to pay the cost of carrying the metal. In a cash-and-carry trade, a bullion merchant or other large-scale holder of gold will pay cash for the prompt delivery of metal and simultaneously sell a future contract. When the due date arrives on the future position, the cash metal is delivered. The income received from selling the future position has covered the carrying charges for holding the metal.

Cash Market. The market for actual gold bullion, as opposed to futures.

Charting. Using charts of the gold market's historical price and/or volume to predict gold's future price (see *Technical Analysis*).

Chervonetz. A gold bullion coin minted by the Union of Soviet Socialist Republics.

Chicago Board of Trade (CBT). One of four U.S. exchanges trading gold futures. Contracts calling for delivery of 32.15 *Troy Ounces* of gold, also known as a *Kilobar,* are traded on the CBT.

Chicago Mercantile Exchange (Merc). One of four U.S. exchanges trading gold futures. The Merc trades contracts calling for the delivery of 100 ounces of gold.

Clearinghouse. An agency associated with a futures exchange which is responsible for matching all transactions during the trading day, as well as for collecting margin payments from each brokerage firm for all open contracts held by their customers. The clearinghouse also is responsible for receiving notices of intent to make delivery from holders of short positions (contracts to sell) and passing them on to brokerage firms whose clients hold the oldest long positions (contracts to buy). The clearinghouse guarantees every contract traded on the exchange.

Clearing Member. A member of an exchange who has shown additional financial capability to pay for all contracts its customers hold. Because this is a substantial amount of money, not every member of an exchange is a clearing member, but all transactions must be handled by a clearing member.

Commission House. A brokerage firm that charges commissions for executing clients' gold futures business.

Commodity Exchange, Inc. (Comex). The world's largest and most influential gold futures exchange. The Comex, which operates in New York City, also handles gold and silver futures options as well as silver, copper, and aluminum futures. Contracts calling for delivery of 100 *Troy Ounces* of gold are traded on the Comex.

Commodity Futures Trading Commission (CFTC). The U.S. government agency charged with supervising and regulating futures exchanges in this country. There are five members, all appointed by the President with the consent of the U.S. Senate. Trading in gold-mining equities and options on equities is regulated by the Securities and Exchange Commission (SEC).

Congestion. A futures market situation marked by little trading or change in price. Congestion may occur when buy orders and sell orders are close in price for a period of time.

Consensus. A survey of gold market investment recommendations from analysts at commodity and stock brokerage houses. This survey forms the basis for *Contrary Opinion* trading.

Contango. A British term common on the London Metals Exchange (where gold is not traded), which is used to describe a normal situation in the gold futures market where the prices of contracts for delivery are higher than those for nearby or prompt delivery. Contango is determined by the storage, insurance, and finance costs incurred by the major bullion houses when they store gold. In the gold markets, even small discrepancies from contango occur only for fleeting moments, because major bullion firms are always quick to profit from such aberrations by arbitrage between the physical and futures markets. The term is used on the metals futures markets in the United States, but is uncommon in other futures markets, such as those involving agricultural products.

Contract. On the gold futures exchanges, contracts are the items traded. Each is a legally binding agreement to buy or sell a specified quantity of gold at a specified price at a specific time in the future.

Contrary Opinion. A technical trading method which determines the *Consensus* of opinion on the gold market, as reflected by recommendations from analysts at commodity and stock brokerage houses, and then takes the position opposite the one recommended. The theory behind contrary opinion is that a number of people following the same advice from analysts will lead to an *Overbought* or *Oversold* market condition, which soon will be followed by a *Correction* or *Reversal*.

Corner. An attempt to control all of a commodity available for delivery in one future month by buying or selling a large number of contracts. This is virtually impossible on gold futures exchanges, because bullion houses, banks, and mining firms have very large inventories of gold. Attempting to corner a market is illegal in the United States.

Corona. A gold bullion coin minted by Austria. The Corona, like its Hungarian cousin, the *Korona*, contains .9802 troy ounce of gold and is 21.6 karats, or 90 percent gold by weight.

Correction. A shift in the direction of the gold market or any other market. If prices have been rising and turn down, it is a "downward correction." If they have been dropping and turn higher, it is an "upside" or "upward correction." Corrections are also known as *Reversals*.

Cover. The process of offsetting a futures contract by taking the opposite position. This is also known as *Liquidating*. When the holder of a short position—a contract to sell—buys that contract back, it is known as "short-covering."

Covered Option. If the writer of an option on gold bullion, equities, or futures owns the underlying asset, it is said to be a "covered option," as opposed to a *Nakèd* one, in which the underlying asset is not owned.

Day Trader. A speculator who assumes a position and then liquidates it at the end of the trading day. This is a short-term tactic that avoids overnight risks.

Dealer. In the gold market, a dealer is someone who buys and sells physical bullion.

Delivery. The transfer of ownership or certificates of ownership from one party to another. Delivery does not necessarily involve the actual physical moving of gold, but usually is accomplished by the transfer of a depository receipt indicating the quantity, brand, and location of the gold bullion.

Delivery Date. The time when a commodity, such as gold, must be delivered in order to fulfill a contract.

Delivery Months. Months designated by each futures exchange as times when delivery notices may be given. On the Commodity Exchange, the delivery months for gold futures are February, April, June, August, October, and December.

Delivery Notice. A notice given by the holders of short gold positions—contracts to sell gold in the future—of the time and place where they will make delivery. Delivery must be made into an exchange-approved depository. For the Commodity Exchange in New York City, this would have to be in New York or the Greater New York area. For the Chicago Board of Trade, all depositories are located in Chicago. The International Monetary Market division of the Chicago Mercantile Exchange and the MidAmerica Exchange in Chicago allow deliveries to depositories in both New York and Chicago. On the Comex, delivery notices may be given up to 12:30 P.M. (New York time) on the second-to-last business day of the contract month.

Delivery Period. The period during which holders of short positions on a futures exchange, or contracts to sell gold, may issue notices of intent to deliver to a futures exchange. On the Commodity Exchange, the delivery period begins with the two days after the last trading day of the month prior to the delivery month, and extends until the day after the last trading day of the current month. The last day of trading on the Comex is the third-to-last business day of the month. Delivery periods often are preceded by heavy liquidation of long positions—contracts to accept delivery—in an attempt to avoid having to accept the physical gold or a warehouse receipt. Once a delivery notice is served, the receiver is obligated to pay the full amount of the gold contract if he or she cannot find a buyer for the long position. The holders of the oldest long contracts are the first to receive a delivery notice, while the choice of when to issue a delivery notice is left to the discretion of the holders of the short positions—that is, contracts to sell. The exchange *Clearinghouse* receives all the delivery notices from the short position holders, and it is the clearinghouse which then distributes them to those brokerage houses holding the oldest long positions.

Delivery Point.   A depository designated by a futures exchange is a place where delivery of gold bullion may be made by the holders of short positions—that is, contracts to sell. For the Commodity Exchange, all delivery points are in the Greater New York metropolitan area, while the Chicago Board of Trade depositories are all in Chicago, and the Chicago Mercantile and MidAmerica exchanges have depositories in both Chicago and New York.

Depository Receipt.   See *Warehouse Receipt.*

Discretionary Account.   An account in which the broker has legal authority to trade without consulting the client. In order to accept a discretionary account, a broker must have been registered with the Commodity Futures Trading Commission for a minimum of two years. In addition, the client must file a document annually granting the brokerage house power of attorney. Many firms will not accept discretionary accounts.

Dore Bar.   An intermediate product in the manufacturing of gold, dore bars contain approximately 60 to 70 percent gold and usually are produced at mines or smelters. The next step in production is refining, either electrolytically or through the use of fire.

Double Top or Double Bottom.   A technical description of a *Bar Chart* formation picturing trading that goes up to the same level twice, but fails to penetrate that level (a double top) or goes down to the same level twice, but fails to penetrate it further down (a double bottom). Double tops form what technicians refer to as *Resistance,* while double bottoms form what is referred to as *Support.* There also can be triple tops or bottoms. Both double and triple formations are signals to technical analysts that there will be a *Reversal* in the pattern of trading shortly.

Doubloon.   A Spanish-American gold coin which was valued at 16 dollars. Doubloons are considered numismatic coins, and are prized for their collector value rather than their gold content.

Electrolytic Refining.   The most efficient method of separating gold from its ore. Using this technique, it is possible to produce gold that is 99.99 percent pure.

Environmental Factors. Influences on the price of gold which arise from the economic environment rather than the fundamental factors of supply and demand. Interest rates, the rate of inflation, and the strength or weakness of currencies are all environmental factors.

Equity. A share of stock in a company. The term "equity" also can refer to the cash value of commodity futures positions or the cash value of stock.

Exchange for Physicals (EFP). The transfer of a long futures contract, or one to buy, for actual gold bullion. EFPs often are accompanied by payments of additional cash by one of the parties. Unlike most futures exchange transactions, EFPs need not be done through open-outcry bidding.

Ex-Pit Transactions. The execution of trades outside the exchange floor. EFPs are always ex-pit.

Fabrication Demand. The need for gold by commercial or industrial users, as opposed to the demand for gold from institutional or private investors.

Fill or Kill Order (FOK). An order on a gold futures exchange which must be executed immediately by the floor broker, if possible, or canceled.

Fine Gold. Pure gold.

Fineness. The amount of pure gold contained in a bar or gold product. Technically, fineness refers to the amount of pure gold contained in 1,000 parts of an alloy. A gold bar of .995 fineness is one that contains 99.5 percent gold and 0.5 percent of some other metal.

Fine Weight. See *Karat*.

First Notice Day. See *Delivery Notice*.

Fix. One of two prices established daily by five major London gold bullion dealers who meet in the office of N. M. Rothschild & Sons to settle on the price at which they will trade bullion. There is a morning fix and an afternoon fix, and the afternoon fix often forms the basis for many bullion contracts around the world. In addition to Rothschild, the other participants are Mocatta & Goldsmid, Ltd., Samuel Montague & Co., Sharps Pixley & Co., Ltd., and Johnson Matthey Bankers, Ltd. They have been meeting in this manner for more than 150 years. Gold prices also are "fixed" daily by dealers in Paris and Zurich, but the London fix is by far the most important.

Flag. A technical formation on a *Bar Chart* that occurs when prices in a market which has been moving higher move lower temporarily (a *Bull Flag*, so called because it is viewed by technicians as an indication that the previous uptrend will quickly resume—a bullish time for gold prices) or when prices in a market which has been moving lower move higher temporarily (a *Bear Flag*, because it is viewed as a signal that prices will again resume their "bearish" downtrend).

Floor. A price level in the gold futures market at which there are no sellers, at least for the time being. The floor is considered the lowest price point for a given move. The term "floor" also can refer to the trading arena of a gold futures exchange.

Forward Contract. An agreement similar to a futures contract, except that it is made in the cash market between the buyer and seller and is not the result of trading on a commodity futures exchange. Forward contracts are not regulated by the Commodity Futures Trading Commission or any other U.S. government agency.

Four Nines. Gold with a fineness of .9999, the purest possible.

Fundamental Analysis. The study of a commodity's supply and demand. In the case of gold, the areas of supply studied by a fundamental analyst are mine production, secondary supply (scrap), and sales by the nations with centrally planned economies. The areas of demand are the fabrication requirements of manufacturers and jewelers and demand from investors in the private sector. Transactions by central banks and official dealings of governments may constitute either supply or demand, depending on whether they are sales or purchases.

Futures Contract. An agreement reached on an organized exchange calling for the delivery of a specified quantity of gold at a specified time in the future for an agreed upon price. Delivery must be made and received at an exchange-approved depository.

Gap. A space left in a *Bar Chart* when prices open higher or lower than the previous day's close. The most significant gap for a technical analyst is a *Breakout Gap*—one that signifies a *Reversal* in the direction of the market. There also are *Exhaustion Gaps*, which occur when a market trend reaches its end, and *Midway Gaps*, which sometimes can appear to be exhaustion gaps but actually are only breathing points in a trend that is quickly resumed.

Gold. A precious (rare) metal that has been used as a medium of exchange, storehouse of value, and decorative item since prehistoric times. Gold's chemical symbol is "Au"—from the Latin "aurora," or dawn. It is an element characterized by its malleability, or softness, and durability. It does not rust and reacts with few other elements. Gold's atomic number is 79 and its atomic weight is 196.967.

Gold Standard. A monetary system based on the convertibility of currency into gold or paper money backed and interchangeable with gold.

Good Delivery. A description of a gold bar that may be delivered against a short futures position. Each exchange designates certain refiners or fabricators whose bullion bars are acceptable for delivery in fulfillment of a futures contract.

Good for the Week. A futures or equity market order that is good for the entire trading week. In both markets, it is customary for a broker to hold an order only for the day in which it was given. In equities, orders can be held longer than a week, although they expire automatically at the end of six months unless renewed. No gold futures exchange will allow floor brokers to hold orders longer than one week, and orders always expire at the end of each week's last trading day.

Grain. The earliest measure of gold weight, a grain is equal to 0.002083 of a troy ounce. Gold is also weighed sometimes in *Grams*. One troy ounce of gold equals 31.103 grams.

Grantor. One who sells an option on gold bullion, mining equities, or future contracts. A grantor, also known as the *Writer* of the option, may write a *Covered Option*—one representing an asset that he or she actually owns—or a *Naked Option*, where the grantor does not own the underlying asset.

Hallmark. A mark or markings stamped on a bar of gold to indicate the producer and the bar's fineness. The first hallmarks were approved by the Goldsmiths' Hall in London.

Hedging. The use of futures contracts, options on futures, or cash forward positions to offset an anticipated cash market transaction in the future. A hedger who expects to sell gold in the future, such as a miner, might hedge anticipated production by selling gold futures contracts or "put options," while a hedger expecting to be a buyer in the future, such as a jewelry manufacturer, might hedge by buying gold futures contracts or "call options." In either case, the hedger "locks in" the price of gold for future sales or delivery and insulates himself from market variations in price during the time horizon of the futures contract or option.

Initial Margin. See *Margin*.

Institutional Customer. A bank, pension fund, or investment company, other than an individual, which engages in fairly large-scale transactions.

In the Money. A *Call Option* is said to be in the money when the *Strike Price* is lower than the price of the underlying asset, while a *Put Option* is in the money when the strike price is higher than that of the underlying asset.

Intrinsic Value. The intrinsic value of an option is the amount it is in the money.

Karat. A unit describing the purity of gold. A 24-karat gold bar is one that is 99.9 percent pure gold. Karatage is expressed in 24ths. Twenty-two-karat gold is $^{22}/_{24}$ths pure, or 91.67 percent gold by weight. "Karat" should not be confused with "carat," which is a unit of weight in gemology.

Karat Gold. Gold of not less than 10 karats fineness.

Kilo Bar. A gold bar that weighs 32.1507 troy ounces.

Korona. A gold bullion coin minted by Hungary and having the same characteristics as the Austrian *Corona*.

Krugerrand. A gold bullion coin minted by the Republic of South Africa and containing exactly one troy ounce of gold. Krugerrands are 22 karats, or 91.67 percent gold. The rest of their alloy is copper, which is added for hardening.

Last Trading Day. The last day on which contracts for delivery in a specific month may be traded. In the case of the Comex gold market, this is four business days prior to the last calendar day of the month. All open positions must be satisfied by the end of trading on the last trading day.

Legal Tender. A term that applies to coins that are minted by a government and guaranteed redeemable for a specified amount by that government. Usually, they carry a face value and have legal-tender value in the amount. However, some gold bullion coins, such as the Krugerrand, are considered legal tender even though they have no face value.

Leverage. The ability to control an investment whose market value is a multiple of the cash one has on deposit. For example, a gold futures contract is considered a highly leveraged investment because the investor pays an initial margin which may be only 5 to 10 percent of the value. Equities purchased on margin also are leveraged investments, and so are options. Sometimes, "leverage" also refers to the degree of volatility of a particular investment asset in relation to a change in the underlying price of gold. An investment that appreciates or depreciates 15 percent for every percentage-point change in the price of gold would be considered a highly leveraged investment; an investment whose price varies by the same percentage as changes in the price of gold is not considered to be a leveraged investment.

Leverage Contract. A contract with a retail bullion firm that calls for an initial down payment of as little as 20 percent of the total value of the gold, with the firm lending the investor the balance in exchange for monthly or quarterly interest and storage payments. The sponsoring firm holds a first lien against the gold. Leverage contracts are not regulated by any exchange or government agency, and can result in the loss of an entire investment. Thus, they are extremely poor investment vehicles.

Life of Contract. The history of a futures contract from the first day it was traded to either the last trading day or the present day, if it is still open. On the Commodity Exchange, contracts have a maximum life span of 23 months.

Limit. The maximum amount by which the price of a futures contract may change, up or down, in one trading day. On the Commodity Exchange, the limit is $25; on the Chicago Board of Trade, it is $50. If the price moves by the limit for two consecutive days on the Comex or three consecutive days on the Chicago exchanges, the limit is raised by 50 percent. On the Comex, for example, it would increase to $37.50.

Limit Order. An order restraining the floor broker from buying at a higher level or selling at a lower level. Limit orders are in contrast to *Market Orders*, which are to be executed immediately upon receipt on the trading floor, without regard to price.

Liquidation. The process of offsetting a futures market position by taking the opposite position. Also, the selling of an asset, such as gold-mining equities or bullion.

Liquid Gold. A solution of gold and various chemicals used for surface decoration of objects.

Liquidity. A subjective term used to describe the facility with which orders can be executed on a market. Because of its high volume, the Comex gold futures market is said to be a highly liquid market, while trading on the International Monetary Market gold futures exchange, which has a very low daily volume, is said to be relatively illiquid.

London Gold Pool. A pool formed in 1961 by the central banks of Belgium, France, Italy, the Netherlands, Switzerland, the United

Kingdom, and West Germany to work with the Federal Reserve Bank of New York in an attempt to stabilize the price of gold at $35.0875 per troy ounce. The pool lasted until 1968, when it was officially dismantled. The inflationary pressures arising from the U.S. financing of the Vietnam War had increased fears that the United States would devalue the dollar by raising the price it would pay for gold, thus increasing the dollar value of its own metal reserves. The London Pool initially was replaced by a two-tiered market in which governments continued trading gold at the official price of $35 per ounce while private individuals and institutions traded the yellow metal at whatever price supply and demand dictated.

Long. As a noun, someone who is holding a contract to buy a commodity; as an adjective, a term used to describe a position that contractually obligates the holder to take delivery in the future, or to describe someone who holds physical gold.

Maple Leaf. A gold bullion coin issued by the Royal Canadian Mint which is 24-karat, or 99.99 percent, gold and weighs exactly 1 troy ounce. The Maple Leaf is legal tender with a face value of $50 (Canadian).

Margin. In the futures market, an amount of money deposited into an investor's account with a brokerage house as evidence of good faith that the investor will be able to satisfy the contract financially. There are three kinds of margins: an *Initial Margin*, which is the first deposit made by a customer; a *Maintenance Margin*, the level at which the cash balance of a futures account must be maintained; and a *Variation Margin*—a margin deposited by the brokerage house with the futures exchange clearinghouse. In the equity market, a margin is a down payment on equities in the stock market. An equity margin is usually 50 percent of the value of the purchased stock, with the brokerage firm lending its customers the difference between the stock purchase price and the amount deposited.

Margin Call. A request from a broker for additional funds to raise a cash position back up to the initial margin level in both the futures and equity markets.

Market Maker. A firm that stands ready to buy or sell a particular commodity such as gold, options, or equities and regularly quotes bid and ask prices to its customers or trading counterparts. In the gold bullion coin market, a market maker is a firm that is obligated by the issuing nation to both buy and sell coins at the prevailing market price, regardless of the level of investor interest. There are no market makers on the futures exchange.

Market Order. An order to a broker to buy or sell gold futures contracts, mining equities, bullion, or options immediately at the going price.

Medal. A metallic object, often shaped like a coin, which is struck to commemorate some person, place, or event or as an award. Unlike a coin, a medal has no relationship to currency. Medals may be struck by a government mint, as was the case of the U.S. Treasury's American Arts Gold Medallions, or they may come from private mints. For the most part, they are numismatic in nature—that is to say, their value is determined largely by collector interest. But some, like the American Arts gold pieces, are priced on the basis of bullion content. A "medallion" is an unusually large medal. Technically speaking, the Treasury "medallions" are really just medals.

Metric Tonne. The metric-system equivalent of the avoirdupois or standard ton: A metric tonne equals 2,204.6 pounds or 32,121 troy ounces. Shipments of gold or sales of gold between central banks often are quoted in metric tonnes.

Mexican One-Ounce. See *Onza*.

MidAmerica Commodity Exchange (MIDAM). The smallest of the four U.S. gold futures exchanges, the MidAm trades contracts for delivery of 33.2-ounce gold bars.

Mine Life. The amount of time left before a gold mine is depleted of workable ore—ore that can be mined commercially.

Moving Average. An average of several days' market closing prices, calculated daily, weekly, or even monthly over a period of time. Moving averages are used by technical analysts to smooth out long-term trend charts that may be distorted by wide daily fluctuations.

Naked Option. When an investor sells an option on gold bullion or gold futures without owning the underlying asset, he or she is said to have sold a "naked" put or call. This is the riskiest option trade possible.

Nearby Delivery. The listed trading month on a futures exchange closest to the present calendar month. *Nearby Active* refers to the soonest actively traded futures contract.

Nominal Price. See *Settlement Price*.

Notice of Intent to Deliver. See *Delivery Notice*.

Nugget. Gold washed from rock and usually deposited in river beds. The largest nugget on record was found in Australia in 1872 and weighed almost 200 pounds.

Numismatic Coin. One that is sought by collectors because of its artistic, cultural, or sentimental value and its rarity, as opposed to the value of the metal it contains. Bullion coins, because they are sought for their precious-metal value, are not numismatic, while medals and medallions usually are.

Offer. The price sought by the buyer of gold; the same as *Bid* and the opposite of *Ask*.

Offset. The act of liquidating existing futures or options.

Onza. A Mexican bullion coin (often listed as the *Mexican One-Ounce*) containing exactly one ounce of 21.6-karat gold.

Open-Face or Open-Pit. A method of mining gold or other minerals by stripping away overmatter that covers an ore body. Open-face mining is in contrast to underground or shaft mining, which involves the digging of underground tunnels in order to reach an ore body. Many of the newer gold mines in North America are open-face operations, while South African mines traditionally are underground.

Opening Range. The range of prices during the first few minutes of trading in a futures market. In the gold futures markets, the opening range is established about five minutes after the start of trading. Orders to "buy market on open" or "sell market on open" can be filled at any price traded during this period.

Open Interest. The number of futures contracts which have not been offset by opposite transactions. The level of open interest is an indication of how active and liquid a gold futures exchange is—or, on a particular exchange, how active a given trading month will be in the time remaining before the last trading day, since all open contracts must be offset or liquidated before their maturity date. Open interest is one measure of a market's *Liquidity*, the other being *Volume*.

Open Outcry. The method of bidding on a futures exchange floor. Although floor brokers often use hand signals to indicate the quantity of contracts being traded as well as whether the transaction is a buy or a sell, every commodity futures trade must be carried out through the open calling out of the price, contract month, and quantity.

Operating Costs. The costs of mining gold, expressed in a given currency (usually U.S. dollars) per ounce. Operating costs are the basis for the fundamental analysis of a gold-mining equity.

Option. The right, but not the obligation, to buy or sell a gold futures contract, mining equity, or bullion (see *Call Option* and *Put Option*).

Ore Reserve. The amount of ore contained in a gold-mining site which can be mined commercially. The ore reserves of a mine are necessarily approximations based upon geological testing, since the size of the reserve cannot be determined exactly until all digging at the mine has been completed and work on the site has stopped. Nonetheless, modern mining engineering has made ore-reserve predictions highly accurate. If gold rises sharply in price, properties previously considered commercially unminable can reach the point where they can be mined at a profit.

Original Margin. Another term for *Initial Margin*. An amount that must be deposited with a brokerage house before any futures trading can begin or stock can be purchased. In the case of futures, original margins are viewed as simply an indication that the investor can afford to make or take delivery of the quantity of gold specified in the futures contract (although this is seldom done). A futures original margin is normally between 5 and 10 percent of the total value of the contract. In the equity markets, the original margin is considered a down payment on the eventual purchase of the stock and normally is 50 percent of the value of the stock.

Oscillator. A technical analytical calculation used to measure how fast prices in a gold market are changing by measuring the daily changes in price and then plotting them on a chart, with advances in price marked above a zero line and price drops marked below the line (also known as a "net-change oscillator"). Oscillator charts can be helpful in predicting *Reversals* in the market's direction.

Out of the Money. Refers to *Put Options* where the *Strike* price is lower than the price of the underlying asset, or *Call Options* where the *Strike* price is higher than that of the underlying asset.

Overbought. A term to describe a market where there is thought to have been too much buying in a given commodity or contract month, and where few new buyers are expected in the near future. Technicians and traders who believe a market is overbought will expect the price to come down from what they think is an unrealistically high level.

Oversold. A term to describe a market where there is thought to have been too much selling, and where few new sellers are expected in the near future. Technicians and traders who believe a market is oversold will expect the price to rise to what they think is a realistic level.

Paper Losses or Profits. Unrealized losses or gains on an investment.

Pennant. A bar chart formation similar to a *Flag*.

Pennyweight. A U.S. unit of weight for gold. Twenty pennyweights equal one *Troy Ounce* (see also *Grain* and *Gram*).

Peso. A shorthand term for the 50-peso gold bullion coin minted by Mexico. In addition to the 50-peso coin, which contains 1.2057 troy ounces of gold, Mexico also mints the one-ounce *Onza*. Both are 21.6-karat coins, or 90 percent gold.

Physicals. Gold bullion bars or coins, as opposed to futures contracts; sometimes referred to as "actuals" in the futures markets.

Pieces of Eight. Spanish silver coins which were equal to eight *Reales*, or "bits." Like doubloons, pieces of eight are prized for their numismatic or collector value rather than their precious-metal content.

Pit. The area on a futures exchange floor where actual trading takes place; sometimes called the ring.

Placer Ore Body. A mine site where the minerals generally are found in their free state, often on a stream bed.

Point-and-Figure. A technical chart that details the buying or selling momentum in a market, identifies *Congestion* points, and can give an indication as to how far prices will advance or decline once the congestion ends.

Position Traders. Traders who deal on a longer term basis on the gold futures market, as opposed to *Day Traders*.

Premium. In options trading, the amount paid by someone buying an option, or received by someone selling one. In the futures markets, an additional payment specified by exchange rules which must be made if the gold that is delivered is higher grade than 99.5 percent pure. In the bullion coin market, the difference between the price of a coin and the value of the bullion it contains.

Present Value. A calculation of the value of a mining firm's gold properties, based on the current or expected price of gold. Present value is one of the factors an investor should consider before buying equity shares in a mining company. The other considerations are operating costs and the extent of the ore reserves.

Price Averaging. The technique of acquiring gold on a regular basis—for instance, by spending $400 per month—in an effort to establish an average price for a portfolio. In a market where the price is rising, this is known as *Averaging Up;* in a falling market, it is *Averaging Down.*

Price Elasticity. The amount by which the prices of gold bullion or futures vary. When there is a high level of elasticity, the differences between the highest and lowest prices in a given period will be large, while low elasticity means that the difference will be slight (see *Range*).

Price-to-Earnings. A measure of the value of an equity share obtained by dividing the price of one share by its earnings per share. This statistic, often referred to as a "P/E" ratio, can be as low as 5 to 1 or as high as 25 to 1 or more. Gold-mining shares often have a high P/E ratio, compared with other equities.

Primary Supply. Gold from mines is referred to as "primary" metal, as opposed to secondary gold, which is recovered from recycling.

P&S Statement. "P&S" refers to *"Purchase and Sale."* Every commodity futures transaction should be reported to a customer by a brokerage firm on a P&S statement on the next trading day. The statement will show the number of contracts involved, whether the transaction is a purchase or a sale, the price at which the transaction took place, the amount of commissions and exchange fees charged, and any profit or loss which may have resulted from the action.

Put Option. The right, but not the obligation, to sell a gold futures contract, bullion, or mining equity at a specific price within a specified time period. The right to "put" the asset to the writer of the option.

Pyramiding. Using the appreciated values of gold investments to pay for increasing the size of those investments.

Rand. The South African unit of currency. Because of that nation's dependency on gold as an export product and source of foreign exchange, the strength or weakness of the rand vis-à-vis other currencies is tied closely to the international price of the yellow metal.

Range. The difference between the highest and lowest prices of transactions in a given trading period, be it a day, week, month, or even year.

Ratios. Technical analysts and traders watch the ratio between the price of gold and that of another precious metal, such as silver or platinum, in an effort to detect any distortions from historic trends. During 1986, the gold-silver price ratio was about 65 to 1; in other words, it took 65 ounces of silver to buy 1 ounce of gold. This was unusually high; within the last 10 years, the ratio has been as low as 15 to 1. The price of platinum has been as much as $100 higher than that of gold. However, the price of gold actually exceeded that of platinum for a time, when the mid-1980s recession curtailed demand for automotive and oil-refining catalytic converters—the two largest market uses for platinum.

Rectangle.   A formation on a *Bar Chart* that results from *Congestion* in the market.

Registered Commodity Representative (RCR).   A person registered with the Commodity Futures Trading Commission and various other exchanges and legally authorized to solicit and accept customer orders. All transactions in futures markets must be handled by RCRs, also referred to sometimes as brokers or account executives.

Registered Representative.   An equities market broker or account executive who has passed an exam administered by the National Association of Security Dealers and is registered with the Securities and Exchange Commission as well as the state in which his or her clients reside.

Relative-Strength Index.   A technical-analysis measure of how strong a given market move is. The higher the relative strength, the greater the possibility that the market is *Overbought* and will reverse and head lower; the lower the relative strength, the greater the chance that the market is *Oversold* and will reverse and head higher.

Reporting Limit, Reportable Positions.   The legal limit of net long or short positions in any given commodity futures market which any one investor may hold without having those positions reported by the brokerage house to the exchange and the Commodity Futures Trading Commission. Reporting limits are designed to prevent any one person from developing too much control over a market without the other participants' being made aware of that individual's position.

Resistance.   A price level high enough to discourage new buying and encourage selling, often serving to establish a temporary ceiling on near-term price moves (see *Support*).

Resting Order.   An order given to a futures or equity market floor broker to be executed at a given price point. Also known as a *Standing Order.*

Restrike.   A gold bullion coin that has been reissued by the minting country. It is a copy of a coin once minted by that country and bears the date of the original issue rather than the date when the coin was actually minted. Restrike coins are not legal tender.

Reversal. A change in the direction of prices, also known as a *Correction*.

Rolling Forward or Rolling Over. The liquidation of one gold futures or options position and simultaneous purchase of the same position in a later month.

Round-Turn. The buying and selling of one contract. Commodity commissions, unlike those paid to stockbrokers, generally are quoted on a "round-turn" basis—that is, the price is the same for both initiating and liquidating the position. However, a P&S statement usually reflects only a "one-way" charge—in other words, half the total commission which will be listed on the statement.

Rule of Multiple Techniques. The theory that all conclusions drawn from technical analysis must be confirmed by several tools of the analyst.

Scalping. The trading of gold futures for very slight gains.

Secondary Supply. Gold recovered through the recycling of obsolete or damaged electronic parts or jewelry. Secondary gold is any gold which has been recovered commercially from any source.

Settlement Price. Often mistakenly referred to as the "closing price," the settlement price is the level determined by an exchange committee at the close of each trading day. Every listed contract month must have a settlement price, even though there may have been no contracts traded that day (in which case the settlement price is known as a *Nominal Price*). The settlement price is the basis for determining changes in a customer's equity and whether there will be any margin calls.

Short. In the futures market, someone who holds a contract to sell a commodity; or an adjective describing contracts to sell (known as "short positions"). Also may be used as an active verb describing the selling of a commodity for future delivery, as in "I shorted December gold today." Equities also may be "sold short"—but in that case, the transaction would entail the borrowing of the underlying security, since there is no contract involved. Stocks may be "shorted" only if the preceding change in price was an increase, while futures may be shorted regardless of previous price moves.

Short Squeeze. Pressure applied to those who have sold the market short to offset their positions. This is done because the price has risen against them and they face margin calls as well as substantial losses. In the physical gold market, when a bullion firm commits itself to selling more bullion than it has in its inventory and is forced to pay more for gold on the open market than its selling price, it is said to have been squeezed.

Slope. A formation on a *Bar Chart* that occurs after a rapid uptrend or downtrend as the angle of the trend becomes less pronounced.

Solid Gold. The U.S. Federal Trade Commission permits the use of this term to describe any article that does not have a hollow center and has a gold content of at least 10 karats.

Speculator. In the gold futures market, one who trades short term in an attempt to profit from changes in price, without actually making or taking delivery of metal. A speculator may be a day trader or a position trader. By contrast, the long-term investor typically may hold a position indefinitely, while a hedger uses the gold futures markets to protect business commitments against adverse price changes. The term "speculators" often is applied to short-term traders in any market.

Spot. The price for immediate-delivery gold in the physical market. In the futures market, "spot" refers to the immediate or current trading month. At the end of a calendar month, even though there may be as many as four business days left, futures trading in that calendar month halts and the next month on the calendar is referred to as the spot month.

Spreads or Straddles. Procedures that involve the purchase of a futures contract in one delivery month and the sale of a contract for the same commodity in another month. Spreads may also be accomplished in the options markets by the simultaneous holding of puts and calls, or they may be established between a futures position and an option contract. Spreads may also be initiated between two different metals, such as gold and silver (for example, by buying gold and selling silver, or vice versa) to take advantage of divergences from the traditional price ratio of the two metals. Spreading is a form of *Arbitrage,* although arbitrage more often refers to buying and selling in two different markets, as in the gold futures and physical gold markets.

Standard Bar. See *Good Delivery.*

Standing Order. See *Resting Order.*

Stop Orders and Stop-Loss Orders. Standing orders placed to liquidate a gold futures market position at a certain point. Stop-loss orders are placed to prevent losses beyond a given point.

Strike Price. The price at which an option may be exercised and the underlying gold asset may be either bought (in the case of a *Call Option*) or sold (in the case of a *Put Option*).

Support. A price level low enough to attract new buying and/or reduce selling, often sufficient to establish a temporary price *Floor* on the market.

Swap. In the physical gold bullion market, an exchange of gold in one location for metal in another, or an exchange between different purities of bullion. In the futures markets, swapping is synonymous with *Rolling Over* or *Rolling Forward*.

Switch. See *Rolling Over.*

Tael. A unit of weight of gold in Asia, particularly in Hong Kong. One tael equals 1.3 troy ounces. Bars of gold in Asia commonly are sold in 1-, 5-, and 10-tael sizes.

Technical Analysis. The use of price history (sometimes also volume and open-interest history) to study a market's past behavior. Technical analysts use price charts, volume and open-interest charts, and the volatility of price changes in an effort to determine future price activity. See *Fundamental Analysis.*

Ten-Tola Bar. A 116-gram (3.73-ounce) bar of fine gold commonly traded in Southeast and Southern Asia.

Time Value. The amount by which an option's *Premium* exceeds its *Intrinsic Value.* Time value reflects the amount of time remaining before the option matures. The greater the amount of time before maturity, the higher the premium. The premium on an *Out-of-the-Money* option is strictly its time value, since this kind of option has no intrinsic value.

To-Arrive Contract. The forerunner of futures contracts, to-arrive contracts were used to set buying and selling terms for commodities to be delivered in the future. Unlike futures contracts, which are arrived at through trading on a formal exchange, to-arrive contracts were agreements between the buyer and seller and resulted from private bargaining. They are similar to forward-delivery contracts.

Trend Line. A line connecting the highest and lowest prices on a *Bar* or *Point-and-Figure* chart in order to determine *Support* and *Resistance* levels.

Triangle. A formation on a *Bar* or *Point-and-Figure* chart which is literally a triangle drawn around a cluster of prices. A *Symmetrical* triangle is one where the top and bottom of the figure converge at some point to the left of the beginning; an *Ascending* triangle is one where the base line indicates price support while the top of the triangle is formed by rising prices; a *Descending* triangle is one where the top line is horizontal, indicating resistance, and the sloping line descends from left to right on the figure. Symmetrical triangles in and of themselves give no technical indication as to which way the market may be heading, while ascending triangles are viewed as technical indicators that the market eventually might move higher, and descending triangles are technical indicators that the market eventually might turn lower.

Troy Ounce. A unit of apothecaries' weight used to measure gold. A troy ounce is equal to 31.103 grams, as opposed to a "standard," "British," or "avoirdupois" ounce, which is equal to 28.349 grams. Thus, a troy ounce weighs 9.7 percent more than a standard ounce.

U.S. Gold. A term used by the U.S. Treasury to describe its American Arts Gold Medallions. This was an effort to improve their marketability by appealing to the patriotic instincts of Americans to buy "U.S. gold," as opposed to South African, Canadian, Mexican, or any other gold.

Variable Limits. See *Limit.*

Variation Margin Call. An order from the clearinghouse to brokerage firms to post additional margin money within one hour. Variation calls are unlike margin calls from brokerage houses to their customers for maintenance margins, which the customers must meet within 24 hours or face possible forced liquidation of a position.

Volume. The total number of contracts or shares traded within a given period on a futures exchange or stock market. On the Commodity Exchange, gold futures volumes may be as high as 90,000 contracts in one day—the equivalent of 9 million ounces of gold—or as low as 15,000. Generally speaking, high volume indicates strong speculator and hedging interest, while low volume is a sign that only the floor brokers and professional traders are involved in the market that day.

Wafer. Gold bullion manufactured in a flat shape and small in size. Wafers range from 1 to 10 troy ounces. Normally, anything larger than that is referred to as a "bar."

Warehouse Receipt. Also known as a depository receipt: A receipt that specifies the quantity, quality, and location of gold in a depository. Such receipts commonly are used as a substitute for actually moving the metal once delivery is made by a short to a long. Any time the holder of a warehouse or depository receipt so directs, an order may be given to the depository to have the metal moved out of storage and shipped to any desired location. The holder of the receipt would be responsible for all costs incurred in such a movement.

White Gold. Gold that has been alloyed with platinum or silver to alter its color and hardness for jewelry applications.

Writer. See *Grantor.*

Yellow Metal. A nickname or slang term for gold, used to distinguish it from the "red metal," or copper, and the "white metal," or platinum. Silver and palladium also are sometimes called "white metals." Because gold often is alloyed with other metals such as silver, platinum, palladium, and/or copper to improve its hardness, color, or other qualities, the "yellow metal" actually may appear red or white in color on occasion.

Information Sources About Gold and Gold Investments

INTRODUCTION

The resources available to interested gold investors are many and varied, ranging from futures markets in major cities to scores of magazines, newspapers, and specialized newsletters; from monitoring organizations and brokers to vast networks of financial and statistical data available through electronic databases. While the scope of this volume does not allow for a comprehensive survey of such a rich lode, I have chosen a few key publications and organizations that may be helpful to readers of this book and serve as a starting point for further study and research.

ORGANIZATIONS

Certain organizations of interest to gold investors defiantly refuse to be neatly categorized. Some of these irksome but necessary nonconformists are listed below. As with the other resources that will be noted, a brief description of each organization's activities and purpose is included.

1. American Bureau of Metal Statistics, Inc.
    400 Plaza Drive (Harmon Meadow)
    P.O. Box 1405
    Secaucus, NJ 07094-0405
Notes: The American Bureau of Metal Statistics publishes statistical reports on all metals on a regular basis.

2. Gold Information Center–Investment Service
   900 Third Avenue
   New York, NY 10022
   Notes: The Center has a wealth of gold investment and other related information which it makes available to the media, the financial community, and the investing public.

3. Industry Council for Tangible Assets
   214 Massachusetts Avenue, N.E., Suite 560
   Washington, DC 20002
   (202) 544-1101
   Notes: ICTA is the trade association of metals and coin dealers and provides information concerning precious metals legislation on a federal and statewide basis.

4. International Precious Metals Institute (IPMI)
   Government Building, ABE Airport
   Allentown, PA 18103
   (215) 266-1570
   Notes: An industry association with a membership from industry, government, mining, academia, trading companies, and brokerage houses. The IPMI regularly holds conferences on subjects of interest to its membership.

5. National Committee for Monetary Reform
   4425 West Napoleon Avenue
   Metairie, LA 70001
   Notes: NCMR is known as an organization of gold advocacy which sponsors seminars and conferences and publishes hard assets newsletters, books, and various magazines.

6. National Futures Association
   200 West Madison
   Chicago, IL 60606
   (800) 621-3570 or (312) 781-1300
   Notes: An organization of futures dealers, dedicated to enforcing standards and investor protections.

7. U.S. Bureau of Mines
   2401 E Street, N.W.
   Washington, DC 20241
   Notes: The U.S. Bureau of Mines publishes regular reports on gold.

FUTURES AND
OPTIONS COMMODITIES EXCHANGES

Each of the gold futures exchanges publishes an annual report outlining activity in the trading of gold futures for the prior year. Some also publish daily statistics on trading activity, including prices for each contract as well as the volume, the open interest for each contract, and the total amount of gold held in exchange-approved depositories. While the annual reports are generally free on request, the daily statistical information is available only upon payment of a fee. The Comex, for instance, maintains a toll-free telephone service which gives an up-to-the-minute price for spot contracts. The number is 1-800-453-2669.

1. Chicago Board of Trade, Market Planning and Support
   LaSalle at Jackson
   Chicago, IL 60604
   (312) 435-3558 or (800) 621-4641 or
      (in IL) (800) 572-4217

2. Chicago Mercantile Exchange
   (International Monetary Market)
   30 South Wacker Drive
   Chicago, IL 60606
   (312) 930-3048

3. Commodity Exchange, Inc. (COMEX)
   4 World Trade Center
   New York, NY 10048
   (212) 938-2900
   (212) 928-2914 (marketing department)
   (800) 255-5202

4. The International Futures Exchange
   1 World Trade Center, Suite 2029
   New York, NY 10048

5. Mid-America Commodity Exchange
   175 West Jackson Boulevard
   Chicago, IL 60604
   (312) 435-0606

6. New York Mercantile Exchange
    4 World Trade Center
    New York, NY 10048
    (212) 938-2222

Note: Many commodity and stock-brokerage firms offer periodic or semiperiodic newsletters for clients. These are often available without charge.

PRINT MEDIA RESOURCES FOR GOLD INVESTORS

What follows is a selective listing of magazines and newspapers that regularly publish articles pertaining to gold and that would interest the gold investor. Publications listed in the first category are general interest newspapers and magazines and are well known to most of us. Some publications, such as *Forbes, Business Week,* and *Fortune,* publish annual surveys ranking the performance of gold relative to other financial assets and carry articles focusing on the relationship between gold and the economic environment. Also, major newspapers, such as the *New York Times* and *The Wall Street Journal,* and the *Journal of Commerce* carry gold and commodities futures prices on a daily basis and also cover gold production and trading. The second category lists publications that deal more specifically and in greater detail with personal investment strategies and money management.

CATEGORY ONE—GENERAL INTEREST

1. *Barron's*
    World Financial Center, Tower A
    200 Liberty Street
    New York, NY 10281

2. *Journal of Commerce*
    110 Wall Street
    New York, NY 10005

3. *New York Times*
    229 West 43rd Street
    New York, NY 10036

4. *The Wall Street Journal*
   World Financial Center, Tower A
   200 Liberty Street
   New York, NY 10281
5. *American Metal Market*
   7 East 12th Street
   New York, NY 10003
6. *The Northern Miner*
   7 Labatt Avenue
   Toronto, Canada M5A3PZ

CATEGORY TWO—PERSONAL INVESTING AND MONEY MANAGEMENT

1. *Fact: The Money Management Magazine*
   305 East 46th Street
   New York, NY 10017
2. *Money*
   Time & Life Building
   New York, NY 10020
3. *Wealth*
   4425 West Napoleon Avenue
   Metairie, LA 70001
4. *Futures*
   219 Parkade
   Cedar Falls, IA 50613

BOOKS

The number of books in print that touch upon gold investment in one way or another could probably fill a small library, but with the amount of printed matter most of us are obliged to deal with these days, who needs another stack of tomes to plough through. The following compilation is accordingly brief and highly selective, concentrating on a few volumes that provide general background on gold and specific information on its special role as an investment commodity. Many of these books contain bibliographies of their own which will point the reader to other titles of potential interest.

The following books/monographs contain valuable information for the seasoned investor and the novice and are recommended reading for general background.

1. Abrahams, Allen E. (Editor)
   Economic Aspects of Precious Metals Feb. 7–8, 1979
   International Precious Metals Institute, 1979
   Texts of papers presented at the International Precious
   Metals Institute seminar on "The Economic Aspects of the
   Precious Metals" at the New York Sheraton Hotel in New
   York City on February 7–8, 1979. Also includes a symposium
   on demand and price forecasting with several of the authors
   participating.

2. Beckhard, Israel (Dr.)
   The Small Investor's Guide to Gold
   Manor Books, 1974
   A compact guide book for the small investor emphasizing
   the positive aspects of gold investment as a hedge against
   inflation, protection against taxation, universally recognized
   value, etc. The book also covers, in some detail, the different
   types of available investment, such as mining stocks, coins,
   bullion, and jewelry.

3. Bernstein, Peter L.
   A Primer on Money, Banking, and Gold
   Random House, 1965
   An introduction to money: how it is created, how it is
   backed up, how it is controlled, the role of gold. Includes
   descriptions of how the Federal Reserve operates.

4. Busschau, W. J.
   Gold and International Liquidity
   South African Institute on International Affairs, 1960
   Text of a series of lectures delivered in Luxembourg in 1960
   presenting arguments for an international reevaluation of the
   gold standard. Specifically, the topics covered are: (1) Barter,
   Credit, and Money; (2) The International Gold Standard; (3)
   Toward a Dynamic Theory of Credit; (4) The Attempt to

Work an International Control of Credit since 1945; and (5) The Restoration of an Effective International System.

5. Busschau, W. A.
   The Measure of Gold
   Central News Agency (South Africa), 1949
The purpose of this 1949 monograph is to "call attention to the main features of gold in its use in modern monetary arrangements," specifically with regard to (1) the price of gold; (2) the influence of gold stocks and movements on incomes; and (3) the international arrangements for gold payments.

6. Chicago Mercantile Exchange
   International Monetary Market: Yearbooks (1981, 1982, 1983)
   Index and Option Market Yearbook, 1983
   Chicago Mercantile Exchange (Statistical Department)
Statistically oriented volumes containing daily price ranges from January through December for the year futures contracts traded on the International Monetary Market/Index and Option Market division of the Chicago Mercantile Exchange. Between them, these volumes include information on membership sales, futures contract records with price range history (open, high, low, and termination prices and dates), date commodity began trading (contract size, limits, trading hours, record total volume, etc.), monthly reviews by commodity and delivery months, exchange closings. Also, futures contract specifications and daily price ranges, summary volume, open interest and delivery tables, cash market prices, economic indicators/fundamentals, charts on daily settlement prices, monthly volume, and open interest.

7. Connell, Norman (Editor)
   World Precious Metals Survey: First Edition
   Metal Bulletin PLC, 1982
Special survey published by the London-based *Metal Bulletin* focusing on world trends and the role of gold in the new global environment.

8. Curley, Charles
   The Coming Profit in Gold
   Bantam, 1974

Although published back in 1974 when the price of gold had just hit $176.74, this book is still valuable, not only for retrospective but because it retains its value as a layman's guide to gold and its place in the world economy. Clearly written chapters explain in sufficient but simple detail such topics as gold production, theory and history of gold and money, and an overview of gold products—gold futures, bullion, certificates, bullion coins, private mints.

9. Gibson-Jarvie, Robert
    The London Metal Exchange: A Commodity Market
    Nichols Publishing, 1983
A history and explanation of the London Metal Exchange, divided into four sections that combine to give a clear understanding of the basis, organization, and mechanism of the exchange. The book reviews the events leading up to the London Gold Futures Market, whose activities are closely related to the LME.

10. Green, Timothy
    How to Buy Gold
    Walker, 1975
Published in 1975 when private ownership of gold had once again become legal in the United States, this is widely considered to be a definitive book on gold investing. Specifically, it details economic conditions to keep in mind when investors consider purchasing gold, the advantages and disadvantages of gold bullion versus gold coins, the best sources for buying gold, and the merit of gold as part of a personal investment portfolio.

11. Green, Timothy
    The New World of Gold Today
    Walker, 1973
This unique reference work examines and explains the gold markets and how they function in minute detail, making it a kind of contemporary bible for investors, traders, and anyone else interested in gold today. Includes a good bibliography and helpful tabular appendices. A major contribution to a growing body of mainstream gold investment literature.

12. Groseclose, Elgin
    Money and Man: A Survey of Monetary Experience
    Frederic Ungar, 1961
This book, despite its early publication date (and even then it is a revision of a 1934 original) contains much valuable and relevant information. It is a general history of money, focusing on the moral issues it poses in history and its influence on men and their governments. The section titled "Bimetallism and the Rise of the Gold Standard" covers the interdependent relationship of gold and money.

13. Holzer, Henry Mark
    The Gold Clause: What It Is and How to Use It Profitably
    Books in Focus, 1980
A handbook and history explaining what gold clauses are, how they have helped protect individuals and corporations against continuously devaluing paper money in the past, and how they can be used as protection today. Although the book is geared primarily toward legal and investment professionals, it is presented in a broad enough style to be of interest to the layman.

14. Jastram, Roy W.
    The Golden Constant: The English and American Experience, 1560–1976
    Ronald Press, 1977
This book examines the relationship between the gold price and various commodity prices in England and America and documents the remarkable stability of the purchasing power of gold over a span of 400 years. The author's stated purpose is to suggest ways to act on current monetary events through an understanding of the historical relationship of gold prices to the prices of other commodities.

15. Lipscomb, Alan H., and Libey, Donald R. (Editors)
    On Gold
    Waterleaf, 1982
A collection of provocative articles by gold experts covering gold investment in general, and focusing also on forecasting and trading. Although each contributor has his or her own point of view, all are recognized authorities in their fields and they favor gold as an investment. The overall approach

to the book is an assessment of gold as a future investment based on its past performance.

16. Ruff, Howard J.
    How to Prosper in the Coming Bad Years
    Times Books, 1979

This "crash course in personal and financial survival" offers a variety of investment techniques to protect individuals against the continuing erosion of the dollar in years to come.

17. Salomon Brothers Center for the Study of Financial Institutions
    The Role of Gold in Consumer Investment Portfolios, 1984

A study applying modern portfolio theory to individual gold investing. In researching gold's recent track record, the prestigious Salomon Brothers Center for the Study of Financial Institutions has provided evidence for the inclusion of a certain portion of gold in investors' portfolios. The authors indicate that although gold has typically been considered a risky investment, the addition of gold to the overall portfolio provides diversification which reduces portfolio risk and enhances returns.

18. Sarnoff, Paul
    Trading in Gold
    Woodhead-Faulkner, 1980 (U.K.)

A comprehensive introduction to the trading of gold in all its forms, focusing particularly on the futures markets of New York and Chicago. Provides a complete overview of gold trading for individual investors, covering the markets, the strategies and mechanics involved, price researching, and forecasting. Includes the author's personal evaluations of available forms of gold ownership such as bullion, coins, jewelry, certificates, delivery orders, futures, options, and gold-mining shares.

19. Sherman, Eugene
    Gold Investment Theory and Application
    New York Institute of Finance
    Prentice Hall, 1986

A comprehensive discussion of supply and demand for gold, price-determining influences, gold prices in relation to U.S. and foreign securities, and gold's portfolio role.

20. U.S. Gold Commission
    *Report to the Congress of the Commission on the Role of Gold
    in the Domestic and Monetary Systems*
    March 1982, Vols. 1 and 2
This report reviews the past role of gold in the U.S.
monetary system, types of monetary standards, existing gold
arrangements, and the commission's recommendations.

21. Reports of Special Issue of *London Times* of Various
    Authors June 20, 1933
    Gold
    London Times, 1934
A volume primarily of historical value, this book collects
various articles on gold that were published in the *London
Times* prior to June of 1933. The subjects of the articles range
from gold deposits, the gold standard, the Bank of England,
and the Royal Mint to the gold mines of Africa, salvage,
coinage, insurance, jewelry, and the subject of gold in legend
and literature.

22. Weil, Gordon L., and Davidson, Ian
    The Gold War: The Story of the World's Monetary Crisis
    Hold, 1970
An account of the international monetary panics of the
1960s, explaining the political and diplomatic conflicts behind
economic and monetary complexities. Starting with the
founding of the International Monetary Fund in 1944, the
authors expose the details of high-stakes games played by
the leading Western nations and explain the effect of the
decline of the dollar, the devaluation of the pound sterling,
the uncertainty of the franc, the rise of the Deutschemark,
the speculative rush on gold and the creation of new
"paper" gold reserves, and other highlights of a political war
fought out on a monetary battlefield.

PERIODIC PUBLICATIONS

1. *Gold*
   Published by Consolidated Goldfields PLC, 49 Moorgate,
   London EC2R 6BQ, England

An annual review of gold supply and demand, as well as important events that may affect these fundamentals. Considered one of the bibles of gold analysts.

2. *Gold Review and Outlook*
   J. Aron & Co./Goldman Sachs & Co.
From time to time, J. Aron, one of the primary bullion coin dealers in the United States, has issued periodic reports on gold. These publications are the U.S. counterpart of the Consolidated Goldfields annual, and are considered another bible for analysts.

3. *Gold Investment Papers*
   Gold Information Center
Research reports focusing on the merits of institutional gold investing, modern portfolio theory, and its impact on gold investing.

ELECTRONIC DATABASES AND CHART SERVICES

Computers are here to stay, and the personal computer (PC) offers many advantages to investors. All manner of software packages and on-line databases are currently vying for your attention (and your dollar) in the electronic marketplace. There are programs to help investors devise "what-if" situations to aid in making more-informed decisions. There are computer "games" based on the commodities market which are designed to help investors better understand its Byzantine workings. And, there are also special chart services that investors and analysts can call to obtain copies of research findings and charts. Most helpful, perhaps, are the on-line services that can be tapped into by means of a modem hookup between your PC and a telephone line. These databases draw on the resources of such sources as *The Wall Street Journal*, U.S. government statistics, the International Monetary Fund (IMF), and others to provide instant access to information helpful to investors. Below is a selective listing of financial database services. Each listing is followed by a brief description of what the service offers to the potential investor of gold.

1. ADP COMTREND
   1345 Washington Boulevard
   Stamford, CT 06902
   (800) 451-1511 or (203) 357-1611
Description: On-line commodities and futures prices,
including precious metals.
2. ADP NETWORK SERVICES
   175 Jackson Plaza
   Ann Arbor, MI 48106
   (913) 995-6400
Description: Includes 10 years of on-line commodities prices
for gold, silver, platinum, paladium, and silver coins. Access
methods vary. Available 24 hours, 7 days a week.
3. COMMODITY COMMUNICATIONS CORPORATION
   420 Eisenhower Lane North
   Lombard, IL 60148
   (800) 621-2628
Description: Provides real-time commodity futures prices as
well as news, charts, and various technical studies.
4. COMPUSERVE
   Information Services Division
   5000 Arlington Center Boulevard
   Columbus, OH 43220
   (800) 848-8199 or (614) 457-0802
Description: This is one of the largest of all database services,
offering a vast range of information, financial and otherwise.
5. DOW JONES NEWS RETRIEVAL
   Dow Jones & Co.
   P.O. Box 300
   Princeton, NJ 08540
   (800) 257-5114 or (609) 452-1511 (in New Jersey only)
Description: Extensive financial news and information
database.
6. INTERACTIVE DATA CORPORATION
   303 Wyman Street
   Waltham, MA 02154
   (617) 895-4300
Description: A wide-ranging information source that includes
information on precious metals.

7. NEWSNET
   945 Haverford Road
   Bryn Mawr, PA 19010
   (215) 527-8030

Description: Features texts of investment newsletters on-line, including a number covering precious metals.

8. PC QUOTE, INC.
   401 South LaSalle Street, 16th Floor
   Chicago, IL 60605
   (800) 225-5657 or (312) 786-5400 (in Illinois only)

Description: Allows user with IBM or compatible computer to access price quotations on precious metals and other commodities as they happen via satellite.

9. THE SOURCE
   1616 Anderson Road
   McLean, VA 22102
   (800) 336-3366 or (703) 821-6666

Description: Wide-ranging database offering many types of information. Their *Investor* series offers information on precious metals.

10. I. P. SHARP ASSOCIATES
    230 Park Avenue
    New York, NY 10169
    (212) 557-7900

Description: A large on-line information broker offering numerous statistical and other data in the areas of finance, economics, energy, etc. Includes access to extensive IMF base, CITIBASE, and many more.